Faulkner and Formalism: Returns of the Text
FAULKNER AND YOKNAPATAWPHA
2008

Faulkner and Formalism: Returns of the Text

FAULKNER AND YOKNAPATAWPHA, 2008

EDITED BY
ANNETTE TREFZER
AND
ANN J. ABADIE

UNIVERSITY PRESS OF MISSISSIPPI
JACKSON

www.upress.state.ms.us

The University Press of Mississippi is a member of the Association of
American University Presses.

Copyright © 2012 by University Press of Mississippi
All rights reserved
Manufactured in the United States of America

First printing 2012

∞

Library of Congress Cataloging-in-Publication Data

Faulkner and Yoknapatawpha Conference
(35th : 2008 : University of Mississippi)
Faulkner and formalism : the returns of the text : Faulkner and
Yoknapatawpha, 2008 / edited by Annette Trefzer and Ann J. Abadie.
p. cm.
Includes bibliographical references and index.
ISBN 978-1-61703-256-1 (cloth : alk. paper) —
ISBN 978-1-61703-257-8 (ebook)
1. Faulkner, William, 1897–1962—Criticism and interpretation—
Congresses. 2. Faulkner, William, 1897–1962—Criticism, Textual—
Congresses. I. Trefzer, Annette, 1960– II. Abadie, Ann J. III. Title.
PS3511.A86Z7832113 2012
813'.52—dc23   2011027309

British Library Cataloging-in-Publication Data available

In Memoriam,

Dorothy (Dot) Falkner Dodson
10 March 1920–23 January 2010

Ruth Elizabeth Ford
7 July 1911–12 August 2009

Howard Barry Hannah
23 April 1942–1 March 2010

James G. Watson
16 June 1939–30 March 2010

Contents

Introduction

Faulkner scholarship is constantly shifting in search of new models of reading and interpretation. In the late 1940s, when Faulkner began to experience national recognition as a major writer, literary scholarship in the U.S. was dominated by the New Critics.[1] Insisting that the author's intentions were neither available nor desirable, the New Critics broke away from biographical, sociological, and historical analyses that had dominated literary study until then. Instead, they argued for a turn to the text itself and the practice of what they called close reading. The "objective status" of the work was at stake, and literary critics fervently investigated its tensions, paradoxes, ironies, and ambiguities.

The New Critical turn to the complexities of the literary text not only influenced generations of scholars to come, but it coincides with the rise of William Faulkner to literary fame. As Lawrence Schwartz argues, New Criticism was a major factor in propelling Faulkner from regional writer to national artist, and Malcolm Cowley's rediscovery of Faulkner's talent in the late 1940s was "perfectly suited to the prevailing formalist aesthetics of the postwar era."[2] Faulkner's experimentation with style and technique—most obviously in *The Sound and the Fury* and *As I Lay Dying*, for instance—began to be investigated and appreciated under the New Critical dictum. This postwar shift in literary practice and aesthetic values—combined with a shift in America's ideological and political climate—contributed to Faulkner's resuscitation and prominence.[3] From the beginning then, the critical assessment of Faulkner's work is closely linked with "a turn to the text."

Returns of the Text begs the question of the status of Faulkner's literary text in contemporary criticism and scholarship. How do scholars today approach Faulkner's texts? How do they characterize the relationship of his texts to the author, the reader, and the world? Questions concerning the status of the literary text are old and venerable; they have been asked since Plato. In recent critical history, the New Critics attempted to separate the text from the world and persisted in a text-world split, whereas poststructuralist critics were busily dismantling this dichotomy: texts make up our world, they claim. Michel Foucault, for instance, alludes to Nietzsche to make this point: "if language expresses, it does so not in so far as it is an imitation and duplication of things, but in so far as it manifests and translates the fundamental will of those who speak it."⁴ Jacques Derrida, whose own work pays microscopic attention to the texts he studies, posits that there is no access to the world, except through language. Our world is a world of texts and texts *are* our world. Another critic to invoke in this discussion is Jacques Lacan, for whom any text is a site of "repression and return" and language users—whether they are creative writers like Faulkner, or his critics—are forever alienated in language.

The title of this volume, *Faulkner and Formalism: Returns of the Text*, alludes to the idea of the repressed and closely echoes Doreen Fowler's book title *Faulkner: The Return of the Repressed*.⁵ The intersections and elisions between the two phrases "the return of the repressed" and "returns of the text" are worth addressing: in our volume, the return has become plural and expressive of an attempt to offer a variety of different ways for constructing the textual field. Here, the text is in the grammatical place of the repressed as if to indicate that the text, long repressed, is now returning. After several decades of Faulkner studies that privileged an ever wider sweep of theoretical angles and aggregate practices of postcolonial studies, cultural studies, gender studies, critical race studies, and so forth, "the text is back," as Theresa M. Towner proclaims in her essay in this volume. There is a slight elision, however, in many of the essays included here: returns *of* the text is read and implicitly understood as returns *to* the text, evidence of slippage indicating the critics' (perhaps long repressed) desires to focus more centrally on the work itself, its language, and its formal characteristics. The ready embrace of this shift away from the "high theory" mode of literary analysis of the 1980s and '90s, and the more recent move away from new historical and cultural studies of the last two decades, so some critics argue, marks a new turn towards a resurgent formalism.⁶

Hailed by some as New Formalism, this movement proves quite controversial in academic circles. While there is no space in this introduction to pursue the points in the debate between formalist and nonformalist modes of analysis, I assert that the practice of "close reading" associated with formalist work never went out of fashion in superior Faulkner scholarship no matter the political direction or ideological slant. As the essays included here demonstrate, reading and understanding the compositional complexities of Faulkner's text forces us to grapple with various paradoxes and inextricable interdependencies of text *and* cultural context. If *Returns of the Text* is read as a contribution to the New Formalism, then it showcases the various interpretive methods drawn from an entire repertoire of literary and cultural studies. As such, the Faulkner scholarship collected here could serve as an example for the diversity of this new movement in contemporary criticism. Marjorie Levinson, in her survey of new formalist work, is judiciously cautious in describing this scholarship as a "movement" rather than a "theory or method" because the "modes and degrees of identification with the movement are so various." [7] The same is true for our collection.

For some of the contributors, including Arthur F. Kinney and James B. Carothers, "returns of the text" is a phrase that raises questions of aesthetics, poetics, and authority. For others, the phrase serves as an invitation to return to Faulkner's language, to writing and the letter itself. Serena Blount, Owen Robinson, James Harding, and Taylor Hagood interpret "returns of the text" in the sense in which Roland Barthes characterizes this shift in his seminal essay "From Work to Text." For Barthes, the text "is not to be thought of as an object . . . but as a methodological field," a notion quite different from the New Critical understanding of the work as a unified construct with intrinsic aesthetic value. [8] The text, by contrast, "is experienced only in an activity of production"; it invites and needs the reader's collaboration. [9] Faulkner's language itself is under close scrutiny in some of the readings that emphasize a deconstructive or a semiological approach to his writing. Historical and cultural contexts continue to play significant roles, however, in many of the essays. The contributions by Thadious Davis, Ted Atkinson, Martyn Bone, and Ethel Young-Minor by no means ignore the cultural contexts, but instead of approaching the literary text as a reflection, a representation of that context, whether historical, economic, political, or social, these readings stress the role of the text as a challenge to the power of external ideological systems. By retaining a bond with new historicist analysis and cultural studies, these essays are illustrative of a kind of analysis that carefully preserves attention to Faulkner's sociopolitical environment. The concluding essay by Theresa Towner issues an invitation to return to Faulkner's less well-known short stories for critical exposure and the pleasure of reading.

The collection opens with two meditations on aesthetics in an early and a late text by Faulkner: *Flags in the Dust* and the Nobel Prize Address. Arthur F. Kinney's essay, "*Flags in the Dust* and the Birth of Poetics," recalls the novel's publication history and its rejection by Horace Liveright. Readers for the publishing house judged the novel's structure haphazard and fragmented because much like many early Faulkner readers in the U.S. they did not yet understand Faulkner's emerging aesthetic. Kinney argues that by contrast, in France, Jean-Paul Sartre grasped the nature of Faulkner's textual experiments early on perhaps because Faulkner's poetic was akin to Balzac's. Like Balzac, Faulkner developed a distinct sense of place and a prose style rich in detail to create "tapestry-like fiction." Kinney shows that what initially seemed haphazard prose, Faulkner had actually carefully designed. "A sequential plot," Kinney argues, "was not what Faulkner ever intended to write." Instead, the plot is made up of "analogous episodes" that slowly accrue meaning and significance as if composed as "an early kind of filmic montage." Kinney argues that Faulkner's third novel, *Flags in the Dust* (shortened, renamed, and eventually published as *Sartoris*), also shares many similarities with *The Sound and the Fury*, a novel often seen as "an early and somewhat failed work and a classic work that sprang from nowhere." By drawing on biography and publication history, Kinney points out that, while *Flags* was on the cutting table for revision, Faulkner composed *The Sound and the Fury*. Kinney underscores this contemporaneous creative process and highlights the close intertextual links and parallels between these two novels' "deliberate and revolutionary poetics."

If Faulkner critics initially had trouble understanding the author's textual experiments, by the time of the Nobel Prize in 1950 they had found their stride. James B. Carothers, in his essay "'In Conflict with Itself': The Nobel Prize Address in Faulknerian Contexts," argues that critics then and today have often expressed doubt at Faulkner's optimism and faith in the endeavor of humanity so famously expressed in the speech. Carothers urges us to reexamine the ostensible irony and possible cynicism in later works like *Go Down, Moses* (1942) and *A Fable* (1950) in light of the affirmative outlook of the Nobel Prize Address. In examining the biographical and literary historical contexts of the speech, Carothers argues that Faulkner sincerely holds the beliefs that he expresses. What gave Faulkner's speech its positive vision, according to Carothers, is not only the conclusion of WWII, but his long career of literary achievements, the increasing financial recognition of his work from movie contracts, and the growing recognition of his global significance as a writer, including success in Europe. In his fifties, Faulkner could look both forward to future projects and back on his achievements, and in the backward glance, he begins to glimpse his own immortality as a writer.

Carothers makes the valuable point that Faulkner, the man, must be separated from Faulkner, the author. "Returns of the text" here means an emphasis on the textual construction of Faulkner as a writer. Even as Faulkner was honored as a person, the celebration of the author in Stockholm and his beginning fame increasingly marked his removal and replacement by his texts. While Faulkner was now able to look both forward and backward on his career, Faulkner, the man, "enter[ed] into his own death."[10] As Roland Barthes argues, "writing is that neutral, composite, oblique space where our subject slips away, the negative where all identity is lost, starting with the very identity of the body writing."[11] Carothers stresses that moment in Faulkner's career that divides the temporality of the author into a "before and after." This crucial divide reminds us of Barthes's critique of the idea that "the author when believed in, is always conceived of as the past of his own book. . . . The author is thought to nourish the book, which is to say that he exists before it, thinks, suffers, lives for it, is in the same relation of antecedence to his work as a father to his child."[12] But even as Faulkner stands at the podium, the text of his famous speech—the enunciation and the language itself—displaces him and opens up a rich network of intertextuality between his speech and his novels.

Veering further into the field of textuality, Serena Blount's essay, "Faulkner's Figures: Speech, Writing, and *The Marionettes*," examines Faulkner's early play as a training ground for an aesthetic intensely concerned with "meditations on language and literary production." The essay probes the dynamics of the characters, Pierrot and Shade of Pierrot, Marietta and the Marionettes, to reveal in each case a complex and contradictory relationship between these figures. In Faulkner's play, Pierrot, a stock character of the Italian commedia dell'arte, is the sad clown whose lifeless mask and silence contrast with the action and voice of Shade of Pierrot. That the "shade" of a clown should be more active than the clown himself points to the artifice of the character, as Blount argues. Much like the Marionettes, who are puppets controlled by a puppeteer, these figures are characters, "two dimensional creations" scripted by Faulkner's hand. In self-referential fashion, the play makes visible their emptiness and status as characters in language. The slippage between character (as in the play) and character (as in the letter or sign) is thereby explicitly and self-consciously foregrounded. The idea is further supported by Faulkner's use of calligraphy and illustration, which, as Blount argues, turns Faulkner himself into a mime of Aubrey Beardsley.

For Blount then, the returns of the text signify the inscriptions and reinscriptions of character: characters from literary traditions such as the commedia dell'arte and characters from the alphabetic tradition, letters rendered in calligraphy. It is helpful to remember that the Greek term calligraphy, consisting of "kallos" ("beauty") and "graphe" ("writing"), refers more idiomatically to the art of writing itself. By actually using calligraphy in the play, Faulkner meditates in form and content on the art of writing itself. Using image and text, he tells the story of writing in all of its dimensions: visually, scripted, canonically, and self-referentially.

Faulkner's fascinating early experiments with texts and textuality are also the topic in Owen Robinson's essay, "'That City Foreign and Paradoxical': William Faulkner and the Texts of New Orleans." In Faulkner's

early sketches we can see the continued concern with characters, especially the textuality and language of the characters that were inspired by
his stays in New Orleans in 1925 and 1926. Robinson points out that,
although William Faulkner's work is primarily associated with the rural
landscapes of northern Mississippi, he offers extensive commentary on
the cityscapes of New Orleans. Faulkner's construction of the city (from
his earliest sketches, written for *Times-Picayune* and the *Double Dealer*,
to its significant appearance in his major work *Absalom, Absalom!*) functions as a polyphonic text; it echoes with multiple voices from margin
and center. Drawing on the work of Mikhail Bakhtin and dialogic criticism, Robinson discovers a veritable heteroglossia in Faulkner's sketches.
For Bakhtin, a text is not a site where meanings are produced "by the
play of impersonal linguistic or economic or cultural forces, but a site
for the dialogic interaction of multiple voices, or modes of discourse,
each of which is not merely a verbal but a social phenomenon."[13] In
these sketches, Faulkner's characters represent different social groups
and classes, and, as Robinson shows, their speech does not express an
individuality so much as the inflection and meaning of a particular social
class. This is particularly apparent in the first part of the essay, where
Robinson discusses various types of characters who populate the pages
of Faulkner's New Orleans. All of these characters are marked by a particular social milieu and many of them are identified by their profession,
such as "The Cobbler" or "The Sailor." Robinson shows that Faulkner
experiments with characters who speak in specific situations and in a plu-
rality of independent voices to produce a genuine polyphony. His essay
highlights the textuality of Faulkner's literary work as constituted by a
rhetorical as opposed to a purely formal dimension. In the early sketches,
he argues, Faulkner is interested in the function of language, especially
the relation between literary language and everyday language produced
in a specific social milieu.

From the Bakhtinian inspired rhetorical analysis of Faulkner's textual
experiments, we move to a stylistic analysis. For James Harding the signal
to return to the text serves as an invitation to examine closely the textual
body of Faulkner's *Sanctuary*. In his essay, "*Sanctuary's* Reversible Bodies," Harding zooms in on Temple's narration of her rape in chapter 23 of
the novel. Temple's testimony of her rape is marked by the repetition of
the singular neuter pronoun "it," which, as Harding argues, seeks to direct
attention way from her body's violation. Faulkner's grammar and syntax,
according to Harding, enacts a semantic conflict in the novel between
the grammatical violence of the body of the text and the material violation of Temple's body. With a careful linguistic parsing of the pronoun
"it," Harding accomplishes two goals: first, he shows how Temple seeks

to deflect from the violence of her traumatic rape. In retelling her story, Temple carefully avoids naming things, instead referring to them anonymously as "it." But the pronouns point beyond a simple denial. Careful analysis of a second passage reveals that Temple attempts to reconstruct the rape in such a way as to reverse her own violation. Harding's analysis reveals that Temple seemingly casually switches the places of victim and violator, woman and man. Temple's texts, more specifically her grammar and her crafty deployment of pronouns, create a confounding ambiguity by hiding and reversing the nouns designating agent and action in order to open up a space for her own female agency. Harding posits that Faulkner—much like his character Temple—attempts to reassess the white female body as a locus of power.

The intersections of language and power are also at stake in Taylor Hagood's reading of *The Sound and the Fury*. Hagood's essay title teases readers with the question "What Is Benjy Compson Really Thinking?" and in attempting an answer he puzzles out the textual fabric of the Benjy section in *The Sound and the Fury*. What, he asks, might be attributable to Faulkner and what to the character he has created? With a careful textual analysis of the opening paragraphs of the novel, Hagood challenges established ways of reading Benjy as Faulkner's famous creation of an "idiot." As he demonstrates, Faulkner's narrative—while admittedly marked by an unusual use of diction and narrative style—actually evidences tight control over a plot that advances the story in rather controlled and economic fashion. The author is clearly constructing and advancing the narrative action with the help of the Benjy section, and in speaking *of* or rather *for* Benjy, Faulkner imagines the inner workings of the mind of a mentally disabled person. For Hagood, at stake in the Benjy section of the novel are Faulkner's poetics and politics of representing "otherness." Benjy is "the other," as imagined and created by Faulkner. And yet, his disability shows no evidence of a mental or lexical handicap; on the contrary, his spelling of words is standard and accurate. This means that, although Benjy occupies a position of marginality, his language (or rather Faulkner's) neither subverts nor questions the hegemony of the Compson family's race and class privilege. Hagood argues that Faulkner uses a narrative maneuver much like Thomas Nelson Page before him to project onto a character of the minority group the desires and the politics of the majority. Specifically, what is projected onto Benjy is a discourse of disability, as imagined by Faulkner. This discourse is subtle because the text works both with and against the grain of an argument about normalcy and disability. Hagood gives Faulkner credit for the nuances of these "projected imaginings" and shows us that his textual work in the Benjy section of the novel is more subtle and complex than critics in the past have allowed. When Hagood turns to Faulkner's text, he focuses on these subtleties of Faulkner's poetics against the background of current-day disability studies, offering the contemporary reader a perspective much different from Faulkner's own.

The body, especially the abject body, is also the focus of Thadious Davis's essay, "Visualizing *Light in August:* Text, Author, Textuality, Authority." Davis begins her essay with an analysis of Doane's Mill as a desolate industrial wasteland that foreshadows the abject or "disposable" human environment offered in the novel. Faulkner's text, Davis argues, centers on those individuals, foremost Joe and Lena, who attempt to resist this economy of waste. In *Light in August* Faulkner "takes on the difficult question of how some humans attempt to dispose of others" because they may be seen as either "inconsequential" like Lena, or "different" like Joe.

Beginning with the opening panorama, the novel is concerned with a mode of specularity that, as Davis argues, resembles early film and that projects the characters as if against a movie screen. Davis sketches an "epistemology of the visual" and its potential for a "social reformation for the eye," including the reader's eye. Faulkner, she argues, "challenges and questions ways of interpreting people, places, and events based on sight," at the same time as he uses film techniques to "intensify the effects of [his novel's] specularity." Davis's essay broadens to include the various visual economies and cultural contexts that surrounded Faulkner, including the Depression economy, the economies of place shaped by WPA landscaping projects, the racial landscape of the Scottsboro trial, the global influence of political figures from Hitler to Ghandi, and even the animated films of the 1930s pop culture industry. Davis's reading opens up Faulkner's textual fabric to include all of these cultural contexts of his time presented in media images and refracted in the visual economies of *Light in August*.

A second essay centering on the visual economies and the racial and social encodings of the bodies in Faulkner's texts is Ted Atkinson's "The Impenetrable Lightness of Being: Miscegenation Imagery and the Anxiety of Whiteness in *Go Down, Moses*." Atkinson examines Faulkner's explicit references to the stereopticon, a 19th-century optical device that provides depth perception for viewing an image. Harkening back to early film history, the device offered an opportunity for viewing "in stereo"—it had literally two lenses, one on top of the other—to produce realistic depth perception. Faulkner uses the image and the technique of the stereopticon, Atkinson argues, to provide readers with the pleasure of such new depth perception in *Go Down, Moses*, where the optical instrument functions figuratively as an image for viewing a person or situation in double perspective. The doubleness produced by the optical device helps to problematize the black/white racial binary in the South of *Go Down, Moses*. Drawing on critical race studies and theories of whiteness, Atkinson renders visible the subtleties of the concept of miscegenation and the anxieties that surround it in his reading of "Was" and "The Fire and the Hearth" chapters. He argues that the stereopticon, both as image and instrument, destabilizes racial difference and by obscuring the binary code yields moments of racial uncertainty for both characters and readers. Atkinson's essay underscores the complexity of Faulkner's text by returning to these double images that engender "a dynamic struggle of domination and resistance waged in large measure through sensory perceptions that influence individual, familial, and social relations." The new historical grounding of Atkinson's essay ensures that this image of doubleness—the stereopticon itself—is anchored in the actual physical and human geographies and the subtle social and racial encodings of Faulkner's time and place. When critics like Davis and Atkinson return to the text, they keep in sharp focus Faulkner's social and historical contexts.

The notion of context also remains relevant in Martyn Bone's essay, "Intertextual Geographies of Migration and Biracial Identity: *Light in August* and Nella Larsen's *Quicksand*." Bone works with a concept of intertextuality that leans on Roland Barthes's reading of every text as "a tissue of quotations drawn from the innumerable centers of culture" to examine the intersections between Faulkner's 1932 novel and Nella Larsen's 1928 novel. When read side by side, Bone argues, these novels interrogate U.S. racial ideology, particularly the "one drop rule" that originated in the South but quickly became a measure of racial identification in the U.S. in the early part of the 20th century. His comparison offers a new look at the intertextual similarities of the two novels: Joe Christmas and Helga Crane were both born in the late 1890s, have mixed ancestry, and become tokens of danger for miscegenation in a culture of clearly drawn racial lines. Bone argues that the characters' discomfort in black and white racial environments arises because both characters have internalized the idea of racial "blood" in a culture that does not offer an identity for racial hybridity. As a result, Joe and Helga are orphaned not so much by their loss of parents, but "by the ways in which their personal histories are inextricable from an ideology in which the specter of *racial* blood (especially 'black blood') trumps familial blood ties." Both characters migrate in an attempt to reclaim their family history and find a place of belonging; in each case, however, this journey is ironically circular leading out of the South and by "a certain grim logic" back into it. What traps the characters within this circle is their adoption of an understanding of racial identity that defines them as "black." Bone argues convincingly that Larsen and Faulkner use the transnational migrations of their characters to Mexico (in Joe's case) and Denmark (in Helga's case) in order to critique specifically "American modes of racial classification" and to show that these identifications that are not universal but culturally specific. Faulkner and Larsen warn against internalizing the either/or definitions of race that lead to tragedy in their respective novels.

Bone's notion of intertextuality is at once geographical—marked by the characters' migrations and transnational notions of race—and literary, marked by genealogies of texts that engage with the specific cultural documents of racial classification. On the macrolevel, the essay establishes an intertextuality of African American and Southern literary traditions; on the microlevel, it offers a kind of "interfigurality" that probes textual relations between characters.[14] Beyond this literary dimension, Bone's essay connects legal and fictional texts engaged in defining and critiquing racial categorizations.

Intertextuality also plays a crucial role in Ethel Young-Minor's essay, "'I Sees De Light, En I Sees De Word': Black Female Transcendence of Racial and Gendered Boundaries in The Sound and the Fury and 'That Evening Sun.'" Young-Minor frames her essay with Langston Hughes's comments on Faulkner. Hughes believed that Faulkner was a "great Mississippi writer," but he was puzzled, like many of his readers, by his treatment of race. Young-Minor probes the question of Faulkner's understanding of race relations in the segregated South of his time; more specifically, she explores the possibility of racial and religious transcendence for Faulkner's black female characters. Faulkner, she argues, reshapes the stereotypical images of black women in the kitchens and churches of the Jim Crow South in order to reveal their hidden cultural and personal complexities. The essay explores how African American cultural practices empower these female characters and encourage them to transcend their positions on the margins of society. Young-Minor questions the generally accepted critical understanding of Dilsey in The Sound and the Fury as an oppressed character who is defeated at the end of the novel. Her reading examines how Dilsey finds power and strength with the help of Reverend Shegog, whose sermon teaches her to transcend the fixed dualities in the segregated South. When Dilsey returns to the Compson household after the sermon, she has a newly gained vision of her own power. Similarly, in "That Evening Sun" Faulkner addresses the awakening of a black female character to the power of self-determination. Nancy's abject self-image changes when she realizes that the Compson family is blind to her personhood. She bravely faces her future and defies the white patriarch's prediction that he will find her in the kitchen tomorrow. Here again, Faulkner uses a religious figure, Jesus and his dual signification in the story, as a way for his black female characters to transcend the confining racial binaries of the segregated South.

The concluding essay models the return of the text as a joyous embrace of close reading. Theresa Towner's essay, "The Weird Stuff: Textual and Sexual Anomalies in Faulkner's Fiction," addresses some of the lesser known stories, including "Hair," "Artist at Home," "Divorce in Naples," and "The Leg." According to Towner, all of these stories feature "oddities" that relegate them to the margins of Faulkner's canon and startle his readers. Some of these stories fail to be engaging because they feature what Towner calls "bad narrators." Faulkner uses these narrators to "reveal the high stakes involved in our attempts to tell our own stories." Indeed, this goal is consistent with some of the effects in his major fiction, which almost always draws spectacular attention to its telling. In these stories, however, especially "Hair" and "Artist at Home," narrators behave "badly" when they introduce careless tense shifts, interruptions, underdeveloped characters, implausible plot development, and chatty asides to the reader. "Artist at Home," Towner argues, features all of these breaches of convention and can therefore be read as "the book on how not to write the book."

The "oddities" in the remaining two stories, "Divorce in Naples" and "The Leg," are of a different order. Here the signification of the term "weird" shifts from "technically bad" in terms of narration, to generically ambiguous; both stories provide complex textual networks of literary allusions and, in the case of "The Leg," literary techniques similar to magical realism. In terms of theme, the "weird" also signals a shift into the "queer" as both stories address themes of (homo)erotic anxiety and desire. No doubt, Towner wants the reader to ponder the relationship between Faulkner's failed stylistics and the sexual anxiety addressed in all of these stories. She ends her essay by addressing the publication history of these stories and Faulkner's choice to include them after all— good and bad—in *Collected Stories*. In this concluding essay, returns of the text quite literally means exposure to the plots of these half-obscure stories.

Together the essays in this volume take up returns of the text as a point of departure from which Faulkner's literature may be read at a wide range of theoretical angles. And yet, it seems to be commonly understood that this return does not signal an emphasis on the privileged status of the literary text the way it was firmly established by the New Critics. This return is not to the self-referential autonomy of Faulkner's texts, nor to his language independent from other forms of discourse. For many of the scholars in this volume, historical, biographical, and cultural contexts remain crucial for reading and understanding Faulkner. Some of these essays explicitly gesture towards the extradiscursive ground of history and social conflict. Other essays in this volume focus primarily on the linguistic choices and textual construction of Faulkner's fiction, but not in the spirit of a depoliticized close reading that recalls the doctrinaire stance of formalism. The text has returned, but it is not isolated from everyday life. The broader arguments about the social function of Faulkner's fiction in the world beyond the text remain and open up a dialectical relation between aesthetics and politics. Even as scholars included here ask about the place of language, aesthetics, and form in contemporary interpretations of Faulkner, they do not foreclose the study of Faulkner's text to ideological or historical questions. Judging by this response to our call for "returns of the text," the contemporary shift that seeks to reaffirm the formal dimensions of literature may have prompted a "return" but not a "revenge" of the text.[15] This volume offers a "turnabout" to the aesthetic subtleties of Faulkner's prose that has always invited sophisticated textual exegesis but keeps on steady course with cultural and historical concerns.

Annette Trefzer
University of Mississippi

NOTES

1. By New Critics I mean those scholars, writers, and poets who developed a formalist aesthetics based on the theories by William Empson, I. A. Richards, and T. S. Eliot. They were interested in explications of the organic unity of literary texts and in correlations of form and theme. This group included, among others, John Crowe Ransom, Allen Tate, Robert Penn Warren, R. P. Blackmur, Yvor Winters, W. K. Wimsatt, René Welleck, and William Van O'Connor. O'Connor is also known as a scholar of Faulkner.

2. Lawrence H. Schwartz, *Creating Faulkner's Reputation: The Politics of Literary Criticism* (Knoxville: University of Tennessee Press, 1988), 203.

3. Ibid., 5.

4. Michel Foucault, *The Order of Things: An Archaeology of the Human Sciences* (New York: Random House, 1970), 290.

5. Doreen Fowler, *Faulkner: The Return of the Repressed* (Charlottesville: University Press of Virginia, 1997).

6. See Marjorie Levinson's review essay "What Is New Formalism?," *PMLA* 122.2 (March 2007): 558–69, 558.

7. Ibid., 558.

8. Roland Barthes, "From Work to Text," in *The Critical Tradition*, ed. David H. Richter (Boston, Bedford, 2007), 878–82, 878.

9. Ibid., 879, 881.

10. Roland Barthes, "The Death of the Author," in *Falling into Theory*, ed. David H. Richter (Boston: Bedford, 2000), 253–57, 253.

11. Ibid., 253.

12. Ibid., 255.

13. This is M. H. Abrams and Geoffrey Galt Harpham's characterization of dialogic criticism in *A Glossary of Literary Terms* (Boston: Thompson, Wadsworth, 2005), 63.

14. Wolfgang G. Müller, who has coined the term "interfigurality," remarks how little attention such interrelations between characters have found in intertextual theory and criticism. He argues that this "lacuna" points to an ideological prejudice towards character study in contemporary criticism. See "Interfigurality: A Study on the Interdependence of Literary Figures," in *Intertextuality*, ed. Heinrich F. Plett (New York: Walter de Gruyter, 1991), 101–22.

15. I am alluding to the title of Michael P. Clark's essay collection *Revenge of the Aesthetic: The Place of Literature in Theory Today* (Berkeley: University of California Press, 2000).

Note on the Conference

The Thirty-fifth Annual Faulkner and Yoknapatawpha Conference sponsored by the University of Mississippi in Oxford took place 20–24 July 2008, with more than two hundred of the author's admirers in attendance. Eleven presentations on the theme "Faulkner: The Returns of the Text" are collected as essays in this volume. Brief mention is made here of other conference activities.

The program began on Sunday with lectures by James B. Carothers and Taylor Hagood. Following a buffet supper at the home of Dr. M. B. Howorth Jr. documentary filmmaker Chris Cranford, of Little Rock, Arkansas, showed his film *Brother Will and Colonel Jim*, a series of interviews with the late Jimmy Faulkner, recalling stories of his famous uncle. Before the film, Richard Howorth, Mayor of Oxford, and Gloria Kellum, Vice Chancellor at the University of Mississippi, welcomed participants and conference director Donald M. Kartiganer introduced Jennie Joiner, a University of Kansas graduate student writing a dissertation on marriages in Faulkner's fiction, as the winner of the 2008 William Faulkner Society Fellowship. Ted Ownby, director of the Center for the Study of Southern Culture, presented the twenty-second annual Eudora Welty Awards in Creative Writing. Stella Day Nickerson of Aberdeen, Emma Richardson's student at the Mississippi School of Math and Science in Columbus, won first prize, $500, for her story "My Candle Burns." Frederick Stacy Parker, Jean Biglane's student at Cathedral High School in Natchez, won second prize, $250, for his poem "Letting Go." The late Frances Patterson of Tupelo, a longtime member of the Center Advisory Committee, established and endowed the awards, which are selected through a competition held in high schools throughout Mississippi.

Thadious M. Davis and Martyn Bone presented lectures on Monday, and John Collins, founder of the Elevator Repair Service Theater Company, talked about his New York production of *The Sound and the Fury* (*April Seventh*, 1928), which consists of nearly every word of the opening section of the novel. The day's program also included sessions during which Seth Berner, a book dealer from Portland, Maine, talked about "Collecting Faulkner"; James B. Carothers and Theresa M. Towner discussed "Teaching Faulkner's Shorter Fiction"; and Nehama Baker, Tim

A. Ryan, and Irene Visser made presentations for the first of two panels featuring short papers selected through an annual call for papers. The day's activities ended with Colby Kullman moderating the eighth Faulkner Fringe Festival, an open-mike evening at Southside Gallery on the Oxford Square.

Tuesday's programs began with Charles A. Peek and Terrell L. Tebbetts leading a "Teaching Faulkner" session on "(Dis)cursed Communities: Faulkner and Texts that Keep on Returning." Owen Robinson and Theresa M. Towner presented lectures, and Serena Haygood Blount, C. F. Sanders Creasy, and James Harding made panel presentations. Following the panel, there was an afternoon party at Tyler Place, hosted by Charles Noyes, Sarah and Allie Smith, and Colby Kullman.

Wednesday's program included lectures by Arthur F. Kinney, Ethel Young-Minor, and Ted Atkinson; a "Teaching Faulkner" panel; and Willie James Faulkner's presentation on his genealogy research, which revealed connections between Falkner family slaves and his own family. Attendees then gathered for the annual picnic at Faulkner's home, Rowan Oak. Guided tours of North Mississippi, the Delta, and Memphis took place on Thursday, and the conference ended with a party at Off Square Books.

Four exhibitions were available throughout the conference. The Department of Archives and Special Collections at the University's John Davis Williams Library displayed items from its new collection of correspondence between William Bacher, a Hollywood film producer, and William Faulkner concerning a screenplay for *A Fable*. The University Museum sponsored an exhibition entitled *William Christenberry Site: Possession*, photographs and drawings of the South. *Katrina: Mississippi Women Remember*, a collection of black-and-white photographs by Mississippi photographer Melody Swaney Golding, was on exhibit at Barnard Observatory's Gammill Gallery. The University Press of Mississippi exhibited Faulkner books published by university presses throughout the United States.

The conference planners are grateful to all the individuals and organizations that support the Faulkner and Yoknapatawpha Conference annually and offer special thanks to James B. and Beverly Carothers for their gift in honor of Faulkner biographer and longtime friend of Ole Miss and the Faulkner Conference, Joseph Blotner, to sponsor the two panels on this year's program. Gifts from the William Faulkner Society and the *Faulkner Journal*, as well as donations in memory of John W. Hunt, Faulkner scholar and emeritus professor literature at Lehigh University, have been made to support the William Faulkner Society Fellows at this year's conference. A special gift has been made by longtime conference registrant Greg Perkins. In addition to those mentioned above, we wish to thank Square Books, Southside Gallery, the City of Oxford, and the Oxford Convention and Visitors Bureau. Also, we thank the family of Phyllis Cerf for use of her photograph of Faulkner to illustrate this year's conference materials.

Faulkner and Formalism: Returns of the Text
FAULKNER AND YOKNAPATAWPHA
2008

Flags in the Dust and the Birth of a Poetics

Arthur F. Kinney

One of the most memorable moments for us in the life of William Faulkner—memorable for what it did, memorable that it even happened—was that time in November 1927 when he sat down for weeks in a room in New York with his literary agent and friend Ben Wasson to write *The Sound and the Fury* while, next to him, Wasson was truncating Faulkner's third novel, *Flags in the Dust*, which would be retitled *Sartoris*. That there is an important lesson represented by this unlikely combination of tasks is what I propose became the secret of Faulkner's success.

Faulkner must have been as surprised as we are. He wrote the publisher Horace Liveright on Sunday, 16 October, "At last and certainly, as El Orens' sheik said, I have written THE book, of which those other things [*Soldiers' Pay* and *Mosquitoes*] were but foals. I believe it is the damdest best book you'll look at this year, and any other publisher. It goes forward to you by mail Monday." Full of the possibilities for *Flags in the Dust*, he continued, "I am enclosing a few suggestions for the printer: will you look over them and, if possible, smooth the printer's fur, cajole him, some way. He's been punctuating my stuff to death; giving me gratis quotation marks and premiums of commas that I dont need. I dont think that even the bird who named 'Soldiers' Pay' can improve on my title. . . . I also have an idea for a jacket. I will paint it and send it up for your approval soon."[1]

It was autumn and Faulkner went hunting only to find Liveright's rejection of the novel on his return the last day of November. "It is with sorrow in my heart that I write to tell you that three of us have read *Flags in the Dust* and don't believe that Boni and Liveright should publish it." He went on: "Furthermore, as a firm deeply interested in your work, we don't believe that you should offer it for publication. Soldier's [sic] Pay was a very fine book and should have done better. Then Mosquitoes wasn't quite as good, showed little development in your spiritual growth and I think none in your art of writing. Now comes Flags in the Dust and we're frankly very much disappointed by it. It is diffuse and non-integral with neither very much plot development nor character development. . . . The story really doesn't get anywhere and

3

has a thousand loose ends. If the book had plot and structure, we might suggest shortening and revision but it is so diffuse that I don't think that would be any use."[2]

Their judgment was, even in a shortened version, generally the judgment of most literary critics since then. But Faulkner was adamant. Two years later he could still recall his reaction: "I was shocked: my first emotion was blind protest, then I became objective for an instant, like a parent who is told that its child is a thief or an idiot or a leper; for a dreadful moment I contemplated it with consternation and despair, then like the parent I hid my own eyes in the fury of denial." He asked for the manuscript back and sent it out again, this time to Harcourt, Brace. "I still believe," he vowed, "it is the book which will make my name for me as a writer."[3]

So Faulkner left Oxford, Mississippi, and went north to see Ben and two old Southern writers and friends, Bill Spratling and Stark Young. For the next weeks, he stayed with Lyle Saxon, aged thirty-seven, another writer from the South, in this case New Orleans, in his apartment over a bookstore on Christopher Street near Sixth Avenue in New York City. He joined Wasson daily, but he stoutly refused to have anything to do with the revision of a book he had worked on so carefully all the previous summer. He argued with Wasson: "I said, 'A cabbage has grown, matured. You look at that cabbage; it is not symmetrical'; you say, 'I will trim this cabbage off and make it art; I will make it resemble a peacock or a pagoda or 3 doughnuts.' 'Very good,' I say; 'you do that, then the cabbage will be dead.'" "'Then we'll make some kraut out of it,' he said. 'The same amount of sour kraut will feed twice as many people as cabbage.' A day or so later he came to me and showed me the mss. 'The trouble is,' he said, 'that you had about 6 books in here. You were trying to write them all at once.' He showed me what he meant, what he had done, and I realized for the first time that I had done better than I knew."

Wasson went ahead, cutting Faulkner's work by 25 percent. As Joseph Blotner recounts in his biography of Faulkner,

> He deleted a long passage of Narcissa's reflections about Bayard as a boy and shortened Bayard's balloon ascent. He did the same thing with other passages in which Narcissa conveyed background material. Several scenes involving Byron Snopes, Virgil Beard, and Mrs. Beard were cut. Long passages were also deleted in which Faulkner had described Byron's twin torments: his anonymous lust for Narcissa and Virgil's blackmail. His final flight from Jefferson to Frenchman's Bend disappeared, as did the brief appearances of I. O. Snopes and his son, Clarence; Horace's role was reduced; his one-time desire to become an Episcopalian minister, his sense of doom, his affair with Belle, a

brief affair with her sister Joan, his prior involvements, his incestuous feelings toward [his sister] Narcissa—all these were removed or drastically cut.[4]

We do not know what role, if any, Faulkner played in these revisions, although he did allow the shortened novel to go forward to Harcourt under a title not initially his own. On its publication, *Sartoris* shared, to some extent, the negative response of Liveright. In the *New York Herald Tribune* Herschel Brickell commented on Faulkner's use of detail to build "uncanny lifelikeness," but he, too, found "certain structural defects" and "a style that at times is overmannered and overdecorated,"[5] while an anonymous reviewer for the *New York Times* found the novel "a work of uneven texture, confused sentiment and loose articulation."[6]

Such assessments were ignorant of the fact that Faulkner had worked tirelessly on *Flags* throughout the summer and early fall of 1927, completing a 596-page typescript on 29 September. For him it was neither haphazard nor digressive. "I wrote *Soldiers' Pay* and *Mosquitoes*," he would say, "for the sake of writing because it was fun. But I found out after that not only each book had to have a design but the whole output or sum of an artist's work had to have a design."[7] One design that set *Flags* apart, and Faulkner on a new course, was that it took place in Yoknapatawpha County, a fictional version of the land he knew best. This was part of his plan long before Sherwood Anderson told him to write about his own little postage stamp of the world. In the *Mississippian* for 17 March 1922, he wrote, "Some one has said—a Frenchman, probably, they have said everything—that art is preeminently provincial: i.e., it comes directly from a certain age and a certain locality. This is a very profound statement; for Lear and Hamlet and All's Well could never have been written anywhere save in England during Elizabeth's reign . . . nor could Madame Bovary have been written in any place other than the Rhone valley in the nineteenth century; and just as Balzac is nineteenth century Paris."[8] This seems to have been a fixation even years before *Flags*. "The beauty—spiritual and physical—of the South lies in the fact that God has done so much for it and man so little. I have this for which to thank whatever gods may be: that having fixed my roots in his soil all contact, saving by the printed word, with contemporary poets is impossible," he wrote in the *Double Dealer* in 1925 while living in New Orleans and went on to praise A. E. Housman in such terms as one who "discover[ed] . . . beauty of being of the soil like a tree."[9] This sense of place was given poetic form by Honoré de Balzac's *Comédie humaine*, a panoramic series of novels which resembles Faulkner's Yoknapatawpha novels "in its overall shape and organizational design"— the word Faulkner used—according to Michael Kreiswirth. "Faulkner's imaginative world, like Balzac's . . . , is fundamentally an interlocking structure, where narratives overlap, characters reappear, and there is substantial cross-referencing between texts."[10] This was clearly Faulkner's fundamental design for *Flags in the Dust*, although Liveright never noticed it.

Like Balzac, Faulkner relishes rich detail—Balzac was known even to add new ones in printer's galleys with his amendments and corrections, because, for him, such detail was not merely ornamental but intensely metaphoric: singly or in constellation, objects, circumstances, and thoughts took on symbolic meanings that constituted the parts of a designed whole.[11] As an American Balzac, Faulkner fills *Flags in the Dust* with detailed descriptions of a Thanksgiving dinner: "with a roast turkey and a cured ham and a dish of quail and another of squirrel, and a baked 'possum in a bed of sweet potatoes; and Irish potatoes and sweet potatoes, and squash and pickled beets, and rice and hominy, and hot biscuit and beaten biscuit and long thin sticks of cornbread, and strawberry and pear preserves, and quince and apple jelly, and blackberry jam and stewed cranberries."[12] This establishment of aristocratic tradition and splendor is enriched by Bayard's Christmas dinner in a sharecropper's cabin: "The woman filled the cup from the coffee pot set among the embers, and she uncovered an iron skillet and forked a thick slab of sizzling meat onto his plate, and raked a grayish object from the ashes and dusted it off and put that too on his plate. Bayard ate his side meat and hoecake and drank the thin, tasteless liquid" (392).

Such passages are meant to be paired, to show the disparity of social and economic class, of race, but they are also the theater of Sartoris operations—what they have to live in, their circumstances seen as opportunities, as limitations, as boundaries. "A substantial portion of the novel," Kreiswirth writes, "seems directed solely toward the accurate rendering of the community's customs and rituals. There are vivid descriptions of tea parties and possum hunts, of tennis matches and the rites of molasses making, of piano recitals and catfish angling."[13] It is decidedly a Balzacian poetics. *Flags in the Dust* records, employs, and makes figural "the region's geographical and architectural variety. Faulkner portrays the fertile 'upland country' of 'gums and locusts and massed vines' which leads to the 'good broad fields' of Bayard Sartoris's valley (*FD*, page 9), as well as the less picturesque parts of the county, where 'waist high jimson weeds' and 'ragged ill-tended fields' surround small 'weathered' houses and 'gaunt' grey barns (*FD*, pages 122–23). The depiction of Hub's dilapidated farm, where Suratt takes Bayard after his fall from the stallion, runs for several pages."[14]

Not only the country but the town is given in striking images.

One street, for example, "bordered by negro stores of one story and shaded by metal awnings," contains "W. C. BEARDS MILL" . . . ; another, across the square, houses the Beard Hotel, "a rectangular frame building with a double veranda," and in the square itself, near the Sartoris bank and the porticoed courthouse with its monument of the Confederate soldier, stands Deacon's "half grocery and confectionary, and half restaurant," with its private room ("or rather a large disused closet") where reliable customers can surreptitiously concoct and imbibe toddies. . . . Typical Jeffersonian sights and sounds are presented with similar care, and much space is devoted to describing such significant features of the local environment as "a blind negro beggar with a guitar and a wire frame holding a mouthorgan to his lips" playing "a plaintive reiteration of rich monotonous chords"; the drowsing "city fathers" dressed in "the grey of Jackson and Beauregard and Johnston" . . . ; and the loafing young men, "pitching dollars or tossing baseballs back and forth or lying on the grass until the young girls in their little colored dresses and cheap nostalgic perfume came trooping down town through the late afternoon to the drug store."[15]

Such descriptions are meant not just for color; they are meant to characterize the county and the town as characters in their own right: all together they absorb the Falkner family on which the Sartorises are based: Dr. Ashford Little transcribed into young Dr. Alford; Stark Young's father, Dr. A. A. Young, transposed into Doc Lucius Quintus Peabody; the Faulkner family retainer Ned Barnett a model for Simon, and—perhaps—Mammy Callie Barr here translated into Elnora. In addition, the novel became a container for earlier printed works that Faulkner found appropriate for reconstruction: Hugh Wiley's *The Wildcat*, a racist novel about the European adventures of a black draftee of World War I, the basis for Caspey's biography, and James Warner Bellah's "Blood," which appeared in the *Saturday Evening Post* during the composition of *Flags* and tells of an aerial battle between twins, the description of which is very close to young John Sartoris's death in Faulkner's novel.

Like Balzac, too, Faulkner deliberately enfolded structural principles into his presentation of luxuriant metaphorical detail. The novel opens with Old Man Falls bringing back to Jefferson a Civil War battle of the past, as if he returned a long-dead veteran to their shared present time; and this introduces one structural design—the homecomings of Young Bayard, which Simon knows of (44), of Caspey (63), and of Horace (190), each return from war taking on its own analogical coloration and together establishing three social classes of Jefferson and Yoknapatawpha. The slow accumulation of detail that first presents members of the Sartoris household (first white, then black in town and, at the plantation home, white, and then by black), followed by the Benbow household in its brick Tudor house (symbolic of an aspiring middle class), then moving from the countryside to the town and on to the town square—a structural organization that is deliberate and telling. The remainder of the novel largely keeps replaying these settings until, near the end, it deliberately eliminates all of them for the MacCallum cabin and the sharecroppers' house. There is yet a third structural plan—what Faulkner would have thought of as his design for *Flags*—in various incidents that are meant to resonate backwards and forward in the novel. One instance is the wild stallion, which Bayard jumps on and nearly kills a child and seriously injures himself. Here the metaphoric value is told us: both stallion and Bayard are "uncontrolled, splendidly uncontrollable" (140), each the representative of the other. Bayard's escapade with the horse is developed into his escapades with the car: "The car was long and low and gray; the four-cylinder engine had sixteen valves and eight sparkplugs, and the people had guaranteed that it would run eighty miles an hour, although there was a strip of paper pasted to the windshield, asking him in red letters not to do so for the first five hundred miles" (81). The auto in turn attracts Aunt Jenny (81–82), threatens Isom (92), and becomes dangerous when Bayard avoids a wagon (124), "filled with negro women asleep in chairs" (124), and shortly after "he swerved and whipped past [a wagon and mules] with not an inch to spare, so close that the yelling negro in the wagon could see the lipless and savage derision of his teeth" (126). Young Bayard's repeated attempts at self-destruction—either in emulation of the Sartoris male myth and his twin, John, or in an attempt to end his failure to undergo brave and reckless exploits—always end in Bayard's managing to save himself. This time, narrowly missing the wagon, we are told, "he felt savage and ashamed" (126), and this twin reaction—to risk danger and to feel shame—will continue in his relationship with Narcissa, Jenny, and Old Bayard and end, as would seem the foregone conclusion of this repeated and escalating thread, with Old Bayard's death and Young Bayard's self-exile. The automobile is surely a means of characterizing Young Bayard, but the others as well: Aunt Jenny, Narcissa, Isom, Simon, and Old Bayard. As a structural thread tying together what might appear to be discrete episodes, it weaves the kind of patterned novel Faulkner was attempting, by which certain motifs—objects, persons, circumstances that constitute life—constitute realistic fiction as well.

All of this tapestry-like fiction is also subjected to, and unified structurally by, history, as Frederick R. Karl has noted:

The historical moment is clouded considerably by the interpenetration of names. . . . Faulkner was able to achieve that doubling and overlapping of parents, children, and grandchildren which fulfill his sense of history as a sequence of interwoven events. Old Bayard's father, John, has acted bravely, fighting in the Mexican War, then in the war between the states, eventually losing his command, though regrouping his forces when he could fight a guerrilla war against Grant (around Vicksburg). . . . But this Bayard is foolhardy rather than simply brave. In this older generation, Bayard Sartoris throws his life away [as young Bayard will eventually do] trying to get hold of some anchovies in the Union camp, where he is shot by an irate cook hiding behind a table. . . . [John] uses his power for white supremacy, harasses and even murders carpetbaggers, and makes certain that Negroes lose the vote. He is part of that movement to roll back Reconstruction, such as it was, and to pave the way for the Klan in its later, racist years. . . . John Sartoris is not just a wild young man—he is a power-hungry, politically obsessed individual whose will is law. . . . This latter John, the grandson of a John and the son of a Bayard, has twin sons, and names them Bayard and John. John, like his great-uncle, Bayard, is killed in the war—only now the war has passed on to World War I, from the Mexican struggle which engaged old John, to the Civil War which had engaged both Bayard and John, and killed Bayard, to the Spanish-American conflict, from whose effects another John has died. When old Bayard dies of a heart attack during a car crash brought on by young Bayard, only the latter survives, the sole Sartoris for the moment. Deaths pass in and out of each other, the clan almost a killing field.[16]

The wide sweep of history, when combined with the limited focus on specific moments and events, making them the significant residue and emphasizing their importance by threading them together, is also Balzacian.

It should be clear by now that what Liveright and Harcourt Brace did not comprehend was not Faulkner's material—he had touched on much of that before in *Soldiers' Pay*—but his fundamentally Balzacian poetics, which he had so carefully "designed." But that may be in part because it was compounded with Faulkner's own techniques. For one thing, he began in medias res, without any explanation:

Old man Falls roared: "Cunnel was settin' thar in a cheer, his sock feet propped on the po'ch railin', smokin' this hyer very pipe. Old Louvinia was settin' on the steps, shellin' a bowl of peas for supper. And a feller was glad to git even peas sometimes, in them days. And you was settin' back agin' the post. They wa'nt nobody else thar 'cep' yo' aunt, the one 'fo' Miss Jenny come. Cunnel had sont them two gals to Memphis to yo' gran'pappy when he fust went away. You was 'bout half-grown, I reckon. How old was you then, Bayard?"

"Fourteen," old Bayard answered.

"Hey?"

"Fourteen," Bayard shouted. "Do I have to tell you that every time you tell me this damn story?"

"And thar you all was a-settin'," old man Falls continued, unruffled, "when they turned in at the gate and come trottin' up the carriage drive."

"Old Louvinia drapped the bowl of peas and let out one squawk, but Cunnel set her up and tole her to run and git his boots and pistols and have 'em ready at the back do', and you lit out fer the barn to saddle that stallion. And when them Yankees rid up and stopped—they stopped right whar that flower bed is now—thar wa'nt nobody on the po'ch but Cunnel, a-settin' thar like he never even heard tell of no Yankees.'" (3–4)

When we return to this opening after reading the novel, we can see how carefully Faulkner makes it do a great deal of work. Old Man Falls is recounting an escapade of the foolhardy Colonel John as if it were a heroic feat, embarrassing his son who has failed to fight a war, who has failed to be a folk hero in any way. Falls incorporates young Bayard into his audience in a moment of personal and local history now turned into legend that excludes him. But what he says is not taken as history or legend, although it uses the present to keep alive the past in order to preserve it for the future, time interrupting and congealing. What he tells, as Bayard calls it, is "this damn story." The account is as true or false as Falls's perspective and memory. What Faulkner meant to convey, even at the outset, is that all we know is what we perceive, clouded by time and reordered by memory, and that is wholly dependent on our conceptual point of view. The legendary account of the Carolina Bayard's coffee raid on a Yankee encampment is called "a hair-brained prank of two heedless and reckless boys wild with their own youth," but when Aunt Jenny recalls the same incident, it has become "a gallant and finely tragical focal-point to which the history of the race had been raised from out the old miasmic swamps of spiritual sloth by two angels valiantly and glamorously fallen and strayed, altering the course of human events and purging the souls of men" (14). "As she grew older," Faulkner's narrative voice, interrupting her, tells us, "the tale itself grew richer and richer, taking on a mellow splendor like wine" (14).

Flags in the Dust, then, is to be essentially a compendium of stories, some more accurate than others. The opening of the novel prepares us for the ambiguity of its closing: is Bayard's death as a test pilot to determine the dangers on behalf of others "a hair-brained prank," or something valiant and glamorous, something "reckless" and selfish, as the raid for coffee was, or something potentially "altering the course of human events"? At a certain level, acknowledging the alternatives and their cross-purposes is a fundamental theme of the novel, and the responsibility of reading it. We will know enough to recognize Caspey's bragging and exaggerations: "Black regiments kilt mo' Germans dan all de white armies put together, let 'lone unloadin' steamboats all day long fer a dollar a day"; but what are we to make of the second observation that is demonstrably true? Where does credibility with Caspey begin and end? When Narcissa and Aunt Sally dispute whether John or his twin, Bayard, jumped off the water tank or went up in the balloon so as not to disappoint those who had come to the show—both of them, after all, were eye witnesses to the same event—whom are we to believe? One technique Faulkner added to Balzac was to filter nearly all of *Flags in the Dust* through individual points of view, through multiple narration, forcing his readers to judge not only the narration, but the narrator. Balzac had not acknowledged that history and historical accounts were personally and partially relayed, turned into stories and even legends. The problem becomes even more complicated when Faulkner seems to validate Aunt Jenny's romantic retelling by his own commentary using her lexicon: Jeb Stuart and Carolina Bayard, he writes, were "two flaming stars garlanded with Fame's burgeoning laurel and the myrtle and roses of Death, incalculable and sudden as meteors in General Pope's troubled military sky, thrusting upon him like an unwilling garment that notoriety which his skill as a soldier could never have won him" (15).

Flags in the Dust starts out, then, by pointing out the insufficiency and unreliability of language itself in a novel that relies entirely on words and on telling. This can be a breathtaking observation, but one that accords nicely with Liveright's objection that *Flags in the Dust* has too many different accounts and too many loose ends. How could any honest novelist, Faulkner might respond, have an authentic work that did otherwise? Indeed, his multiple incidents with Bayard's car have distinct parallels with Bayard's need and inability to verbalize his twin brother's death. At many points, since it is the main criterion for judging the Sartorises as well as Bayard, he confronts this very problem, conscious that it is an act of storytelling for himself and for others. For each time he is relegated to storytelling to make sense of potentially senseless events, as in the following episode:

"He was drunk," young Bayard answered harshly. "Or a fool. I tried to keep him from going up there, on that damn Camel. You couldn't see your hand, that morning. Air all full of hunks of cloud and any fool could a known that on their side it'd be full of Fokkers that could reach twenty-five thousand, and him on a damn Camel. But he was hell-bent on going up there, damn near to Lille. I couldn't keep him from it. He shot at me," young Bayard said. "I tried to head him off and drive him back, but he gave me a burst. He was already high as he could get, but they must have been five thousand feet above us when they spotted us. They flew all over him. Hemmed him up like a damn calf in a pen while one of them sat right on his tail until he took fire and jumped. Then they streaked for home." (46)

It is, in a sense, a forced confession, explaining to his family not only why and how John died but why and how Bayard—given the Sartoris family tradition of dying risky and glamorous deaths—is still alive. It is significant that in this rendition Bayard attempted to stop his brother, but his brother was outmanned and outflanked; once in the air, glamour and risk were lost in unfair competition.

But John's death becomes the obsession that haunts Bayard. Drinking alone in town with his childhood buddy Rafe MacCallum, the emphasis of the story changes. Now we learn from Bayard that John "'never could learn to fly properly'" (134). In his sharply abridged version to Rafe, "'He shot at me'" becomes "'he gave me a burst. Right across any nose'" (135). This was not an accidental shot; it sounds more like deliberate twinship in deliberate deaths. But there is a striking absence of detail with Rafe, something Bayard may not wish to share. Such details come racing forth in the story he tells to his wife, Narcissa, neither a Sartoris nor a man:

"He was zig-zagging: that was the reason I couldn't get on the Hun [that is, John prevented Bayard from aiding him]. Every time I got my sights on him, John'd barge in the way again. Then he quit zig-zagging. Soon as I saw him side-slip I knew it was all over. Then I saw the flame streaming out along his wing, and he was looking back at me. The Hun stopped shooting then, and all of us just lay there for a while. [This account differs from that given his family where John was surrounded by the enemy shooting at him.] I couldn't tell what John was up to until I saw him swing his legs outside. Then he thumbed his nose at me like he always was doing and flipped his hand at the Hun and kicked his machine out of the way and jumped. He jumped feet first. You cant fall far feet first, you know, and so pretty soon he sprawled out flat. There was a bunch of cloud right under us by that time, and he smacked on it right on his belly, like what we used to call gut-busters in swimming. But I never could pick him up below the cloud. I know I was below it before he could have come out, because after I was down there his machine came diving out right at me, burning good. I pulled away from it, but the damn thing did a split-turn and rushed at me again, and I had to dodge. And so I never could pick him up when he came out of the cloud. I went down fast, until I knew I was below him, then I looked again. But I couldn't find him, and I thought maybe I hadn't gone low enough, so I dived again. But I couldn't pick him up. Then they started shooting at me from the ground——" (280–81)

Thumbing his nose at Bayard, John thought this a joke, or at least the reckless and glamorous fulfillment of the Sartoris legend that Bayard did not yet enjoy; the shot John fired at Bayard is gone now. The damaged plane is a dangerous risk of death that Bayard avoids; the first avoidance will come later on the wild stallion and, after that, in the speeding car.

The last time Bayard recalls the incident he likens it to his own biography as he lies restless at night in the MacCallum cabin:

> Perhaps he was dead, and he recalled that morning, relived it again with strained and intense attention from the time he had seen the first tracer smoke, until from his steep side-slip he watched the flame burst like the gay flapping of an orange pennon from John's Camel and saw his brother's familiar gesture and the sudden awkward sprawl of his plunging body as it lost equilibrium in midair; relived it again as you might run over a printed tale [a telling simile for Faulkner], trying to remember, feel, a bullet going into his body or head that might have slain him at the same instant. That would account for it, would explain so much: that he too was dead and this was hell, through which he moved forever and ever with an illusion of quickness, seeking his brother who in turn was somewhere seeking him, never the two to meet. He turned onto his back again; the shucks whispered beneath him with dry derision. (368–39)

The sense of derision and of death are Bayard's, but for us to understand what he deems hell can handily account for that wealth of detail of time and place in which his story and his slow recognition of its significance has its meaning, to him and to his readers. Rather than a loose end, Bayard's determination to become a test pilot in a dangerous plane is what pulls together the narrative that Liveright found so confusing. Alongside this self-revelation, others—such as the confessional thoughts and letters of Horace Benbow and the crude letters and thoughts of Byron Snopes—take their compositional place, including the need for Old Man Falls to find stature alongside Colonel Sartoris, and Aunt Jenny's need to remember her valse with Jeb Stuart. Through such stories, they find their own senses of being.

Memory may change details or emphases. "Memory believes before knowing remembers," Faulkner would write in *Light in August* just two years later.[17] That is, memory of the past—which we depend on for identification and understanding—grows out of belief aided by, but not

conquered by, knowledge. This gives point to the many limited narrative perspectives we can find in a single Faulkner novel, another major
departure from Balzac. At the same, time, though, "memory is always
repetition even when it revises what it repeats," David Minter tells us in a
study of Faulkner.[18] Summarizing *The Use and Abuse of History*, Minter
writes that "Nietzsche distinguishes among three modes of memory: an
antiquarian mode that glories in the past's particularities, sometimes for
the purpose of escape and sometimes for the purpose of locating origins
or making connections, and thus satisfying our need to feel historically
rooted; a *monumental* mode that turns to the past searching for examples
of heroic action that can instruct and inspire heroic action in the present;
and a *critical* mode that views the past as a burden and therefore seeks
to judge it or reject it in order to justify casting it off in the name of being
free to move on."[19] We do not know if Faulkner ever read Nietzsche, but
if Aunt Jenny and a whole line of Sartorises adopt the antiquarian mode,
Bayard must learn to work his way through the monumental in order to
arrive at a resolution through the critical mode. His very choices need the
vast circumstantial details of *Flags in the Dust* if we hope to understand
his acknowledged position and judge his reactions and the reactions (and
stories) of those around him. Minter sees in the great novels of Faulkner
"both fidelity and distortion," for he would portray in his various narrative perspectives, his storytellers, "minds caught up in disremembering
and reconstructing. Musing over life, these minds discard and reclaim,
displace and recreate."[20]

A sequential plot, then—what Liveright was looking for—was not
what Faulkner ever intended to write; *Flags in the Dust* deals with discrete events narrated by individuals who often differ in what they recall,
what in *Absalom, Absalom!* he would call the "rag-tag and bob-ends"
of old tales.[21] *Flags* therefore is constructed episodically, out of narrative building blocks; or, as Kevin Railey told this conference a few years
ago, "a series of snapshots, a frieze on which figures stand next to one
another, collectively representing a distinct moment in history."[22] "*Flags
in the Dust* is divided into numerous sections and subsections," Kreiswirth reminds us, "and there is the same abrupt cutting from scene to
scene and incident to incident with little regard for transition or narrative
summation" (121). What Faulkner strives for, however, is not discrete,
stand-alone episodes but analogous episodes that speak to each other
and accumulate into meaning and significance. We have already noted
this in the three scenes of homecoming, with the scenes of an apparently
death-wishing Bayard on the wild stallion, in the car, testing a dangerous
new biplane. We can place people by comparing the antebellum home of
Sartoris (11–12, 13) with the Tudor brick house of the Benbows (177–79)

with the cabin of black sharecroppers (323). Each one is partly defined by the other two. Bayard's streaks of wildness prepare us for the passionate responses of the generally calm Narcissa when she finds one of Byron's letters, and they prepare us for Horace's suddenly passionate affairs with Belle and with Joan. Old Man Falls's narrative introduces Aunt Jenny's. Old Bayard's "ceremonial" opening of the Sartoris chest of treasured family relics (93–96) remeasures his reverence when we place it alongside Young Bayard's fiery destruction of his twin brother's personal possessions (240), the "frogged and braided coat of Confederate grey" against a photograph of a Princeton eating club. Such acts, which employ an early kind of filmic montage when they are connected in the reader's engaged mind, differ widely from the narrative revelations to which Liveright was accustomed. "By cutting back and forth [among the incidents]," Karl writes, "Faulkner indicates a greater weight and gravity than they [would otherwise] achieve" (278).

This art of montage is reinforced not only by an invitation to correlative episodes that once appeared discrete, but the striking juxtapositions that lead us to thinking of them. Thus Old Bayard does not hesitate to place "a gown of sprigged muslin scented faintly of lavender and evocative of old formal minuets and drifting honeysuckle among steady candle flames" into the chest with the Confederate uniform and "a huge, brassbound Bible" (96). Faulkner deliberately puts "the essence of spring" (397) alongside young Bayard's suicidal death and Aunt Jenny's visit to the Sartoris graves. "In a small alcove" of the speakeasy where Bayard agrees to test the bi-plane, "Harry Mitchell sat" (416), and as Bayard passes him on the way out "he saw that the diamond was missing from Harry's tie" (416): two outcasts, two victims. Aunt Jenny recalls Colonel John's attempt to capture anchovies just before we meet Elnora, his mulatto bastard by Euphony, who

> stood barelegged in the center of the kitchen floor and soused her mop into the pail and thumped it on the floor again [singing]:
> "Sinner riz fum de moaner's bench,
> Sinner jump to de penance bench;
> When de preacher ax'im whut de reason why,
> Says 'Preacher got de women jes de same ez I'" (25).

We know whom she may be thinking of. Other juxtapositions are more obvious, as if to remind us of Faulkner's design: the three visitors who come to Narcissa's home the same night (164–65); the Mitchell tennis game next to the Mitchell daughter's recital, which the mother joins in (196–219); the futile attempt at farming by Young Bayard next to his car accident (231–32). Nothing seems to happen, but thinking makes it so: external and social moments are indivisible from internal and psychological ones. Juxtapositions alert us to the possibility of analogies, call into action our own memories, making our own reading of past pages the present reading of related ones.

In a brilliant aperçu, Frederick R. Karl calls *Flags in the Dust* "an act of retrieval."[23] The past keeps intruding on the present—in the thoughts of the Sartorises, in the pattern of our readings. This is because the present is not only the heir to the past; the present must learn to embody the past as a part of itself. Faulkner tells us this metaphorically by the intrusion of Colonel John in the thoughts and actions of Simon: "Quite often these days Isom could hear his grandfather talking to John Sartoris as he labored about the stable or the flower beds or the lawn, mumbling away to that arrogant ghost which dominated the house and its occupants and the whole scene itself across which the railroad he had built ran punily with distance but distinct, as though it were a stage set for the diversions of him whose stubborn dream, flouting him so deviously and cunningly while the dream was impure, had shaped itself fine and clear now that the dreamer was purged of the grossness of pride with that of flesh" (120). The novel opens with Colonel John's ghostly presence as well: "As usual old man Falls brought John Sartoris into the room with him" (5). But young John's ghost displaces him, becoming even more prominent, not only to Young Bayard in his progressive recountings of his twin's death, but also to Aunt Sally and Narcissa (72–73), to Rafe MacCallum (132), to Mandy (381), and to Buddy MacCallum (366–67). At the novel's end both ghosts join: "the dusk was peopled with ghosts of glamorous and old disastrous things. And if they were just glamorous enough, there would be a Sartoris in them, and then they were sure to be disastrous" (432). Faulkner "augmented the technical resources of the novelist by showing how unnecessary it is to tell a story covering several generations by the linear method," Willard Thorp alone saw of the truncated earlier version. "*Sartoris* has an extraordinary depth because events widely separated in time, but spiritually akin, are made to seem simultaneous."[24] This was the new poetics of Faulkner: simultaneity displacing linearity. This, too, is part of the act of retrieval.

Yet we do not, cannot retrieve everything. Karl saw this too: *Flags in the Dust*, he contends, is "the first of [Faulkner's] novels to work through concealment, withdrawal, withholding, silences" (304–5). Faulkner is silent on Colonel John during Reconstruction, silent on Elnora's lineage, and relatively silent on Young Bayard's first marriage to Caroline, and Harry's and Horace's marriage to Belle Mitchell. Characters such as Old Man Falls and Caspey can disappear on us. Most strikingly, perhaps, key scenes, what might dominate a novel by anyone else in the period, are omitted: the courtship of Narcissa by Bayard, his car accident, the death of Old Bayard and how Jefferson—and the MacCallums—found out about it and what they thought about it, the death of young Bayard. Such absences are profound. All we have are gravestones. One of Faulkner's first French supporters, Jean-Paul Sartre, saw this even with *Sartoris*: "Acts are the essential element of the novel. . . . But Faulkner does not name them, does not ever speak of them and, consequently, suggests that they are ineffable, beyond language. He will only show their results: an old man dead in his chair, an auto overturned in the river and two feet which appear above the water. Motionless and brutal, as solid and compact as the Act is fleeting, these results appear and unfold definitive, inexplicable, in the midst of the fine, dense outpour of everyday gestures."[25] Thus for Sartre, perhaps the greatest cause of mystification is what we finally make of Bayard's suicide: is he heroic? charitable? desperate? escapist? mocking?

It is time now to return to where we began: with Ben Wasson cutting *Flags in the Dust* and Faulkner beside him writing *The Sound and the Fury*, and with what is seen as an early and somewhat failed work and a classic work that sprang from nowhere. We should now see how closely related the two works are, as closely related as the two men sitting beside each other. Like *Flags in the Dust*, *The Sound and the Fury* is set in Jefferson and is a discontinuous account of the Compson family, two families studied in their decline. Like *Flags in the Dust*, *The Sound and the Fury* talks about a family's self-destruction, obsession with the past, the failure of parents, and (with Horace and Narcissa, Quentin and Caddy) notions of incest as a way of binding up a disintegrating family. What may appear jumbled—at least in the Benjy section—is structured by the days of Easter weekend, just as *Flags in the Dust* follows through the seasons of one year, from planting time to Christmas. Both novels begin abruptly, in medias res: surely Benjy's allusions and observations are no easier to follow than the first scene of *Flags* but, like *Flags*, Faulkner manages to introduce, from the call of "caddy" onward, most of the major themes of the work to follow. There are multiple narrators. This too is a novel of storytelling, where there is also an absent center: John never appears in the present of *Flags* as Caddy never appears in the present of *The Sound and the Fury*. Horace seems to anticipate Quentin; as Bayard felt helpless and partial without his twin brother, so Benjy and Quentin feel helpless and partial without Caddy. Like Horace, Benjy and Quentin and Jason are all three narcissistic; like Bayard, Quentin can appear homosocial and incestuous, and necrophiliac; Bayard's longing to join John is comparable to Quentin's thoughts of Little Sister Death. Just as Young John's absence causes an unbridgeable void, so does Caddy's departure. In both novels, the external family circumstances give rise to internal dynamics. Both novels seem, at a distance, long journeys to the cemetery, and both novels all but end there: Aunt Jenny's visits to the Sartoris graves is her penultimate appearance, and Benjy's trip to see the graves of his ancestors is cut short by Luster's devilment and Jason's reprimand.

But these are somewhat surface parallels. What we can now also appreciate is that Faulkner's deliberate and revolutionary poetics produced both novels. The overlapping Johns and Bayards become the overlapping Quentins and Jasons. The novel is not at the start chronological nor sequential, but built through narrative perspectives—through recounting stories as they are individually perceived—and presented as narrative building blocks of discrete moments alternating with discrete memories. Faulkner seeks development not through causation but through analogies and juxtapositions. By returning again and again in the monologues of Benjy, Quentin, and Jason to the suffering of a diminished aristocracy, the demise of the family fortune, and the loss of Caddy (and Quentin IV), even though emphases change, such recurrences provide a sense of simultaneity to the three narrators' accounts, although they are not narrated simultaneously. One narrator, in fact, has been dead for some time. The novel abounds in analogies, such as the brothers' failure to find customary sexual relationships. Quentin's suicide precedes Jason's self-destructive attempts to extort Quentin IV for her money and Earl Triplett in not fulfilling his responsibilities at the hardware store. Juxtapositions are most frequent in Benjy's section where key words or events trigger his associative mind. But Quentin also relates Dalton Ames to Spoade, Caddy to the little Italian girl. The past incessantly interrupts the consciousnesses of Benjy, Quentin, and Jason while Dilsey puts her suffering present alongside the blessedness of eternity, allowing her to endure. Major events are missing, too, as in *Flags in the Dust*, chief among them Benjy's emasculation and Quentin's suicide. Finally, the failure of *Flags in the Dust* to be unambiguously conclusive is repeated in *The Sound and the Fury*, where it is not clear that Bayard's death can be countermanded by naming Narcissa's and his child Benbow Sartoris rather than John or Bayard. It is not clear that Jason can overcome the loss of Quentin IV's money or who might care for Benjy following Dilsey's death.

Faulkner's latest biographer, Jay Parini, writes that "with *The Sound and the Fury*, Faulkner made a startling breakthrough, not only for himself. This was something new in American fiction, something strange, complex and disruptive, a work that attempted to articulate grief and loss while acknowledging, at every turn, the impossibility of recovery, the limits of articulation, as well as the pleasures afforded by repetition and incomplete reconstruction, the pleasures of the text itself."[26] We know now, if Liveright did not know then, that he could just as well have been talking about *Flags in the Dust*.

NOTES

1. *Selected Letters of William Faulkner*, ed. Joseph Blotner (New York: Random House, 1977), 38.

2. Joseph Blotner, *Faulkner: A Biography*, 1-vol. ed. (New York: Vintage Books, 1991), 205–6. The following account is from Blotner, 206–7.

3. This account is also from Blotner, 206.

4. Ibid., 222–23.

5. Herschel Brickell, *New York Herald Tribune*, 24 February 1929, Section 9, 5; reprinted in *Critical Essays on William Faulkner: The Sartoris Family*, ed. Arthur F. Kinney (Boston: G. K. Hall and Company, 1985), 124, 123.

6. Unsigned, *New York Times*, 2 March 1929, Book Review Section 8, 9, col. 1; reprinted Kinney, 125.

7. Martin Kreiswirth, *William Faulkner: The Making of a Novelist* (Athens: University of Georgia Press, 1983), 105.

8. *William Faulkner: Early Prose and Poetry*, ed. Carvel Collins (London: Jonathan Cape, 1963), 86; *Mississippian*, 3 February 1922, 5.

9. *Early Prose and Poetry*, 116–17; *Double Dealer* 7 (April 1925), 129–31.

10. Kreiswirth, 106.

11. For an independent commentary on Faulkner and Balzac, see Arthur F. Kinney, *Faulkner's Narrative Poetics* (Amherst: University of Massachusetts Press, 1978), 46–48.

12. William Faulkner, *Flags in the Dust* (New York: Vintage Books, 1974), 329. Subsequent references are cited parenthetically in the text.

13. Kreiswirth, 113.

14. Ibid., 114.

15. Ibid., 114–15.

16. Frederick R. Karl, *William Faulkner: American Writer* (New York: Weidenfeld and Nicolson, 1989), 292–94.

17. William Faulkner, *Light in August* (New York: Vintage Books, 1990), 119.

18. David Minter, *Faulkner's Questioning Narratives: Fiction of His Major Phase, 1929–42* (Urbana: University of Illinois Press, 2001), 41.

19. Ibid., 145.

20. Ibid., 88.

21. William Faulkner, *Absalom, Absalom!* (New York: Vintage Books, 1990).

22. Kevin Railey, "*Flags in the Dust* and the Material Culture of Class," in *Faulkner and Material Culture: Faulkner and Yoknapatawpha, 2004*, ed. Joseph R. Urgo and Ann J. Abadie (Jackson: University Press of Mississippi, 2007), 68.

23. Karl, 297.

24. Willard Thorp, "Four Times and Out," *Scrutiny* 1:1 (September 1932), 172–73; reprinted in Kinney, 128.

25. Jean-Paul Sartre, "William Faulkner's *Sartoris*," *Yale French Studies* 10 (1952), 95–99; originally in French, *Novelle Revue Française* (February 1938); reprinted Kinney, 144.

26. Jay Parini, *One Matchless Time: A Life of William Faulkner* (New York: HarperCollins, 2004), 127.

"In Conflict with Itself": The Nobel Prize Address in Faulknerian Contexts

James B. Carothers

On 10 December 1950 William Faulkner read an address to the Swedish Academy accepting the Nobel Prize for Literature. No one heard him; his voice was soft and Southern, he spoke even more softly as he went along, and he was distant from the microphone. Upon publication immediately afterward, however, the speech was greeted by widespread popular acclaim, with special emphasis on Faulkner's assertion that writers should ground their work in "the old eternal verities and truths of the heart, the old universal truths lacking which any story is ephemeral and doomed—love and honor and pity and pride and compassion and sacrifice." "I decline to accept the end of man," Faulkner famously concluded. "I believe that man will not merely endure: he will prevail."[1] Many experienced Faulkner readers of that time, however, expressed astonishment at the speech and questioned its sincerity, arguing that the optimism expressed therein was inconsistent with what they variously described as the pessimism, despair, and cynicism of Faulkner's earlier fiction. Although phrases and sentences from the speech, and to some extent, the speech in its entirety, now hold iconic status with the general public, later Faulkner critics, for the most part, have continued to doubt the Nobel address as authentic Faulkner, not only questioning the writer's refusal to accept the end of man as an accurate description of, for example, *The Sound and the Fury*, but also lamenting that the speech marked Faulkner's turn toward a more rhetorical and conservative mode in his subsequent fiction.

One of Faulkner's biographers, Richard Gray has said: "The first reaction to published versions of that speech, in the United States especially, was surely the right one. It might be splendidly stirring, the response was, but how did all those references to 'the old verities and truths of the heart, the old universal truths' fit in with a book like *The Sound and the Fury*? The fame of the Noble Prize acceptance speech has, by now, perhaps blinded us to the fact that it is, at best, a glorious piece of windy oratory; that tries to make up in terms of rousing cadences for what it lacks in substance." Gray links the Nobel speech with the subsequent fiction and allies himself with those who disparage the later fiction. "Too often

20

in the later novels," he writes, "intimacies of character and intensities of feeling are submerged under great waves of rhetoric."[2] Gray's views of the Nobel speech and of the fiction that followed it are by no means unique; in fact, they represent a consensus that is seldom questioned: the Nobel speech is insincere, it does not represent Faulkner's "real" view of the world, it is inconsistent with the views expressed or implied in his great earlier fiction, and the fiction he wrote after the speech is radically impaired, perhaps even corrupted, to the extent that it manifests the beliefs and values articulated at Stockholm.[3]

In returning to the Nobel speech, I wish to reconsider its text in various Faulknerian contexts, reviewing its origins and development in the immediate circumstances of Faulkner's life at the time of the award itself, as well as in both his earlier and later fiction. I propose a reading of the Nobel Prize address as an authentic expression of Faulkner's views of the artistic endeavor in general, and of his own achievement in particular, both in the immediate moment and multiple contexts of the Nobel award, and in the extended contexts of his continuously developing career. So, while most critics would agree that the key phrase in the first section of the speech, "the problems of the human heart in conflict with itself," accurately describes Faulkner's characteristic subjects and methods in the entire range of his fiction, I seek also to demonstrate that several developments in both global and personal contexts may have encouraged Faulkner to express a more positive assessment of his own achievement and of the world around him, which, in turn, enabled him to complete the substantial projects of his fiction from *Requiem for a Nun* to *The Reivers*. The most controversial part of the Nobel speech, in which Faulkner declines to accept the end of man and asserts instead that man, sometimes helped by the artist, will endure and prevail—his newly articulated *credo*, if you will—can be understood as a consequence of his own surprise and delight that he, as an artist, has been able to endure and prevail in a profoundly threatening world. The Stockholm podium, often marked as the unfortunate divide between far greater and embarrassingly lesser Faulknerian binaries, ought, rather, to be seen as a pinnacle from which the author looked back at his own artistic and personal past and forward to his continuing career.

Even while his possible selection by the Swedish Academy was still in the rumor stage, Faulkner was wary of the Nobel Prize award. Privately he expressed his ambivalence on the subject well before he was notified of his selection. "I don't know anything about the Nobel matter," he wrote Joan Williams in February 1950: "Been hearing rumors about it for about three years, have been a little fearful. It's not the sort of thing to decline; a gratuitous insult to do so but I don't want it. I had rather be in the same pigeon hole with Dreiser and Sherwood Anderson, than with Sinclair Lewis and Mrs. Chinahand Buck."⁴ When, on 10 November, the rumors were confirmed by a phone call from Sven Åhman, New York correspondent of Stockholm's *Dagens Nyheter*, Faulkner chose his words carefully. Acknowledging that "one must feel flattered that his work has been considered worthy of this distinction," he told the reporter that he would be unable to travel to Stockholm to receive the prize. "It's too far away," he said. "I am a farmer down here and I can't get away,"⁵ and he gave similar comments to other reporters.

The language of the speech began to appear in his correspondence and interviews even when he was still trying to avoid going to Stockholm. He wrote Åhman on 16 November, expanding on his response in what can be read as a first draft of the eventual acceptance speech: "I hold that the award was made, not to me, but to my works—crown to thirty years of the agony and sweat of a human spirit, to make something which was not here before me, to lift up or maybe comfort or anyway at least entertain, in its turn, man's heart. That took thirty years. I am past fifty now; there is probably not much more in the tank. I feel that what remains after the thirty years of work is not worth carrying from Mississippi to Sweden, just as I feel that what remains does not deserve to expend the prize on himself, so that it is my hope to find an aim for the money high enough to be commensurate with the purpose and significance of its origin." Faulkner asked Åhman to convey this message to the Swedish Academy, if he thought it appropriate, but promised to "do nothing to violate its canons or show anything but respect to the Academy and the Swedish people." Uncomfortable with the attention of journalists local and national, Faulkner began to anneal himself in whiskey and took off for his annual hunting camp. While he was in camp, many people, including numerous government officials, publishers, friends, and family, marshaled further arguments hoping to convince him to go to Stockholm.⁶

Faulkner returned to Oxford on Monday, 27 November, and capitulated, wiring Swedish Ambassador Erik Boheman "returned hunting trip today. received your letter nov 21st. will be pleased to journey stockholm."⁷ It is impossible to say precisely why Faulkner finally agreed to accept the prize in person, whether out of a sense of courtesy to the Swedish Academy and the Swedish people, a sense of duty to his own country, a sense of responsibility to the publisher who had supported him through difficult financial times. He may have finally been persuaded by Estelle Faulkner's suggestion that she could stay home, while Jill Faulkner, then sixteen, accompanied her father. It may have been some combination of these. Whatever his motives, he put aside his own ambivalence, reluctance, and strong personal preferences and he was on his way.

Granted his lifelong resistance to interviews, publicity, speeches, and the like, why, in this particular case, had he been so reluctant to go? His comments doubting the justice of the awards to Sinclair Lewis and Pearl Buck, as well as the Swedish Academy's failure to honor Theodore Dreiser and Sherwood Anderson surely provide part of the answer. He especially wished to honor Anderson, his early friend and mentor, whose assistance he variously acknowledged in his dedication of *Sartoris*, his essay "A Note on Sherwood Anderson," and in his *Paris Review* interview, but whom he had offended with his early parody, *Sherwood Anderson and Other Famous Creoles*, as Hemingway had parodied Anderson in *The Torrents of Spring*.[8] Characteristically, he was also reluctant to subject himself to the persistent reporters who sought him out in Oxford and continued to assail him throughout the journey to Stockholm and back. Faulkner was, of course, a very private man, who avoided publicity rather than seeking it, and who was usually uncomfortable and querulous with interviewers. He was always uncomfortable, moreover, in "literary" company, insisting that he was a farmer or a writer, rather than a "literary man."[9] By late 1950 he was feeling tired and exhausted, and he was not writing to his satisfaction. His long stint in Hollywood, marital discord, and too much alcohol contributed to his exhaustion, as did the temporary uproar connected with the premiere of the film of *Intruder in the Dust* in Oxford, which he had attended with great reluctance, and then only out of deference to his Aunt 'Bama.[10] He had been engaged in what would become *A Fable* off and on since 1943, the end was nowhere in sight, and he frequently doubted its merits. Although he had recently published both *Knight's Gambit* (1949) and *Collected Stories* (1950), these two volumes were compilations of previously published short stories, a form he had now virtually abandoned.[11] He had also begun what he imagined as a play, partly to offer young Joan Williams an opportunity to collaborate with him, but their relationship had not developed as either of them would have liked and had caused serious problems between Faulkner and Estelle. Alcohol, as so often the case, compounded his plight; even after his return from hunting camp, he continued to drink, negotiating a "tapering off" period for himself.[12]

But during this time he also began work on the acceptance speech, dictating to Estelle's son-in-law, Bill Fielden. He mentioned other writers of his time, including Hemingway and Dos Passos, and included some of the "last ding-dong of doom" language. Other phrases that would find their way into the speech appeared in an interview that he gave to the Memphis *Commercial Appeal* before he left Oxford. Again he distinguished between the man and his work, saying that the human individual who makes the book is not important, "so long as the work uplifted, strengthened or did something to other hearts."[13] In this last phrase he was recalling the preface by Henryk Sienkiewicz, himself a Polish Nobel laureate, whom Faulkner had mentioned in a letter to Malcolm Cowley in 1946. Now he again invoked the names of Dreiser and Anderson, and said that the award to him was a "recognition of all the writers of my time," specifically acknowledging Hemingway and Dos Passos among his contemporaries. He expanded on some of the material he had dictated to Bill Fielden, including more language that would appear in the Nobel speech: "There are no longer any problems. Man is faced with one question: Whether he's going to get blown up. There used to be problems of courage, honor, chastity, virtue." Nevertheless, he expressed confidence in man's immortality. "When the last ding dong rings his voice will continue to be heard in the ruins and ashes."[14]

So, by the time Faulkner and Jill flew from Memphis to New York on 6 December, although he had not personally written a line of it, the main components of the speech were tentatively drafted, in his correspondence, in his interviews, and in his dictation. In New York, father and daughter went immediately to the Algonquin, where the next day Faulkner, according to Åhman, referred to "a twenty-minute acceptance speech, though it was still too formless to talk about."[15] Faulkner had little time in New York to do any writing on the speech. He went to parties and suffered a relapse of a bad cold, which he treated with antibiotics, whiskey, and tobacco. So it was probably Friday morning, 8 December, when, now aboard the SAS DC-6, he took out sheets of Algonquin stationery. According to Blotner, "he was probably working from a single typed sheet composed of three paragraphs of equal length"—perhaps the product of his dictation to Bill Fielden. The opening paragraph of this draft began with the argument that the Nobel award could have been made to "any one of a hundred others," including Hemingway, Dos Passos, Thomas Wolfe, and Erskine Caldwell, "all of us children of Sherwood Anderson." As he wrote, in pencil, he not only reworked the typed draft, but expanded on comments made in letters and interviews, and the speech began to take much of the shape we know today. In one place, however, he included a personal anecdote to clarify one of his main points: "A few years ago I was taken on as a script writer at a Hollywood studio. At once I began to hear the man in charge talking of 'angles,' story 'angles,' and then I realized that they were not even interested in truth, the old universal truths of the human heart without which any story is ephemeral—the universal truths of love and honor and pride and pity and compassion and sacrifice."[16]

This Hollywood story is important because there has been a good deal of speculation about just which writers write as though they "stood among and watched the end of man," who "labor under a curse" and write "not of the heart but of the glands." Faulkner, as he revised the speech into the form in which it was delivered at Stockholm, removed all references to identifiable individuals and events, leaving readers to speculate about his more particular sources. Thus, some have seen a competitive reference to Hemingway, perhaps echoing the title *Winner Take Nothing* in the passage describing one who writes "of defeats in which nobody loses anything of value, of victories without hope and, worst of all, without pity or compassion." It would, however, be absurd to assume that Faulkner would offer even a veiled insult to the man whom he considered his greatest contemporary and rival in a speech that contained *in this draft* an explicit acknowledgement of Hemingway as his peer. Others have thought the allusion might be to "Spillane and the toughs," the writers of the hard-boiled school of sensational detective fiction, but Faulkner's subsequent single reference to Spillane occurred a number of years after the Nobel address, and is not developed to any extent.[17] A more frequent, and more problematic, conjecture is that Faulkner is here talking about his own earlier work, that he is, in some sense, announcing a new view of the human condition by rejecting what were thought to be the implications of the great fiction for which the Nobel award had been conferred on him. His Hollywood anecdote, however, constitutes a plausible source for the remark, and some of the Nobel language can be discerned in his film scripts, particularly *Battle Cry*. I do not contend that Faulkner's Hollywood experience constitutes the absolute and comprehensive explanation of the phrase "not of the heart but of the glands," even though there is as much or more immediate, concrete, and relevant evidence for that view than there is for any of the other explanations. The "Hollywood angles" reference was eventually excised from the successive drafts of the speech, as were the references to Hemingway, Dos Passos, Dreiser, and Anderson. The version delivered at Stockholm and the slightly revised final text published in the New York *Herald Tribune* and heard in the subsequent Caedmon recording shows no trace of these more specific references. The speech as we know it displays that elevated style that Faulkner once described to Cowley as "studbook style: 'by Southern Rhetoric out of Solitude' or 'Oratory, out of Solitude'"[18] or, as Gray and others would have it, "windy." The last part of the pencil draft, for example, makes explicit the connection between the writer's duty and the survival and triumph of the human spirit: "I believe he is immortal not just because he will endure, but because he will prevail: because he has a soul and a spirit capable of honor and pride, compassion and pity, endurance and duty and sacrifice if only there be one to remind him of these."[19]

In Stockholm there were more interviews and more parties. Here, also, Faulkner revised the speech again, reading his pencil draft while the American ambassador's press attaché's secretary typed.[20] The speech was shortened and punctuation was added, and Faulkner began to rehearse it. Although slight changes would eventually be made after the speech was given and published, the speech, as we know it, was done. In drafting and revising the speech that would mark great changes in his career, Faulkner incorporated, sometimes consciously, and sometimes, perhaps not, allusions to a variety of other authors: Sienkiewicz, Conrad, Housman, and, as I shall argue, Byron.[21] In addition, he drew significantly on phrasing and imagery from the fiction he had written over the range of his career. As Michael Grimwood has shown, the imagery of the last paragraph of the Nobel speech—"the lone man standing upon the last rocky island in an apocalyptic seascape"—appeared in various forms, including the short story "The Leg," probably written by 1928, Reverend Shegog's sermon in *The Sound and the Fury* (1929), the "Old Man" section of *The Wild Palms* (1939), and, especially, in "Delta Autumn" (1940).[22]

Grimwood, in his sustained and thoughtful critique, argues, however, that the Nobel speech "presents only one side of the internal debate that occupied Faulkner from the late thirties into the fifties." This debate, he asserts, deals with Faulkner's struggles with vocation, his uncertainty about whether human history has meaning, and about whether it is meaningful for Faulkner to write. Putting the address in Faulkner's personal context, he states that "under the onslaught of middle age, commercial failure, critical obscurity, marital discord, disappointment, and international upheaval, he reactivated the debate that had remained relatively dormant within him through the years of his masterpieces. The Nobel address expressed only the hopeful half of that debate." In the Nobel speech, he concludes, Faulkner "ignored the conflict within himself, which his books continued to reveal whether he wished them to or not.[23]

This is serious criticism indeed, and in order to respond to it in terms of the text and immediate contexts of the Nobel address, and in terms of Faulkner's earlier and later fiction, we shall need to consider a variety of elements. For one thing, we must note that Grimwood's overarching thesis is that Faulkner's career began and ended in ambivalence toward the efficacy of writing, or the artistic endeavor in general, and in relation to himself in particular. While it would, in one sense, be convenient for me to accept this hypothesis entirely—to posit that Faulkner's fiction is primarily or exclusively "writing about writing"—I prefer to consider this reading as one possibility among many, one of the multiple interpretations that Faulkner's works and career invite, demand, and sustain, precisely in the ways that these several interpretations sometimes contradict each other.

At the very outset of the Nobel speech Faulkner insists on the separation between himself and his fiction: the Nobel award is made "not to me as a man, but to my work." Faulkner, as we know, strongly preferred not to discuss his personal life in the context of his fiction. He wished he had published his works anonymously, he wrote once.[24] He said repeatedly that no one had the right to information about his personal life unless he committed a crime or ran for public office. He wrote Joan Williams in 1953, again distinguishing between himself and his work, and wondering "if you had ever had that thought about the work and the country man whom you know as Bill Faulkner—what little connection there seems to be between them."[25] Much earlier he had written his Aunt 'Bama from Paris, "I have just finished the most beautiful short story in the world. So beautiful that when I finished it I went to look at myself in a mirror. And I thought, Did that ugly ratty-looking face, that mixture of childishness and unreliability and sublime vanity, imagine that? But I did. And the hand doesn't hold blood to improve on it."[26] This distinction accounts, I think, for a good deal that has always seemed problematic in reading "Faulkner," rather than in reading Faulkner's texts: the man might say anything, especially in interviews or in letters in which he was trying to gain advances from publishers or affection from women, or when he had been drinking, and, perhaps, when he was making public speeches. It also explains why he did not wish to profit personally from the Nobel award. Privately he asserted to his family what he had told Sven Åhman, "there is not much more in the tank." He had written, he maintained, "not for glory and least of all for profit." Cynics might reject this assertion, or call it hypocrisy, citing Faulkner's Hollywood stints, his assertion that the original *Sanctuary* was "a cheap idea designed to make money," and all the self-proclaimed potboiling and "whoring" he did for the *Saturday Evening Post* and others. His aim, he said, was rather "to create out of the materials of the human spirit something which did not exist before." And there could be no doubt at this moment that he had, in fact, done that. These creations, his work, were being honored. "So," he continued, "this award is only mine in trust. It will not be difficult to find a dedication for the money part of it commensurate with the purpose and significance of its origin." In fact, Faulkner put the Nobel money in an actual trust, which was used for a variety of purposes, including college scholarship money for black Mississippians. The subsequent Faulkner Foundation also sponsored an award for the best first novel by an American and a later award for the best book of short fiction.[27] This promise and these actions validated his "least of all for profit" assertion.

"But I would like to do the same with the acclaim too, by using this moment as a pinnacle from which I might be listened to by the young men and women already dedicated to the same anguish and travail."[28] Having announced his intention to dispose of the money part of the award in an ethical fashion, Faulkner seeks to do the same with the glory of the moment. He advises young writers by talking, albeit implicitly, about the qualities of the work that has been honored. To do so, he moves abruptly from aesthetics to the current geopolitical situation: "Our tragedy today is a general and universal physical fear so long sustained by now that we can even bear it. There are no longer problems of the spirit. There is only the question: when will I be blown up?" There is no need to dwell extensively on the international events of the immediate historical context of the speech: the relief and elation at the successful conclusion of World War II was followed immediately with the Russian establishment of hegemony among Eastern European states, memorably acknowledged and described in Winston Churchill's "Iron Curtain" speech in 1946; the announcement that Russia had successfully tested its own atomic bomb, 29 August 1949; and the 25 June 1950 North Korean invasion of the republic of Korea. Faulkner, clearly aware of these events, and of the realpolitik created by them, thus describes the extraordinary intersection of the artistic endeavor and the world which contains both artist and audience.[29]

One consequence of the threat of nuclear annihilation, Faulkner reasons, is that "the young man or woman writing today has forgotten the problems of the human heart in conflict with itself which alone can make good writing because only that is worth writing about, worth the agony and the sweat." There are many ways to explain "the problems of the heart in conflict with itself" and to explain why "only that is worth writing about," but few would dispute the authenticity of these components of Faulkner's aesthetic. "These sentiments," Grimwood stipulates, "he had long felt,"[30] and before we turn again to Grimwood's (and others') objections to the latter portion of the speech, it may be useful to consider some possible meanings of the "heart in conflict" phrase. One of the earliest formulations of it was by Keats, long a favorite of Faulkner's: "what quality went to form a Man of Achievement especially in literature & which Shakespeare possessed so enormously—I mean *Negative Capability*, that is, when a man is capable of being in uncertainty, Mysteries, doubts, without any irritable reaching after fact & reason."[31] The New Critics preferred the term "paradox," while Eric Auerbach called it "the problematic"; Faulkner himself called attention to the "discrepancies and contradictions in his fiction," proof that "his entire life's work is part of a living literature. "It is only in literature," the narrator of Faulkner's short story "Monk" asserts, "that the paradoxical and even mutually negativing anecdotes in the history of a human heart can be juxtaposed and annealed by art into verisimilitude and credibility."[32] However we choose to label it, Faulkner's "heart in conflict with itself" describes an internal conflict in basic human values that is inevitable and insoluble, consisting of authentic alternatives, as Grimwood posits the efficacy of writing against the inefficacy of writing and Daniel J. Singal examines the conflict between Victorian desires for a traditional morally ordered community and modernism's subversive challenges to that ideal. On a fairly elementary level we see such a conflict in Miss Emily Grierson of "A Rose for Emily," who is torn between her desire to conform to the patriarchal values that dictate what is respectable in Jefferson and her desire to acquire, by whatever means, a husband. Sarty Snopes of "Barn Burning," likewise, is "pulled two ways," between his desire to protect the peace and dignity of de Spain's mansion, and "the old fierce pull of blood" that draws him to try to protect his father from de Spain's wrath. Neither Miss Emily nor Sarty, as far as we know, is explicitly conscious of this division, but Quentin Compson of *The Sound and the Fury* most certainly is. As John T. Matthews summarizes Quentin's dilemma, "Like his eventual suicide, Quentin's memories betray the unsolvable contradictions of his predicament. Just as he smears mud on Caddy to express his outrage at her befoulment—trying to undo by redoing—he also tries to restore her virginity by taking it himself, to preserve his own by losing it to her, to purify their lives by ending his, to defend honor by contemplating an act of perfect shame, to gain his father's respect by defying him, and to confirm his identity by dissolving it."[33]

Up to this point in the Nobel speech, then, Faulkner stands on familiar ground, and he admonishes the young writer to "leave no room in his workshop for anything but the old verities and truths of the heart lacking which any story is ephemeral and doomed—love and honor and pity and pride and compassion and sacrifice." The writer who has not relearned these things "labors under a curse." Faulkner here may have been recalling his own earlier views of the human condition, expressed in interviews or correspondence, and by particular characters in his fiction: Life is "a moment between dark and dark," the narrator of "All the Dead Pilots" says, and Faulkner had put it to Cowley a few years before: "Life is a phenomenon but not a novelty, the same frantic steeplechase toward nothing everywhere, and man stinks the same stink no matter where in time."[34] Faulkner, the man, as his speech had already stipulated, was not to be honored or specially trusted. He well knew his own unreliability in expressing his ideas. He was a writer, not a literary man, and he had no special use for theory. So, if Faulkner the man had earlier expressed an apocalyptic vision, Faulkner the man now was repudiating it. He was not, however, repudiating the work.

The last paragraph of the speech represents a conscious choice for Faulkner, a manifesto against the despair, cynicism, pessimism, and solipsism he recognized in the Cold War *zeitgeist*. One writer who needed to relearn these things, one who had written "as though he stood among and watched the end of man," was William Faulkner. In the peculiar phrase "stood among," Faulkner was quoting Byron, specifically the 113th stanza of Canto 3 of *Childe Harold's Pilgrimage*:

> I have not loved the world, nor the world me;
> I have not flattered its rank breath, not bow'd
> To its idolatries a patient knee,—
> Nor coin'd my cheek to smiles,—nor cried aloud
> In worship of an echo; in the crowd
> They could not deem me one of such; I stood
> Among them, but not of them; in a shroud
> Of thoughts which were not their thoughts, and still could,
> Had I not filed my mind, which thus itself subdued. [35]

The telling phrase is "stood among," rather than the more usual "stood alone"—*Time* magazine misquoted it this way in its story on Faulkner's death, and it continues to be so misquoted in a variety of contexts. Faulkner, however, knew his Byron well enough; he quoted Byron, if somewhat elliptically, in "Divorce in Naples" and humorously in "A Courtship," and the protagonist in "Carcassonne" reflects that there was "something of the rat about Byron: allocutions of stealthful voracity."[36] Among his characters there are two very different Byrons (Snopes and Bunch), as well as *Manfred* de Spain, the artist Gordon (a sculptor) in *Mosquitoes*, the aristocratic Gordon family in the Memphis stories "Rose of Lebanon" and "A Return," and at least six Georges and a "Georgie." But the salient point here, I submit, is the resemblance between Childe Harold, at this moment, proud, scornful, and alienated, and the isolated, saturnine, brooding William Faulkner from the young Count No 'Count of the Ole Miss days to the distracted Oxford pedestrian of the later years whose pride and haughtiness were a byword among Oxonians. The Byronic pose was one that Faulkner struck, and he may well have believed that he was standing among men (but not *of* them) and watching their individual and collective marches to oblivion. By abandoning the Byronic attitude, with its sneering, condescending isolation, Faulkner chose to reenter humanity. In doing so, he gave himself the wherewithal not only to "do right" by the Nobel ceremony, as so many family and friends had urged him to do, but also to reinvigorate his writing career.

How (and why) could Faulkner discard the Byronic pose and return, refreshed, to his writing? To answer these questions I want to call attention to a number of factors from Faulkner's life from 1945 to 1950 that may have given him a more positive evaluation of himself, his achieve-ment, and the human condition, all of which culminated at the "pinnacle" of Stockholm. The global factor, surely, was the satisfactory conclusion to World War II, made specifically possible by the American and Allied resistance to Hitler and Mussolini and Tojo. "Delta Autumn" in its origi-nal (1940) publication expressed doubts about American willingness to fight. Don Boyd's pessimism—he asked if Americans proposed to fight Hitler "by singing God Bless America in bars at midnight and wearing dime-store flags in our lapels"—is juxtaposed with more optimistic views expressed by Ike McCaslin, but the issue was by no means a foregone conclusion in Faulkner's own mind, and his various unsuccessful efforts to get himself into uniform in some fashion attest to his own willingness to commit himself to the cause for the duration.[37] Instead, he had to confine himself to producing short stories like "Two Soldiers," "Shall Not Perish," and "The Tall Men," and he languished in Hollywood where he worked on, among other properties, a script entitled *Battle Cry* that was never produced.

His eventual escape from Hollywood in March 1946 was a more per-sonal improvement. He had been under what seemed to be perpetual contract to Warner Bros., which had claimed rights in any fiction he wrote while he was working for them. Faulkner chafed miserably under this arrangement, which he finally escaped by showing them a draft of what would eventually become *A Fable*. When Warner Bros. turned down the project, Random House came to Faulkner's rescue by agreeing to advance him money so he could work on the book at home in Missis-sippi. Another significant event in his relations with Hollywood occurred in 1948 when the film rights to *Intruder in the Dust* were bought by MGM for $50,000, a sum that gave Faulkner relief from the debts and tax obligations that had worried and depressed him for over ten years.[38] Although Faulkner could very well have done without the carnival-like atmosphere of the Oxford world premiere of the film, and especially with the attention that was directed at him personally, he had become more nearly solvent and prosperous than ever before in his life. This com-parative affluence gave him the means to sustain the principle behind his later refusal to benefit from "the money part" of the Nobel award.

Another source of encouragement for Faulkner in the 1940s was the beginning of several new fiction projects, principally "the fable," for which Faulkner had extraordinarily high hopes, but also *Intruder in the Dust*, the collection of the Gavin Stevens detective stories in *Knight's Gambit* (1949), and the critically and commercially acclaimed *Collected Stories* (1950). Faulkner sought a different kind of inspiration in his slowly developing relationship with Joan Williams, a young writer who appeared at Rowan Oak in the summer of 1949 seeking advice about writing and soon found herself importuned by a man thirty years her senior, who sought her as muse, collaborator, protégé, and lover. At Faulkner's insistence, they worked sporadically together on another new project, which would eventually issue under Faulkner's own hand, as *Requiem for a Nun* (1951).[39]

An overarching factor in developing his confidence and optimism was the recognition of his work, with the Nobel Prize providing him a pinnacle and a platform. It had not been so long ago that Faulkner labored in obscurity in Hollywood, while, according to Sartre, "the reading of novels by Faulkner and Hemingway became for some a symbol of the resistance."[40] "What a commentary," Faulkner wrote Harold Ober in 1946: "In France, I am the father of a literary movement. In Europe I am considered the best modern American and among the first of all writers. In America, I eke out a hack's motion picture wages by winning second prize in a manufactured mystery story contest."[41] As every schoolboy Faulknerian knows, the rescue of his reputation in America was launched when Malcolm Cowley proposed *The Portable Faulkner* for Viking. Faulkner saw the opportunity immediately: "I would very much like to have the piece done. I think (at 46) that I have worked too hard at my (elected or doomed, I don't know which) trade, with pride but I believe not vanity, with plenty of ego but with humility too (being a poet I give no fart for glory) to leave no better mark on this our pointless chronicle than I seem to be about to leave."[42] Faulkner collaborated with Cowley on the *Portable*, to the extent that the critic would let him, providing what we persist in calling the "Compson Appendix," discussing possible selections, and finally imploring Cowley to omit references to World War I combat experiences Faulkner had invented for himself as much as twenty-five years earlier. Cowley's introduction and the two-part review by Robert Penn Warren proclaimed Faulkner's work "the most challenging single task in contemporary American literature for criticism to undertake."[43] Cowley's work and Faulkner's contributions, combined with Warren's review, led to a revival of interest in Faulkner among academics and influential reviewers, and Faulkner himself was both surprised and pleased with the *Portable*. "The job is splendid," he wrote Cowley. "Damn you to hell anyway. But even if I had beat you to the idea, mine wouldn't have been this good. By God, I didn't know myself what I had tried to do, and how much I had succeeded."[44]

In this last comment, we see Faulkner revising his understanding and estimation of his work. In a few short years, he had gone from obscurity and critical neglect to the pinnacle at Stockholm. The Nobel speech confirms his understanding of that fact. So, at Stockholm also, he articulated another discovery of what he had tried to do, and how well he had succeeded. In his present moment he could, like so many poets, see the human condition in his own, and, amazingly, here he could infer mankind's triumphant endurance in his own. From this pinnacle, he could foresee his own immortality through his art. If he could do it, flawed though he was, others artists could as well, and through their art each could be "one of the props, the pillars" for other people who struggled, hoped, and believed. By declining to accept the end of his artistic vocation, he could, by extension, decline to accept the end of man as well. In the remainder of the speech he implicitly juxtaposed himself at this pinnacle with his earlier cynical portrait of the last human survivor, "when the last ding-dong of doom has clanged and faded from the last worthless rock hanging tideless in the last red and dying evening, that even then there will still be one more sound: that of his puny inexhaustible voice, still talking." Again, he specifically repudiated that apocalyptic vision. "I refuse to accept this"; and he explained his faith: "I believe that man will not merely endure; he will prevail. He is immortal, not because he alone among creatures has an inexhaustible voice, but because he has a soul, a spirit capable of compassion and sacrifice and endurance."

The Nobel speech, Grimwood maintains, "is not completely sincere. Faulkner did not fully believe what he was saying." In the end, the speech "presents only one side of the internal debate that preoccupied Faulkner from the late thirties into the fifties. It therefore provides a false resolution to a question Faulkner was still struggling to answer, a question that touched him personally in a way the Speech conceals: not only 'Will mankind prevail?' (that is, does human history have meaning?) but also 'Is it meaningful for me, William Faulkner, to write?' (is *my* voice 'inexhaustible'?)."[45] This formulation, however, ignores Faulkner's powerful articulation of the contemporary international geopolitical situation early in the speech: "Our tragedy today is a general and universal physical fear so long sustained by now that we can even bear it. There are no longer problems of the spirit. There is only the question: When will I be blown up?" Surely this assertion sufficiently acknowledges the other half of the external debate that frames the internal debate for Faulkner. If there is only the question "When will I be blown up?," mankind will neither endure nor prevail, and Faulkner's voice, and the voices of the young man or woman writing today, are not only exhaustible, but "ephemeral and doomed." Faulkner's subsequent pronouncements are strongly positive precisely because the evidence for the apocalyptic view has been so overwhelmingly emphasized by contemporary analysts, and so eloquently articulated in his own earlier fiction. And, as Grimwood notes, the debate continues in Faulkner's subsequent fiction and in his own mind as well.

Faulkner and his fiction did not became suddenly and permanently "happy" at Stockholm—far from it; rather, the Nobel speech provides a lens through which Faulkner and his readers can see backwards and forwards into his continuously evolving career.

In arguing Faulkner's lack of complete sincerity in the Nobel speech, Grimwood pays special attention to scenes in the fiction—one before the Nobel award and one after, that have obvious relevance to the "endure and prevail" pronouncement. In *Go Down, Moses* (1942) McCaslin Edmonds invokes Keats's "Ode on a Grecian Urn" as part of his effort to get young Isaac McCaslin to reconsider his determination to relinquish the McCaslin property. *"He was talking about truth,"* Edmonds says: *"Truth is one. It doesn't change. It covers all things which touch the heart—honor and pride and pity and justice and courage and love."* While Isaac silently resists Edmonds's appeal to words, even or especially those of Keats, Edmonds continues: *"McCaslin watched him, still speaking, the voice, the words as quiet as the twilight itself was: 'Courage and honor and pride, and pity and love of justice and of liberty. They all touch the heart, and what the heart holds to becomes truth, as far as we know truth.'"*[46] Grimwood reads this disagreement as an argument for and against the efficacy of words and writing. In this reading he says "Faulkner entrusted his optimism about the human race to a man who belittles the value of writing [Isaac] and his defense of literacy to a man who accepts a bleak vision of history [Edmonds]—a confusion he only artificially disentangled in the Nobel Speech."[47] To endorse Isaac's position and to discredit Edmonds's, however, makes the novel into the kind of allegory that Faulkner usually avoided. Isaac and McCaslin Edmonds both invite approbation and criticism; to reduce or limit either character to an unequivocal and unassailable moral position ignores "the heart's driving complexity" and diminishes the power of the text. If we can agree that Edmonds is an equivocal advocate for the words he speaks, we must also remember that Isaac himself is neither a simple and unquestionably trustworthy Faulknerian spokesman, nor is his high-minded relinquishment of the McCaslin property an efficacious corrective to the crimes of his family.

The same kind of confrontation is repeated, with a difference, in *A Fable*, when the Old General—in a "paraphrase of the Nobel Speech, amounting almost to an act of self-quotation or—parody," according to Grimwood[48]—attempts to dissuade the Corporal from allowing himself to be executed. Foreseeing nuclear catastrophe, the General nevertheless predicts that man will "endure" and even "prevail" "because he has that in him which will endure even beyond the ultimate worthless tideless rock freezing slowly in the last red and heatless sunset, because already the next star in the blue immensity of space will be already clamorous with the uproar of his debarkation, his puny and inexhaustible and immortal voice still talking still planning; and there too after the last ding dong of doom has rung and died there will still be one sound more his voice."[49] In the phrase "It is easy enough to say" the Nobel speech signals a parodic tone that we might well recognize in the General's speech, and we can agree with Grimwood that the General's addition of "prevail" marks him as cynical rather than optimistic. The General speaks, however, to advance the cause of war; his career commits him to carnage and destruction. Faulkner's career, by contrast, encompasses creation. Putting the Stockholm words in the General's mouth does not necessarily imply their repudiation. The General addresses the Corporal for reasons radically at variance with the reasons Faulkner addressed the Swedish Academy. "By placing these words in the mouth of a character who utters them in the quite literal role of devil's advocate," Grimwood suggests, "perhaps Faulkner was revealing his suspicion of their inauthenticity in his own mouth."[50] Perhaps, but, alternatively, the passage perhaps constitutes one of Faulkner's characteristic scenes in which the Devil quotes scripture.

Gavin Stevens in *The Town* and Mink Snopes in *The Mansion* are surely as equivocal in their ways as McCaslin Edmonds and the Old General are in theirs. Gavin and Mink each looks at the world that surrounds him, reflects on his place in it, and finds himself exalted by the experience. These "pinnacle" moments, meditative-descriptive prose lyrics rather than dramatic exchanges, constitute tableaux of Faulkner's Stockholm experience. In the passage beginning "There is a ridge," Gavin Stevens articulates a transcendent and comprehensive vision of Yoknapatawpha County. In this silent interior monologue marked by his objectification of himself—"suzerain and solitary," "detached as God himself," "you, the old man, already white-headed . . . and pushing forty"[51]—Gavin contemplates the world in which he finds himself, within Faulkner's contemplation of the world he has made. The echoes of the Nobel address are unmistakable, but perhaps less obvious is that Faulkner here finds a way to incorporate the language of Stockholm within the language of fiction. If it is true enough that McCaslin Edmonds and the Old General are ambiguous and perhaps cynical and manipulative characters whose appropriation of the Stockholm speech's language might lead us to suspect or discount it, Gavin Stevens himself is also a problematic figure in *The Town*. One must often hear Gavin's voice, juxtaposed with and contradicted frequently by Ratliff's, as part of Faulkner's penchant for self-parody. Gavin's moment here, however, also transcends and qualifies the often painful, grotesque, and tragic events of a novel that is sometimes wildly or savagely comic. When he finished *The Town*, Faulkner found himself reassessing his achievement in this particular text, as Cowley's *Portable* and the Nobel award had given him a new perspective on the totality of his work. Gavin's richly complex passage, at once a gorgeous set piece, a description of an extraordinarily significant interlude, and, if you will, "windy," represents not only Gavin's interiority and also demonstrates Faulkner's continuing reconsideration of the "little postage stamp of native soil" on which his characters act and live in myriad ways that surprised even Faulkner himself.[52]

At the end of *The Mansion*, on the last page of the last novel Faulkner thought he would write,[53] Faulkner provides Mink Snopes with a similarly transcendent passage amounting to a benediction: "himself among them, equal to any, good as any, brave as any, being inextricable from, anonymous with all of them: the beautiful, the splendid, the proud and the brave, right on up to the very top itself among the shining phantoms and dreams which are the milestones of the long human recording—Helen and the bishops, the kings and the unhomed angels, the scornful and graceless seraphim."[54] Thus, Mink lies down to sleep, perhaps forever. Unlike Gavin, he has no earthly community to sustain him, and he has already accomplished his nearly lifelong ambition by murdering Flem Snopes; also unlike Gavin, Mink apprehends life directly and unselfconsciously, without thinking of himself as a divisible being; he cannot and does not comprehend the divisions Gavin distinguishes within himself and among his relations with others. Appropriately, therefore, Mink's narrative is told through omniscient narration, while Gavin's is told in a highly sophisticated interior monologue. Mink, at least as equivocal as McCaslin Edmonds, the Old General, or Gavin Stevens, is granted the ultimate "pinnacle" moment. Although the exact language of the Nobel address appears nowhere in the passage, its narrative places Mink precisely where Faulkner found himself in Stockholm, "equal to any, good as any, brave as any, being inextricable from . . . the shining phantoms and dreams which are the milestones of the long human recording."

Faulkner transposed particular words and concepts from the Nobel address into his subsequent fiction and found encouragement from the Nobel experience to continue and complete that fiction. He also discovered in that experience a matrix within which he could transfigure and redeem otherwise profoundly mixed and troublesome characters. The immediate and continued refusal to acknowledge the Nobel speech as an authentic and worthy expression of Faulkner's assessment of his own aims and beliefs constitutes, in my opinion, one of the longest-standing efforts of his expositors—be they advocates, detractors, or both—to locate and isolate his work within the boundaries of their own values.

One consequence of this sort of reading is to impose a certain consistency and even simplicity on what we identify as Faulkner's "project," although we should acknowledge that his "consistency," his "simplicity," and the blueprints of the ostensible project are of our construction rather than of his. One result of this sort of reductive reading is a kind of *a priori* censorship that limits the Faulkner texts we can read with "approval." Whatever form it has taken in the long period of his critical reception, from the cult of cruelty to cultural studies, the critical project of reducing Faulkner's achievement to a matter of theory or ideology is predicated on the assumption that we need not bother with much of his fiction, as so much of it fails to meet whatever standards we currently seek to enforce. For fifty years, the standard practice of Faulkner studies has been to slight, ignore, dismiss, or even condescend to any fiction he wrote after 1942 and especially anything he wrote after the Nobel Prize address. I refuse to accept this. Faulkner's fictions, including the late ones, endure because they have a soul, the spirit of a writer who also had a heart in conflict with itself, a writer who crafted his fictions through his agony and sweat, and in spite of his own manifest imperfections. His Nobel address, the pinnacle from which he reconsidered his life's work, celebrates his own sense of having endured and prevailed.

NOTES

1. "Address upon Receiving the Nobel Prize for Literature, 1950," in *Essays, Speeches, and Public Letters*, ed. James B. Meriwether (New York: Random House, 2004), 120. Hereafter cited as *ESPL*.

2. *The Life of William Faulkner* (Cambridge [UK] and Oxford [U.S.]: Blackwell, 1994), 310.

3. See, for example, *Faulkner: After the Nobel Prize*, ed. Michel Gresset and Kenzaburo Ohashi (Kyoto: Yamaguchi, 1987), passim. Melvin Backman, in *Faulkner: The Major Years* (Bloomington: Indiana University Press, 1966), identified 1929–42 as the essential period in Faulkner's career. Joseph Gold, in *William Faulkner: A Study in Humanism from Metaphor to Discourse* (Norman: University of Oklahoma Press, 1966), was among the first to describe the formal changes in the rhetoric of Faulkner's fiction over his entire career. Daniel J. Singal extends the discussion in *William Faulkner: The Making of a Modernist* (Chapel Hill: University of North Carolina Press, 1997).

4. *Selected Letters of William Faulkner*, ed. Joseph Blotner (New York: Random House, 1977), 299. Hereafter cited as *SLWF*.

5. Joseph Blotner, *Faulkner: A Biography* (New York: Random House, 1974), 1338. Hereafter cited as *FAB*.

6. *SLWF*, 309; *FAB*, 1345–47.

7. *SLWF*, 309; *FAB*, 1347–49.

8. The dedication to *Sartoris* reads "to sherwood anderson/through whose kindness I was first published, with the belief that this book will/give him no reason to regret

that fact" (New York: Harcourt, Brace, 1929); "A Note on Sherwood Anderson," *ESPL*, 3–10; "[Anderson] was the father of my generation of American writers and the tradition of American writing which our successors will carry on. He has never received his proper evaluation," *Lion in the Garden*, ed. James B. Meriwether and Michael Millgate (New York: Random House, 1968), 249–50; William Spratling and William Faulkner, *Sherwood Anderson and Other Famous Creoles* (1926; Austin: University of Texas Press, 1966); for the background of Hemingway's deliberate break with Anderson, see James R. Mellow, *Hemingway: A Life without Consequences* (Boston: Houghton Mifflin Company, 1992), 317–21.

9. Faulkner made this distinction frequently, beginning at least as early as 1948. See *Lion in the Garden*, 59, and *passim*.

10. See *FAB*, 1297.

11. Faulkner had last published a story, "A Courtship," in 1948, though the story was written in 1942. Shortly after this publication, he sold *Intruder in the Dust* to the movies and ceased writing short stories to augment his income. See Theresa M. Towner and James B. Carothers, *Reading Faulkner: "Collected Stories"* (Jackson: University Press of Mississippi, 2006), 194.

12. On Faulkner's developing relationship with Joan Williams, see, for example, *FAB*, 1306–28 and *SLWF*, 296–301. On his drinking during this period, see *FAB*, 1349–50.

13. *FAB*, 1351.

14. Ibid., 1351–52.

15. Ibid., 1355.

16. Ibid., 1357. In Oxford, he had also told the "angles" anecdote to a Memphis *Commercial Appeal* reporter. See *FAB*, 1351–52 and n.

17. Faulkner's criticism of Spillane, however, resembles his criticism of Hollywood's preoccupation with "angles": "It's successful but it ain't worth doing." His conclusion here echoes the language of Stockholm: "That's what I mean by to write from the heart. That it's the heart that makes you want to be brave when you are afraid that you might be a coward, that wants you to be generous, or wants you to be compassionate when you think that maybe you won't. I think that the intellect, it might say, Well, which is the most profitable—shall I be compassionate or shall I be uncompassionate? Which is the most profitable? Which is the most profitable—shall I be brave or not? But the heart wants always to be better than man is." See *Faulkner in the University*, ed. Frederick L. Gwynn and Joseph L. Blotner (New York: Vintage Books, 1965), 26.

18. *SLWF*, 216.

19. Unnumbered page of holograph manuscript on "Hotel Algonquin" stationary. My thanks to Robert W. Hamblin for providing a copy of this document from the Brodsky Collection.

20. *FAB*, 1361–62.

21. *FAB*, 1358 and n.

22. Michael Grimwood, *Heart in Conflict: Faulkner's Struggles with Vocation* (Athens: University of Georgia Press, 1987), 301. See also his earlier essay "The Self-Parodic Context of Faulkner's Nobel Prize Speech," *Southern Review* 15 (1979): 366–75.

23. Grimwood, *Heart in Conflict*, 302.

24. "I am more convinced and determined than ever that this is not for me," he wrote Malcolm Cowley in 1949. "I will protest to the last: no photographs, no recorded documents. It is my ambition to be, as a private individual, abolished and voided from history, leaving it markless, no refuse save the printed books; I wish I had had enough sense to see ahead thirty years ago and, like some of the Elizabethans, not sign them. It is my aim, and every effort bent, that the sum and history of my life, which in the same sentence is my obit and epitaph too, shall be them both: He made the books and he died." *SLWF*, 285.

25. Ibid., 345.

26. Ibid., 20.

27. On portions of the proceeds dedicated to scholarships, see, for example, *FAB*, 1370–71. For information about the writing awards, see www.penfaulkner.org.

28. With the inclusive reference to both genders—repeated shortly thereafter in "the young man or woman writing today"—Faulkner shows his awareness of the difficulty of gendered nouns (and pronouns). Although he subsequently reverts to "man" and "he," his references seem comprehensive and his attitude quite contemporary.

29. Faulkner's Nobel speech could be read as, in part, responding to Churchill's "Iron Curtain" speech, which expresses sympathy for "the myriad cottage or apartment homes where the wage-earner strives amid the accidents and difficulties of life to guard his wife and children from privation and bring the family up in the fear of the Lord, or upon ethical conceptions which often play their potent part." In these circumstances, Churchill concluded, "humble folk are confronted with difficulties with which they cannot cope. For them all is distorted, all is broken, even ground to pulp." *The Sinews of Peace: Post-War Speeches by Winston S. Churchill*, Randolph S. Churchill, ed. (Boston: Houghton Mifflin Company, 1948), 94–95. For an extended discussion of Faulkner's relation to post–WWII American international politics and policies, see Lawrence H. Schwartz, *Creating Faulkner's Reputation: The Politics of Modern Literary Criticism* (Knoxville: University of Tennessee Press, 1988).

30. Grimwood, *Heart in Conflict*, 300.

31. Letter to George and Thomas Keats, 21 December 1817, published in *The Norton Anthology of English Literature*, ed. Stephen Greenblatt, et al., 8th ed. (New York: W. W. Norton & Co., 2006), 942–43.

32. "Discrepancies and contradictions" appears in Faulkner's prefatory note to *The Mansion* (New York: Library of America, 1999), 331; The "Monk" quotation is from William Faulkner, *Knight's Gambit* (New York: Random Vintage, 1978), 39.

33. *"The Sound and the Fury": Faulkner and the Lost Cause* (Boston: Twayne Publishers, 1991), 52

34. William Faulkner, *Collected Stories* (New York: Random House, 1950), 512. *SLWF*, 185.

35. Published in *The Norton Anthology of English Literature*, ed. Stephen Greenblatt, et al., 8th ed. (New York: W. W. Norton & Co., 2006), 634.

36. *Collected Stories*, 882, 362, 898.

37. William Faulkner, *Uncollected Stories* (New York: Random House), 269. On his efforts to secure a military appointment, see *FAB*, Ch. 50.

38. *FAB*, 1257.

39. See Lisa C. Hickman, *William Faulkner and Joan Williams: The Romance of Two Writers* (Jefferson, N.C.: McFarland & Company, 2006.

40. *FAB*, 1222.

41. *SLWF*, 217–18.

42. *SLWF*, 182.

43. "Cowley's Faulkner," rpt in *William Faulkner: The Critical Heritage*, John Bassett, ed. (London: Routledge & Kegan Paul, 1975), 327.

44. *SLWF*, 233.

45. Grimwood, *Heart in Conflict*, 300–301.

46. *Go Down, Moses*, in *William Faulkner: Novels 1942–1954* (New York: Library of America, 1994), 220.

47. Grimwood, *Heart in Conflict*, 302.

48. Ibid., 304.

49. *A Fable*, in *William Faulkner: Novels 1942–1954*, 994.

50. Grimwood, *Heart in Conflict*, 305.

51. *The Town*, in *William Faulkner: Novels 1957–1962*, 278.

52. "Just finishing the book," Faulkner wrote Jean Stein on 22 August 1956. "It breaks my heart, I wrote one scene and almost cried. I thought it was just a funny book but I was wrong." *SLWF*, 402. Three days later he wired Saxe Commins, "finished book today. will break the heart. thought it was just funny but was wrong." *SLWF*, 403.

53. See, for example, his letter to Else Jonsson 13 December 56: "Am now working on the third volume, which will finish it, and maybe then my talent will have burnt out and I can break the pencil and throw away the paper and rest, for I feel very tired." *SLWF*, 407.

54. *The Mansion*, in *William Faulkner: Novels 1957–1962*, 720–21.

Faulkner's Figures: Speech, Writing, and *The Marionettes*

Serena Haygood Blount

"The ability to write great poetry is an excellent preparation for the writing of great prose," Willard Huntington Wright wrote in 1917.[1] Whereas the "greatness" of William Faulkner's rather rough and obscure verse is doubtful, his attempts at it were certainly excellent preparation for his later work. It would seem prudent for the serious scholar to begin tracing Faulkner's artistic ambitions through careful study of these efforts; certainly it was Faulkner's opinion that the early work should count. *A Green Bough* (1933)—following publications of *Sanctuary*, *The Sound and the Fury*, *As I Lay Dying*, and *These 13*—can be called nothing other than a mature publication. It is a collection of poems written in the early to mid-1920s, many of them revised and all of them artfully arranged, which Faulkner insisted on publishing at the height of his career.[2] In Faulkner's judgment, these are important pieces, and the genetic history evidenced in these early texts demonstrates the extent to which he looked toward nineteenth-century European avant-garde movements for his primary artistic models.

These compositions in verse constitute important steps toward establishing Faulkner's own aesthetic, and Judith Sensibar is correct in her assertion that they should be viewed as "a comprehensive body of work," reflecting a logical pattern of Faulkner's concentrated reading and study, which encompassed related movements, texts, and authors.[3] Such study informed his poetry and later his prose, and propelled Faulkner toward an artistic theory of his own. As Wright wrote, "Every man of genius has at some early period played the plagiarist to more than one master."[4] Indeed, Lothar Hönnighausen's book-length study of the early work, *William Faulkner: The Art of Stylization*, clearly establishes Faulkner's artistic ancestry as it is evidenced in the early work and outlines Faulkner's affinities with other American artists of his time.[5] Hönnighausen argues that elements that may seem esoteric or anomalous in Faulkner's writing are actually genetic and permeate his work as well as that of his modernist contemporaries. Also, Hönnighausen echoes Wright when he declares, "Establishing a manner of writing and painting in imitation of an already

41

existent mode of perception and style is of primary importance for most artists."[6] As Faulkner became a more accomplished writer, he stripped his work of this obvious mimicry while he kept intact theoretical ideas about the relationship between speech and writing in literary discourse, which he developed from his early reading and experimentation. Returning to his early compositions gives us a sense of the literary debts that Faulkner said little about, and it helps us to contextualize the later work; it is here, in the early work, that we see Faulkner's initial logic of literary production, a logic that is replayed throughout the Faulkner canon and at its core remains unchanged.[7]

Faulkner's literary and artistic interests during the early years are readily apparent in compositions dating from that period. In about 1918 Faulkner seriously began to commit himself to careers in both writing and the visual arts. Under the guidance of Phil Stone, he looked toward nineteenth-century European avant-garde movements, particularly the French Symbolist and British Aesthetic movements, while he also read the work of their heirs—A. E. Housman, T. S. Eliot, Conrad Aiken, and James Joyce. In one effusive essay Faulkner admits, "Surely if one be moved at all by Swinburne he must inevitably find in Swinburne's forerunners kinship."[8] This comment explicitly establishes his interest in a particular artistic tradition, the most striking feature of which is the consistent rejection of literary realism by the artists whom Faulkner admired.[9] Among near contemporaries, his unfettered admiration for Conrad Aiken (a follower of the same tradition) is presented in Faulkner's essay "Books and Things: Turns and Movies" in terms of Aiken's "impersonal," scientific composition, his knowledge that "aesthetics is as much a science as chemistry, that there are certain scientific rules which, when properly applied, will produce great art," and in opposition to "our national curse" of realist art that fills "each and every space, religious, physical, mental, moral."[10] Indeed, Faulkner's work evolved along parallel lines with that of his modernist contemporaries in an intellectual climate that included the philosophical ideas of Sigmund Freud and Ferdinand de Saussure, and at a time when a self-conscious vocabulary of literary and linguistic analysis emerged. Faulkner aligned himself early with movements that focused foremost on examining the frontiers of aesthetic experience. His early compositions—in all of their capacious mimicry of the Symbolist masters, the Decadents, and the established Modernists—constitute important steps toward creating new artistic forms and establishing Faulkner's own aesthetic.

In his essay "Verse Old and Nascent—A Pilgrimage" Faulkner admits that upon his first discovery of Swinburne he "was not interested in verse for verse's sake," implying that in 1925 when he penned this essay, a mere three years before the composition of *The Sound and the Fury*, Faulkner now was thoroughly interested in this conception of art.[11] His interest in the "art for art's sake" movement ("With a man it is—quite often—art for art's sake") and his lack of interest in such writers as Twain ("a hack writer who would not have been considered fourth rate in Europe") set him on a distinctive path, at the same time as it aligned him with modernist contemporaries.[12] Hönnighausen concurs, noting that Faulkner's Symbolist play *The Marionettes* "can hardly be dismissed as the idiosyncratic product of a *fin de siècle* mannerism which Faulkner soon outgrew," and he cites Wallace Stevens's "Domination of Black" as a contemporary product of the same ancestry.[13] Hönnighausen opposes the notion that Faulkner's tastes were local, suggesting that his "interest in Swinburne and Verlaine, for example, appears in a different light when we bear in mind that Fitzgerald, Wallace Stevens, and Joyce all turned to the same sources for inspiration."[14]

What Faulkner learned early from his reading was that, for him, serious art is engaged in a careful study of its own status. Faulkner then pursued the refinement of a theoretical ideal through his efforts in both literary and visual arts, focusing chiefly on issues of authorship, speech, and writing. These artistically articulated theories, which exist as prescient, original forecasts of twentieth century poststructuralist ideas—particularly those that Jacques Derrida would articulate in philosophical terms only several decades later—stand as a testament to Faulkner's brilliance as a writer and thinker. His early achievement should not be underestimated, and the way we best arrive at our own recognition of his particular efforts is through intense technical study of his early work in verse, prose, and the graphic arts. Here we find him performing the algebraic laboratory exercises that later on lead him to the successes of his most important novels and short stories.[15]

Prescient in Faulkner's early work is the recognition that in art every appearance of vitality must be characterized by absence. Faulkner tested this idea of absent epiphany in his early prose sketch "Landing in Luck" (1919). In this sketch, the nervous pilot, Thompson, despite having vowed to "pull a perfect landing," loses control of his plane and makes a graceful crash landing that preserves his dignity before a throng of onlookers. The moments before the actual crash are characterized by a singularity of movement as the plane nosedives and rushes toward the ground. What early occurred to Faulkner, however, and what distinguishes his early writing, is that in art such moments must ultimately be characterized by absence, stasis, and silence. Thompson, flying toward the ground, loses his nerve and is "unable to make any pretence of leveling off, paralyzed"; by the time he regains "dominion over his limbs," the moment is over.[16] Ultimately, Thompson's landing is considered exceptional, and he takes credit for it despite his paralysis during it. That Thompson is not the agent of his own landing and that he maintains no control over his body suggests the kind of inscribed automatons that Faulkner carefully develops in later work.[17] Throughout Faulkner's work these paradoxical moments of both presence and absence are consistently attached to the experiences and productions of artists.[18] Thompson, for example, is mastering the art of flying. Later, military strategists, painters, sculptors, writers, storytellers, and other "artists" (and, by extension, authorial figures) of different kinds populate Faulkner's fiction; they experience similar moments, yet do so with increasing acceptance of the absence of vitality that must accompany them. These figures parallel the role of the author himself, who is present only by proxy in his own works. Eventually, in fact, the epiphany becomes the recognition of such absence, as when Nancy Mannigoe laughs in the street in "That Evening Sun," shortly before she hangs herself in jail. After the attempted suicide, Nancy's presence in the story becomes as ghostly as the dead Quentin's, while at the same time she assumes an authorial role akin to his; she tells a story to the children. Finally, Faulkner's interest in these ghostly artistic, and authorial, presences and their strange and increasingly literary epiphanies—Nancy and Quentin are both storytellers—connects to a study of writing and speech, where speech seemingly correlates with presence and writing with absence or proxy.

Faulkner looked for ways to delineate these functions of language and insisted upon inscription as predominating literary discourse. He therefore constructed two principal modes of textual existence, which he introduced in the late teens and early twenties. Reading his work, we are confronted repeatedly by marble fauns, who remain motionless and silent, and by marionettes, who appear to move and speak. In fact, *The Marble Faun* (published in 1924 but composed about 1919–20) and *The Marionettes* (1920) stand out as remarkable early meditations on the status of written language. Noel Polk has called *The Marionettes* one of Faulkner's "most ambitious productions" during his early career, a "remarkable synthesis of his reading up to that time," and "an organic part of the whole, a frame of reference, if not quite a controlling metaphor, rather than mere decoration." [19] This early work presents an orderly concept of composition principles that underscores everything else Faulkner wrote and that should be familiar to any advanced reader of Faulkner; to elaborate, *The Marionettes* exists as a philosophical skeletal system that he fleshes out and naturalizes in later work. The pains that Faulkner took with it are clear: the several slightly varied copies known to exist are each painstakingly lettered, illustrated, and bound by hand. In reading this highly stylized drama, it is good to remind ourselves of Jean Moréas's words concerning the work of the Symbolists: "Inimical to pedantry, to declamation, to false sensitivity, to objective description, symbolist poetry tries to house the Idea in a meaningful form not its own end, but subject to the Idea."[20] Indeed, for Faulkner, they will be described for the sake of explaining the relationship between speech and writing through the modes of literary language and graphic art.

The Marionettes revolves around a few key concepts familiar from Faulkner's other early works such as *The Marble Faun*: motion and motionlessness, nature and artifice, sound and silence. These concepts are directly related to Faulkner's meditations on language and literary production.[21] In the narrative at the beginning of the play, for example, we are given a detailed description of a garden scene, a setting adorned with a "marble colonnade," "sections of wall," and a pool and fountain. The formal order is further reflected in the backdrop, which includes descriptions of stars in "regular order" and a "regular band of black trees" (1). The depiction of a cultivated garden against a backdrop of nature rendered unnatural (via its "regularity") prepares us for the dialogue between the Lilac and Grey Figures. In the opening scene, they debate the setting's stillness via an extended series of similes and metaphors. These initial elements of the setting allude to authorial control over the elements of any piece of writing, and the "slightly unnatural rhythm" in which the Figures move further alludes to the idea of artifice. Moreover, their dialogue deliberates upon the complexities of literary production itself.

As the Grey and Lilac Figures comment on the stillness of the setting, a revelation unfolds for readers of *The Marionettes*. From the outset, the Figures (identified only as "First Figure" and "Second Figure" in the text) notice paradoxical elements in their surroundings. The First Figure comments, "How still it is," remarking that the "air does not stir," but he then declares, the "air is like a candle flaming." The Second Figure qualifies this comparison, asserting that the sky is like a flaming candle and a "curtain of thin blue silk" and that "the wind stirs it gently like a white hand" (4). The First Figure then disagrees, claiming that the sky is still and that the wind only stirs the Second Figure's hair (4). The similes continue through descriptions of the stars as "apples pasted on thin blue silk," and as "gardenias before they turn brown from the heat of a human body." Additional descriptions are of the "breathing" sky and of the moon as a "Roman coin," as a "dismembered breast upon the floor of a silent sea," and as "the bloated face of a scorned woman who has drowned herself" (5, 6). The First Figure again remarks, "How still it is!" and the Second Figure maintains, "It is not still" (6, 8). In the two Figures' extended debate over the stillness of the setting, Faulkner very carefully delineates and insists upon the illusion that fiction makes of "life"—or motion or action—while, through highly figurative language, he reveals this animation as absent. The train of metaphors demonstrates that, in such composition, all language occupies the restricted role of metaphor. That the characters here are called "Figures" refers to their metaphoric roles, and their abstract conversation, maintaining itself in the idiom of simile, metaphor, and repetition throughout the play, echoes the idea.[22]

As the "action" of the play unfolds then, the reader learns that it actually does not unfold, for Pierrot sleeps through the entirety of the play, while only the Shade of Pierrot takes the stage. More specifically, Faulkner's written words, and Faulkner himself in the figurative role of a puppeteer, never engender any actual movement or life. Like the marble faun, the dreaming Pierrot occupies the position of the artist figure.[23] One of Faulkner's early declarations about recursive art is pertinent here; his essay "Verse Old and Nascent, a Pilgrimage" presents his particular admiration for "Ode on a Grecian Urn": "I read 'Thou still unravished bride of quietness' and found a still water withal strong and potent, quiet with its own strength, and satisfying as bread. That beautiful awareness, so sure of its own power that it is not necessary to create the illusion of force by frenzy or motion."[24] Indeed, when we find "frenzy and motion" in Faulkner's work, it is always suspect; generally, lurking somewhere about the periphery of such scenes we find a sleeping Pierrot or a marble faun.[25]

In contrast to the snoozing Pierrot, the wakeful marionettes in this play do appear to speak and move about; Marietta's first line is "I cannot sleep," and we find that this is due to the "singing voice" that she has heard (10, 11). Additionally, she makes "sudden gesture[s]" and "sudden movement[s]" (9, 14). The Shade of Pierrot is called "Voice" in the drama, emphasizing audibility, and, indeed, Marietta hears his voice before she sees him. The Shade of Pierrot is further characterized by action verbs; he "leaps," "strums," "sings," and so forth (18). The contrast between motion and motionlessness is emphasized by the initial description of the sleeping Pierrot who is an embodiment of silence and stillness: "He appears to be in a drunken sleep, there is a bottle and an overturned wine glass upon the table" (2). Faulkner sets up the play as a dreamscape, the action as a dream, and thus, as an artistic creation of sorts. While Pierrot is silent and still, the Shade of Pierrot, a figure characterized by poetic speech and motion, complicates the picture, and together the two echo the vacillations of the traditional Pierrot: the active, social Pierrot and the contemplative, melancholy Pierrot.

The Shade, however, while characterized by motion and speech, is certainly not frenzied. The same sense of control is exerted over his role as is over the entire drama; he speaks in verse and his motion is controlled dance. For example, he explains, "I am not calm but, to and fro/ I sing and whirl and leaping dance," and the Chorus echoes: "We sing and whirl and leaping dance/ To mandolin's high dissonance" (16). Pierrot seeks "music for our revelry" in the garden and begs with the chorus for Marietta to "come dance with us" (17, 18). That he enters from without the garden would at first glance suggest that he is not part of the rigid order established within, but when we recall that in the play the world outside of the garden is ordered, too, the ungoverned freedom that this Pierrot seems to represent is undone. His apparent freedom from the kind of constraints that keep Marietta from participating in his antics seems at first to cast him in stark contrast to her contemplative mood. Finally, however, Pierrot exercises under the same kind of order. His speech is regulated verse, and he dances to music issuing from a lute and a mandolin. The term "dissonance" seems to suggest that his music and dance are ungoverned and perhaps even chaotic; however, in the musical term that describes the intentional interweaving of discordant sounds, a technique associated with modernist literature, we discover again design in Pierrot.

Ultimately, the Shade acts the role of "life," but there is nothing of life in him. The Pierrot character is in fact by tradition simply a mask; he is inscribed with certain traits and qualities prior to Faulkner's use of him, and his hailing from "Paris town" asserts his position within the particular continental sophistication of the commedia dell'arte form (15).[26] Additionally, marionettes, by definition, are not living persons, but they appear to speak, move, and act via the puppeteers who control them. They are, in effect, perfect figures for the characters we encounter in literature: two-dimensional creations who ultimately have no life, who fail to speak or move, despite their apparent animation. Marionettes, and all fictional personae, are by necessity scripted characters, and this idea surfaces in Faulkner's choice of genre for *The Marionettes*. The concept is enhanced by Faulkner's calligraphic writing and his use of illustration throughout; he obviously points us toward the graphic elements of his work. His admiration for the work of Aubrey Beardsley, along with his concentrated mimicry of Beardsley's drawings, is particularly important. Beardsley, after all, created line drawings; his primary point of interest was the line. The signature on his mature work comprised of three stylized lines that varied from piece to piece emphasizes and underscores this point quite nicely, and the import of this was not lost on Faulkner. In a letter to his mother on 12 November 1921, Faulkner plainly expresses his interest in the line: "I want to learn something about line, as you know . . . all my ideas on the subject of line drawing are purely personal."[27] The illustration on pages 6 and 7, for example, demonstrates

Faulkner's attention to line quite nicely. The drawing incorporates two vertical images; on the left is a dark and slender tree whose top tapers into a full white moon. On the right stands Pierrot, significantly wider than the image at the left, and acting almost a photographic negative in the inversion of white and black that Faulkner uses. While Pierrot fades into the white background, the tree, emphasized in black, stands out, suggesting more vitality than the character to its right. Returning to the text, we find that Faulkner's black calligraphy is what stands out—not the white field. In turn, the black ink creates (via line drawings and inscribed language) only an illusion of "life." Finally, we are forced to acknowledge a certain lack of vitality in everything that we see within *The Marionettes* and, thus, to acknowledge the play as a visual artifact rather than as a litany of voices comprising liveliness and speech. Thus, the reasoning behind Pierrot's claimed kinship to the moon (called a "dead leaf") is revealed. In Faulkner's later work, such graphic elements become more subtle and are typographically rendered in a variety of ways. Some critics have correctly suggested that the combination of text and illustration is the chief importance of *The Marionettes*, but they have failed to carefully examine why this combination is so important and they have overlooked the importance of the graphic elements as part and parcel of the play's literary qualities.[28] Faulkner's approach, however, communicates his idea of speech's subordination to written language and the author's position of a puppeteer or ventriloquist who supplies scripted and inscribed "voices" to his characters.

While it would seem that the Shade of Pierrot makes his first appearance as an audible voice—again, he is called "Voice" in the text—in actuality we do *see* him first, both in illustrations and in the calligraphic writing that constitutes him. In fact, it cannot be said that we ever *hear* Pierrot. Furthermore, the character himself articulates throughout *The Marionettes* an extraordinary self-awareness and recognition of his inscribed literary existence, as when he declares that "all the far world lies/ A stage for our revelries" (26). When he sings, "Every month, when comes the moon/ I leave my musty garret room," we get through a fairly common trope, the notion that Pierrot, both sleeping and wakeful, comprises a cerebral entity. Later, this is reinforced when the Second Figure observes that the "statues in this garden are not cold: they are all head" (15, 41). The Shade of Pierrot then exhibits an awareness of his own and Marietta's existence as inscribed literary discourse, by referencing the component of poetic feet when he sings, "Your little white feet have crossed my heart, Love!/ Your little white feet,/ And now I am a garden sprung beneath your footsteps" (19). Furthermore, Pierrot recognizes his own silence: "Then we shall be one in the silence, Love! The pool and the flame,/ Till I am dead, or you have become a flame" (20).[29]

Pierrot characterizes Marietta herself as poetry through the metaphor of her feet, and a few pages later we find she is indeed governed by her poetic existence: she is "like one hypnotised," who moves "step by step, as though in a trance," or "like a sleepwalker"; and when she begins speaking in verse it is without volition (22, 24). Marietta, the marionette (and the similarity between the name "Marietta" and the term "marionette" is not lost on the reader), is inscribed; this means she is written before she ever speaks, and we find that she, like Pierrot, is the product of a poetic tradition: "Then she returned, my mother sweet,/ And slow and sad were her white feet;/ Yet slower still, till from her grave/ There sprang a flower sweet and brave" (23). Marietta evolves into a figure for poetry. At the end of the play, she stands a self-described inscription, in a "sea of ink," where "the wind combs the sky from grey to black," and she laments, "I shall sit on a grey wall, and I shall swing my painted legs through intricate figures . . . and my peacocks will follow me in voluptuous precision" and "their cold feet [will] mark my body with thin crosses" (52, 53, 54). Ultimately, Faulkner creates a text in which he devises a poet who, assisted by "Figures," then creates a poem (43). Pierrot, in both his aspects as sleeping and silent, moving and speaking, provides an accomplished depiction of how literary language functions and how his own position as a poet who "weav[es] his song like a net about [Marietta]" creates yet another poetic speaker and marionette, which doubles the point (24).

The marionettes' inky blackness against the moon, the description of the moon as a "dead leaf," Pierrot's consistent role—he "stamps [his] feet," "spin[s] and weave[s]," creates "dreams" even as "the voices slowly die away"—along with Marietta's unchanged aspect create for us finally a perfect illustration of how literary language functions (41, 27, 28, 43). The Spirit of Autumn, itself a rendition of life and lifelessness, reiterates the point by citing Marietta on the muteness of such art, "Never the nightingale/ Oh my dear,/ Never again the lark/ Wilt thou hear," and he repeats, "Though ever love call and call/ He will not hear at all" (33, 36).[30] We learn that the ordered garden "will not change," that it is populated by "ghosts," and the overriding silence of literary sound is again presented to us through similes such as this: "the passing days scatter like petals on the ground as quietly as shattered roses, like a sweet and sad endless repetition of a name" in a "muted world" (38, 39, 40, 41). The play closes with the same highly metaphorical language issuing from the First and Second Figures that opens it, and at last, in the midst of such overbearing silence, the Second Figure's instruction at the beginning of the final scene to "Listen!" strikes the attentive reader as a climactic exposé of literary artifice (41). In the end, we are left with an artifact, a handcrafted volume that incorporates calligraphy, prose, verse, and illustrations. The Figures tell us this: "A leaf: it is a dead leaf. There, another one" (29). We must conclude, as Sensibar does, that Faulkner's admiration for the Symbolists and their successors is directly attached to their status as "artists of masks, but also poets whose subject was always themselves: 'The worm that gnaws at Pierrot's white breast is consciousness being conscious of itself.'"[31]

It is fruitful to consider *The Marionettes* in specific relation to Faulkner's course of reading under the tutelage of Phil Stone. As part of their discussions on "the theory of fiction," Stone and Faulkner discussed Willard Huntington Wright's *The Creative Will: Studies in the Philosophy and Syntax of Aesthetics*, which Stephen B. Oates has called "Stone's literary bible."[32] Their deliberations and discussions are striking, in that Wright, too, found interest in a "science" of aesthetic analysis.[33] Stone later remarked that "the aesthetic theories set forth in that book . . . constitute one of the most important influences in Bill's whole literary career."[34] Faulkner's perusal of Wright's most important volume agrees with his forays into the work of the Aesthetes, the Symbolists, and his Modernist contemporaries, and, as Joseph Blotner points out, it appears that Faulkner absorbed and modified Wright's ideas early on. Further, it appears that he was particularly interested in positivist ideas, in a science of composition, and in the limits of two-dimensional graphic qualities of both easel painting and literary inscription. Thus we have Faulkner's review of Aiken's *Turns and Movies*, in which he derides authors of literary realism as (significantly) "so many puppets fumbling in windy darkness," while he praises Aiken's "impersonality" and "impersonal sincer[ity]" as catalysts for creating great art.[35] The broad lack of pathos among characters in Faulkner's own corpus surely derives from his respect for this type of art. Finally, Faulkner seems most impressed with Aiken's ability to create "abstract three-dimensional verse" based upon musical forms. This last observation is highly pertinent to our study of *The Marionettes* and, by extension, perhaps to all of Faulkner's work. At the heart of his project is Faulkner's interest in how two-dimensional art both becomes and fails to become three-dimensional via a reader's ideation or mental realization of text on a page. And he focuses his scrutiny particularly on inscribed "music" or "speech"—images that are perceived as acoustic. Indeed, whereas Wright dismissed in *The Creative Will* a "synthesis of all arts," Faulkner clearly embraced the idea, because he recognized that to suggest "three-dimensional verse" on a two-dimensional plane was nothing less than a feat. The sort of synaesthesia of sight and polyphonic sound that Aiken employs to this effect also surfaces in Faulkner's work. *The Marionettes'* renderings of music, dance, visual art, and literature—all upon the flat pages of a book—works toward this end.

As Faulkner's career progressed, the effect became more sophisticated and seemingly three-dimensional when he naturalized these formalist ideas within his novels, tempting us to succumb to the illusion of literary realism. In achieving this effect, however, Faulkner carefully and consistently reminds his reader that these are always mere illusions.

The Marionettes, then, is by no means anomalous within the Faulkner canon; its thematic content is found throughout Faulkner's work. In his earliest texts, however, Faulkner dwelled transparently upon the idea of inscribed marionette characters and authorial ventriloquism by supplying "voice" to an array of literal puppets, while studying the two-dimensional plane upon which literary art "happens." Noel Polk relates the play to two other Faulkner poems, "Claire de Lune" and "Fantoches," as well as to the poem fragment "Two Puppets in a Fifth Avenue Window."[36] Additionally, several other poems employ the Pierrot mask, along with other Italian comedy masks. In the unpublished poem fragment "Scaramouch," for example, we encounter an active and vocal cursing protagonist, cast in present tense verbs, who by the end of the poem is reduced to silence.[37] That the title character *sees* ships "loudly boarded," rendering the audibility of passengers boarding a ship a visual phenomenon, exposes us initially to the nature of poetic speech. By the end of the poem, Scaramouch is presented to us as a dead man via past tense verbs. Following this, visual images and familiar tropes predominate; we find an ocean "bluely running" (like ink), a shadow at Scaramouch's "feet," and "filigrees" woven by "clear interstices." Taken together, the language and imagery of the poem evoke the notion that literary speech is subordinate to and governed by the preexisting inscriptions.

In "Fantouches" [*sic*], Faulkner's loose translation of Verlaine's "Fantoches," we encounter Pucinella [*sic*] and Scaramouches [*sic*].[38] While there is no speech in the poem, there is action; the doctor of Bogona "seeks simples"; his daughter "glides trembling"; and her lover "thrills her." Faulkner, in his adaptation, however, makes one important alteration. While in Verlaine's poem Scaramouche and Pulcinella gesticulate in the moonlight, in Faulkner's poem they merely "Cast one shadow . . . and kiss against the sky" (lines 2–3).[39] The movement of the figures throughout the poem is underscored by the dark silhouette of Scaramouches and Pucinella, and the result is the idea that movement in the poem issues from the silent and still kiss of shadows on the "mellow night." The initial characters' presence is an inscription upon the sky, and in this first stanza we are given a brief overview of how to read the rest of the "characters" in the poem. While they seem animate, they are just as inscribed as the commedia dell'arte figures—the buffoonish Scaramouch and the quarrelsome Pulcinella—that we begin with. Furthermore, the poem itself is inscribed: Faulkner "translates" Verlaine's poem while borrowing the final line from T. S. Eliot's "Rhapsody on a Windy Night" (1917), in which the words are "spoken" by a streetlamp, and which Eliot had already adapted from LaForgue's "Complainte de cette Bonne Lune" (1885), a poem constructed as a drama in verse, in which the stars and moon "speak." The intertextuality here reinforces Faulkner's explicit literary lineage and highlights the complexities of speech and writing integral to his own career, for speech and writing are also at the crux of the game in both Eliot and Laforgue's poems. That this final line is cited again in *Soldiers' Pay* only compounds the idea. Citation itself, in fact, as a mode of repetition and inscription is important to Faulkner's project. If characters are inscribed before they "speak," then citation is a necessary component of this "speech," and his work here and in later fiction proves an ongoing fascination with the idea.[40]

Finally, Faulkner's use of Italian masks, particularly in the calligraphic *The Marionettes*, is also indicative of his ongoing attention to issues of "character." His calligraphy emphasizes that his inscribed characters are particularly formed by the strokes of the pen. Faulkner takes a material view of his characters; he demonstrates not only that they are formed of characters—that is, of letters—but evidences as well a particular difficulty faced by any major author, that of building characters upon existing characters. In Faulkner's formulation of his unique calligraphy, he expands upon "the rigidity of an alphabet" that "presents a never-ending artistic challenge: How do you do something new and still preserve the letters' essential forms?"[41] Furthermore, in his deliberate comparison of alphabetic characters with "human" characters, Faulkner insinuates himself into a procession of authors with similar interests.[42] Beyond his interest in inscription, Faulkner also demonstrates the difficulty of coming up with a "new" character and the ease of falling into clichés; authors most often build their characters on and out of existing characters (in both senses of the word). The major author, however, brings something additional to the table; in building, he introduces additional concepts, and in Faulkner's case, this added interest attaches to self-aware inscriptions and notions of speech and writing. He seems to accept that an original character cannot be born in the author's imagination (thus, his early years comprise a revelry in capacious mimicry) and that the author must start with a form (here, Faulkner presses the issue in two modes—the comedic masks and the least forms available, alphabetic characters).

The concepts of character, inscription, and Poe-esque "lifelikeliness" outlined in *The Marionettes* repeat throughout the Faulkner canon, and this repetition is of the utmost importance to Faulkner, for in his figuratively posited conclusions about textual and authorial functions,

Faulkner arrives at a theory of literary language as repetition, literary speech as citation.[43] He writes about a great variety of subjects in a great variety of styles, and he can do so because he develops a systematic way of achieving this virtuosity through study, mimicry, and experimentation with literary discourse. His marionettes, his marble faun, and his pilot, who move, speak, and land without volition, exemplify this idea. In his efforts to represent language in stories and poems with speaking characters, Faulkner delineates the linkage between them and the automatic, repeated, inscribed marks on the page that yield their utterances. In *The Marionettes*, he does this both through illustration and calligraphy, pushing his pen into the reader's face, forcing us to acknowledge the text as a written artifact.

NOTES

1. Willard Huntington Wright, *The Creative Will: Studies in the Philosophy and the Syntax of Aesthetics* (New York: John Lane Company, 1916), 259.

2. The galley copy of *A Green Bough* held at the University of Texas demonstrates the care Faulkner took in producing the volume. In this manuscript, poem groupings are separated by blank pages, and some poems bear titles. In the published volume, titles were replaced with Roman numerals.

3. Judith L. Sensibar, *The Origins of Faulkner's Art* (Austin: University of Texas Press, 1984), xvi.

4. Wright, 195.

5. Lothar Hönnighausen, *William Faulkner: The Art of Stylization in his Early Graphic and Literary Work* (New York: Cambridge University Press, 1987).

6. Ibid., 5.

7. In concert with his increasing silence about literary influences (the enthusiasm that we see for Swinburne, Keats, and Aiken in the early essays does not surface in later interviews and essays), it appears that Faulkner also took very few reading notes; the volumes of his library are remarkably lacking in marginalia. Regarding his book borrowing arrangements with Phil Stone, William Van O'Connor in *The Tangled Fire of William Faulkner* (Minneapolis: University of Minnesota Press, 1954) writes that volumes "were always returned with the margins as clean and untouched as when Stone handed the books to him" and the contents of Faulkner's library held at the University of Virginia are also devoid of notes and markings (18). Instead, rather stunningly, Faulkner seems to exhibit a kind of total recall in regards to his favorite authors. This state of affairs is pertinent to Faulkner's overall project, in which the idea of inscribed and repeating recordings is a predominant theme.

8. "Verse Old and Nascent: A Pilgrimage," in *William Faulkner: Early Prose and Poetry*, ed. Carvel Collins (Boston: Little, Brown and Co., 1962), 115.

9. Faulkner became acquainted with the work of these forerunners through the introductions of Phil Stone and specifically, it appears, through his perusal of Arthur Symons's *The Symbolist Movement in Literature* (New York: E. P. Dutton and Co., 1919). Importantly, as Alexander Marshall insists, we "know that he was reading the Symbolists long after his initial apprenticeship was over—Faulkner called Verlaine and LaForgue 'old

friends' he came back to again and again" (389). See "William Faulkner: The Symbolist Connection," in *American Literature* 59:3 (October 1987): 389–401.

10. *Early Prose and Poetry*, 74–76. The proliferation of poems written by Faulkner that clearly mimic the work of T. S. Eliot speak further to his formalist interests; Eliot's interest in Wyndham Lewis, in turn, betrays similar concerns: Kenneth Rexroth writes that Eliot's "narrative style is LaForgue reduced to a formula: 'Describe human beings as though they were machines, landscapes as though they were chemical formulas, inanimate objects as though they were alive'" (155). See "The Influence of French Poetry on American," in *World Outside the Window: The Selected Essays of Kenneth Rexroth*, ed. Morrow Bradford (New York: New Directions, 1987). 143–70.

11. *Early Prose and Poetry*, 115.

12. Ibid., 115, 94.

13. Hönninghausen, 142.

14. Ibid., 6.

15. Rather than retrospectively working from Derrida's ideas and applying them to Faulkner's work, it seems more valuable to follow the chronological trajectory of Faulkner's own career. His own efforts guide us toward an understanding of his original ideas.

16. Ibid., 48.

17. Some examples include the speaker of "The Lilacs"/Poem I in *A Green Bough*, Alec Gray in "Victory," the marching soldiers in "Crevasse," and Donald Mahon in *Soldiers' Pay.*

18. Faulkner's perusals of Joyce perhaps led him to tie this sort of absence to language itself. In *Portrait of the Artist as a Young Man*, for example, Stephen Dedalus composes in his mind a few lines and then experiences a revelation: "The word ['ivory'] now shone in his brain, clearer and brighter than any ivory sawn from the mottled tusks of elephants" (178).

19. William Faulkner, *The Marionettes*, ed. Noel Polk (Charlottesville: University Press of Virginia, 1977), ix, x, xi.

20. Jean Moréas, "The Symbolist Manifesto," in *Manifesto: A Century of Isms*, ed. Mary Ann Caws (Lincoln: University of Nebraska Press, 2001), 50–51.

21. Noel Polk names several more thematic touchstones found in the drama: "time, change, frustrated sexuality, the relationship between the wilderness and civilization, sterility and fecundity" (ix). I would suggest, however, that these topics might all be located beneath the related headings I have given.

22. The colors associated with the Figures further underscore the strange status of the text. "Lilac" implies the traditional death symbolism of purple lilacs (another example of this usage by Faulkner occurs in the c. 1919 poem "The Lilacs"), and "Grey" suggests the twilit moment of the "living text"—a text that appears to sound even while it remains silent. Faulkner's consideration of this hue surfaces elsewhere, as in poem XXX, c. 1924, of *A Green Bough* and in his character Alec Gray in "Victory." His fiction demonstrates an enduring fascination with symbolic twilight and dusk.

23. Indeed, Judith Sensibar terms the marble faun "the pierrotique Marble Faun," 9.

24. *Early Prose and Poetry*, 117.

25. Hönnighausen concurs that Faulkner, as a disciple of the aesthetes, was interested in a "particular state of pure concentration." He further writes that "Pater, Wilde, and the early Yeats all differentiated between action and contemplation in a similar way, making contemplation their ideal" (143).

26. In *The Marionettes*, however, the mask is compounded, with both Pierrot and the Shade of Pierrot making appearances.

27. *Thinking of Home: William Faulkner's Letters to his Mother and Father, 1918–1925*, ed. James G. Watson (New York: W. W. Norton & Co., 1992), 159.

28. See Michael Millgate, *The Achievement of William Faulkner* (Athens: University of Georgia Press, 1989), Hönnighausen, and Polk.

29. This remark is also striking in its implication that Pierrot will remain silent until he is dead, and that only then will he speak. This idea reverberates throughout the Faulkner canon, in such pieces as "The Hound," "Carcassonne," and most notably in Addie Bundren's section of *As I Lay Dying*.

30. As the seasons change in the play, and we are finally left with the cold, dead garden (just as in *The Marble Faun*), and as Faulkner carefully calcifies his ideas over the course of the play, he adjusts the familiar trope wherein changing seasons parallel human life and death so that the Spirit of Autumn ultimately serves as an echo for the literary "truths" that Faulkner posits.

31. Sensibar, xviii.

32. Stephen B. Oates, *William Faulkner: The Man and the Artist: A Biography* (New York: Harper & Row, 1987), 35.

33. Joseph Blotner, *Faulkner: A Biography* (New York: Random House, 1974), 320. See also Oates, 35.

34. James Meriwether, "Early Notices of William Faulkner by Phil Stone and Louis Cochran," in *Mississippi Quarterly* 17 (1964): 136–164, 141.

35. *Early Prose and Poetry*, 75, 76. Faulkner's penchant for "fumbling in windy darkness" surfaces later in descriptions of his own work—his dedication of *The Wishing Tree*, to his step-daughter, for example, uses the same words. It is instructive also to compare these observations on Aiken to Faulkner's evaluation of Swinburne's work: "I do not mean . . . that I ever found anything sexual in Swinburne: there is no sex in Swinburne. The mathematician surely; and eroticism just as there is eroticism in form and color and movement wherever found" (*EPP* 115). This commentary is important when we consider that Faulkner's work up to this moment is as algebraic as anything Swinburne wrote.

36. See Polk's introduction to *The Marionettes*.

37. "Scaramouch," Wynn Faulkner Collection, University of Mississippi: Folder 4, #20–21.

38. *Early Prose and Poetry*, 57.

39. This image occurs also in *The Marionettes*.

40. We might consider, as an additional example, the biblical citations in the short story "Victory."

41. Virginia Postrel, "Playing to Type," in *Atlantic Monthly* 301:1 (January/February 2008):143–46, 143.

42. This comparison happens as well in "Miss Zylphia Gant," the title of which typographically adapts Faulkner's unique calligraphy, in which the letter /s/ is uniformly printed backwards, so that it looks much like the letter /z/. Zilphia's name begs comparison with the more traditional name "Sylvia." Melville's chapter in *Moby Dick* on the carpenter takes up the same problem of material character.

43. Drafts that incorporate lines from both *The Marionettes* and *The Marble Faun* begin to make sense, not only in terms of Faulkner's experimentation during his early writing years, but also in terms of his greater sense of literary production. See Polk, and Judith Sensibar's catalogue, *Faulkner's Poetry: A Bibliographical Guide to Texts and Criticism* (Ann Arbor: UMI Research Press, 1988).

"That City Foreign and Paradoxical": William Faulkner and the Texts of New Orleans

Owen Robinson

William Faulkner's fiction is primarily associated with his apocryphal Yoknapatawpha County, the principal setting for all but five of his novels and many of his short stories. But the intricate construction of this rural, troubled, northern Mississippi world is balanced by engagement with similarly complex others, perhaps the most intriguing of which is New Orleans. The physical fragility of this city is famous, of course—indeed, Hurricane Gustav is approaching the Gulf Coast literally as I write—and with its complex colonial history and position at the cusp of the Caribbean and mainland North America, its identity likewise has a peculiarly resonant contingency. New Orleans is both unique and plural, both problematically "Southern" (in U.S. terms, at least) and "American" in the widest connotations of that term; that is, it is a place impossible to pin down to a firm identity. And if, to use the famous description offered in *Absalom, Absalom!*, New Orleans is "that city foreign and paradoxical," then so might Faulkner's own place in American letters perhaps be considered similarly: the place and the writing constitute polyphonic, shifting, highly complex cultural fields.

Faulkner lived in New Orleans for six months in 1925, returning for part of 1926, writing his first novel and numerous sketches there, and participating in its thriving literary and artistic scene; beyond this, its significance to his career might be gauged by the point that all five of those errant non-Yoknapatawpha books have some claim, in one sense or another, to be considered New Orleans texts. *Mosquitoes* (1927) is explicitly set in and around the city, *Pylon* (1935) is set in the New Orleans stand-in New Valois, both story strands of *The Wild Palms* (1939) include the city as an important site, and *A Fable's* (1954) tall tale of the three-legged racehorse is founded there. Even Faulkner's very first novel, *Soldiers' Pay*, frequently seen as a practice run for Yoknapatawpha, was, as the plaque outside what is now Faulkner House Books in Pirate's Alley proclaims, written there, at the same time as the usually overlooked sketches of the city that he wrote for the *Double Dealer* and the *Times-Picayune*. Thus, New Orleans is Faulkner's other great literary construct after his county and constitutes a fairly substantial body of work to stand in relation to the much larger Yoknapatawpha series, in terms of its depiction of and inspiration from *place*, albeit with some important differences. It is also feasible to trace a dialectic between Faulkner's New Orleans and Yoknapatawpha, though for the most part this must be one traced implicitly, as the two are rarely juxtaposed in the texts themselves—with, of course, one very important exception: *Absalom, Absalom!*

I have explored elsewhere the extreme dialogic factors that energise and indeed construct Yoknapatawpha County[1]; my intention here is to suggest that New Orleans, and Faulkner's increasingly complex portrayal of it, is similarly infused. While the New Orleans material does not feature among Faulkner's greatest works until the novels of the mid-1930s, both the later triumphs and the early career experiments benefit from being seen as part of a developmental engagement with the city, along dialogic lines. Seen from this perspective, the mid-1920s sketches gain much resonance, particularly when considered collectively and in conversation with other texts, while the later work is even richer through building on the already intricate foundations of the sketches and early fiction. I hope to show that there is greater depth and sophistication throughout Faulkner's New Orleans texts than is often allowed and that the city is a crucial part of his body of work, in terms both of form and content. I will begin with a closer look at Faulkner's very first New Orleans texts and then briefly examine two scenes from *Mosquitoes* and *Pylon*. In the latter parts of this essay, I will discuss the treatment of New Orleans in *Absalom, Absalom!* as a crucial Faulknerian place where the city is at its most "myriad."

1. Faulkner's First Texts of the Myriad City: *New Orleans Sketches*

The material now best known through the collection edited by Carvel Collins, *New Orleans Sketches* (1958), consists of a series of brief character sketches written for the "little magazine" the *Double Dealer*, edited and published in the city, and a longer and more disparate set of short stories that appeared in Sunday editions of the New Orleans *Times-Picayune*. The sketches and stories were written and published between January and September 1925, during Faulkner's own major period of residence in the city and soon after, and serve as the most direct product of his work for and association with the editorial and creative forces behind those publications. Even when we apply the most generous appreciation to them, they scarcely rank among Faulkner's most significant achievements, though to be fair, that bar is set high. Much of the comparatively scarce (for Faulkner) criticism on *Sketches*, from Collins himself to more recent work, considers them primarily as precursors to the later, greater writing.[2] I will do this myself, indeed, and I am not about to suggest that *Sketches* be moved up the Faulknerian pecking order (or at least not far up it), but I do think that they also have further value beyond this stepping-stone function. Granted, in many cases, the individual pieces are sometimes insubstantial, with trite or contrived plots and characters that cross the line into stereotype, but these are frequently countered with an alertness to how these contrivances relate to the greater fabric of the city. Indeed, I suggest that the book form, the collection, rather than the weekly series of stand-alone pieces, suits them well, as their greatest value overall is cumulative: placed together in a single volume, they present a suitably dialogic array, to use Bakhtin's model, of myriad people, images, and places in and of New Orleans. Bakhtin's theories of dialogism, heteroglossia, and the chronotope are, of course, applied more specifically to the novel form; however, they can clearly be applied to, or discerned in, *Sketches* when collected together in Collins's volume—particularly if we take into account the fragmentary nature of Faulkner texts that *are* perhaps problematically deemed novels, such as *The Unvanquished* or *Go Down, Moses*. In his writings on heteroglossia, Bakhtin shows the potentially liberatory power of prose by demonstrating the continual interaction and stratification of languages, speech, and voices. Bakhtin suggests that each voice is as valid and constitutive of society as any other and that, through its particular ability to render them artistically and plurally, prose has the ability to wrest power from those who assume narrative control over people's lives. This ability applies both to authors and narrators within texts and to authorities and the otherwise dominant in society at large. Through the understanding that every moment consists of essentially limitless voices, Bakhtin posits that each literary moment, as such, allows for the possibility of different voices speaking to, against, and through each other: "Every concrete utterance of a speaking subject serves as a point where centrifugal as well as centrapetal forces are brought to bear. The processes of centralization and decentralization, of unification and disunification, intersect in the utterance; the utterance not only answers the requirements of its own language as an individualized embodiment of a speech act, but it answers the requirements of heteroglossia as well; it is in fact an active participant in such speech diversity."[3]

The first section in *New Orleans Sketches* consists of the very brief character sketches published in the *Double Dealer* in January and February 1925, collected in the volume under the title "New Orleans." They

vary in quality, to be sure, but they also give something like a representative spread of the voices that constitute the myriad city (in *Pylon's*
useful phrase); that they are in the first person, even if this is not always
completely realized, serves to emphasize their status as a collection of
"utterances," of speech acts, that attempt to represent the speaker but
also contribute to the greater complex dialogue that is "New Orleans,"
in the way that Bakhtin describes. There is some justification, then, in
Daniel Singal's contention that "one finds in these sketches Faulkner's
first experiments with what would soon be a dominant feature of his
novels—the dramatic reversal of social and racial stereotypes. Nothing,
it seemed, delighted him more than turning conventional perceptions
inside out, exploding widely held myths, images, and identities in an
effort to establish more complex and authentic ones in their place."[4] The
characters chosen to represent aspects of New Orleans life do not necessarily serve this subversive purpose. Earlier writing of the city, perhaps
most notably that of George Washington Cable, is replete with figures we
might identify with Faulkner's labels: "Wealthy Jew," "The Priest," "The
Sailor," "The Beggar," "The Artist," and so on. However, their apparently
unmediated juxtaposition, as well as, frequently, the sensitivity to the
complexities of their own lives, shows that behind each of these labels lies
a shifting, often multilayered identity. In a city often represented through
its population of (stereo)types, which such an array as this might initially
seem to be reinforcing, this miniseries attempts to explore the humanity
behind these social faces; through their narrative promixity to each other,
there is also implied their interaction, even if this is not direct.

The results are varied. Some portraits situate both the individual and
the city in global contexts, claiming New Orleans as a juncture in the
worldwide scope and potential of man; the tenor in these pieces is expansive. The "Wealthy Jew," for instance, suggests that this city is no more
foreign to him than any other place: "No soil is foreign to my people,
for have we not conquered all lands with the story of your nativity?"
This reference registers Jews as one of many New Orleanian diaspora,
of course, and this individual explicitly attempts to reach out to other
inhabitants of the Creole city to place his narrative alongside theirs just
as "your sons and my sons lay together in the mud at Passchendaele and
sleep side by side beneath foreign soil," but the portrait remains clumsy,
at best, the reference to conquest perhaps unfortunate.[5] Another form of
conquest is claimed by "The Sailor," a transient, temporary inhabitant of
the city, a man who has seen the world but who differentiates its regions
not through religion or movements of people, but through the women he
has slept with. "A sound footing is good," he reasons of his New Orleans
sojourn, "and wine and women and fighting; but soon the fighting's done

and the wine is drunk and women's mouths don't taste as a man had thought, and then he'll sicken for the surge and sound of the sea, and the salt smell of it again."[6]

Other portraits, while similarly alluding to personal or conceptual existence elsewhere in the world, rather posit the lives of the speakers in terms of restriction. "The Beggar" has a jadedness, a trammelled hope, that perhaps points forward to the bleaker, claustrophobic views of the city in some of the 1930s writing. It begins with a recollection of childhood idealism that almost combines the varying worldliness of the Wealthy Jew and the Sailor: "When I was a boy I believed passionately that life was more than just eating and sleeping, than restricting a man's life to one tiny speck of the earth's surface and marking his golden hours away to the stroke of a bell. What little of the world the ant can see is good to him; and I, with his vision magnified an hundred times . . . what would it not be to the ant with my vision! Then multiply the limit of my sight by the size of the earth . . . and there you are." But there he isn't, alas, as he finds himself "in the dusty road," having to "whine and snarl with others whose steeds have failed."[7] Rather than a port of call in a global voyage of individual or collective opportunity, New Orleans here is the site of his disillusionment, of his failure, the "one tiny speck" that enshrines his own bitter insignificance. This sense is even more poignant in the portrait of "The Cobbler," which begins: "My life is a house: The smell of leather is the wall of my house. Three sides are dark, but from the other side there comes faint light through dingy unwashed windows. Beyond these windows the world grows loud and passes away. I was once part of the world, I was once a part of the rushing river of mankind; but now I am old, I have been swirled into a still backwater in a foreign land, and the river has left me behind. That river of which I was once a part. I do not remember very well, for I am old: I have forgotten much."[8] The Cobbler identifies himself entirely with his house, which itself serves as the prison of his old age, at least as he conceives of it. The darkness and isolation of his current existence are then set against romantic visions of youth and long-lost love in Tuscany. It is telling that life and house are apparently inextricable from each other: the stories of his life are contained by, enshrined in, and, it seems, limited to this place.

Interestingly, the sketches briefly discussed so far do not mention New Orleans by name, and one could probably transplant many of these pen portraits to any number of other world cities—particularly port cities—with little difficulty. This does not make them any less a collective picture of the city, as their association-through-collection, under the title "New Orleans," creates a loose, uneasy, and fractious dialogue both of the Crescent City and, implicitly, between it and other such places. The final two sketches in the *Double Dealer* series, however, form a pair that do bring things more specifically and uniquely home to New Orleans, though, still, the name appears only in the very last one. Both present versions of the much-invoked image of the courtesan. In the first of these, "Magdalen," without directly identifying her profession (and this is the only portrait to have a personal name, rather than a designation of position, as such), laments that "Men aint what they used to be, or money aint, or something. Or maybe its I that aint like I was once. God knows, I try to treat 'em like thay'd want I should. I treat 'em white as any, and whiter than some . . . not calling no names. I'm an American girl with an American smile I am, and they know it."[9] In this very slight way, Magdalen touches here on some of the complex issues of race and cultural identity that New Orleans is suffused by and to which Faulkner will return in a serious and involved way in *Absalom, Absalom!* Magdalen's lament is pained, though this is in effect a pain of absence of feeling: like the Cobbler, she seems to exist in a malaise, such extremes as love and grief now "forgotten" and "long ago." Hers is a personal account in spite of itself, a testimony of individual struggles in a set of social codes seeking to deny such individuality: just as "thay" need to be treated "white," so she is likewise defined by how she conducts herself in relation to "them." This, as she perhaps wryly notes, is part of her fate as "an American girl with an American smile," and "American," here, surely carries connotations from beyond the borders of the United States. This page-long piece initially reads melodramatically and seems overwritten, but when read closely it is suggestive of greater complexities to come: it evokes through very sparse detail the difficulties of a particular life lived in a role frequently used emblematically to evoke the city itself.

And the very last of the series does just that. "The Tourist" presents two visions of "a courtesan," each beginning with the words "New Orleans" and "a courtesan." The first of these has the city's name as a point on an itinerary, as the place of writing; "——New Orleans." It describes "a courtesan, not old and yet no longer young, who shuns the sunlight that the illusion of her former glory be preserved," who "does not talk much herself" but "seems to dominate the conversation." The aura of decadent decay that the woman projects, in this perception of her, and the combined neglect and esteem that are directed towards her resonate with Magdalen's lament immediately preceeding, though we are not told that this is she. Living "in an atmosphere of a bygone and more gracious age," it is also implied that she represents the city in which she "reclines gracefully." This representative duty is made explicit in the second of the tourist's visions: "New Orleans . . . a courtesan whose hold is strong upon the mature, to whose charm the young must respond. And all who leave her, seeking the virgin's unbrown, ungold hair and her blanched and icy breast where no lover has died, return to her when she smiles across her languid fan . . . New Orleans." In terms of its imagery, this vision is reminiscent of the first, but here, like Magdalen but unlike the unnamed woman of the first paragraph, this courtesan has a name: New Orleans. This vision of New Orleans as an aging but seductive beauty, antithetical to propriety yet urgent in her irresistability, is, of course, one of the most overused, albeit inevitably tempting, metaphors for the city. The juxtaposition of the city as courtesan here with an individual, "actual" courtesan serves both to drive home the potential richness of the metaphor and to show how it arguably cheapens both its constituent elements. Indeed, when taken together with Magdalen's narrative, we might reflect on how it is just such insistence on the part of others—usually men—that circumscribes and defines the lives of real people through the imposition of codes. But before we lambast Faulkner himself for further progating a potentially damaging myth, we should note that this is the voice of "The Tourist," an acknowledged outsider imposing his outsider's perspective. Faulkner himself is an outsider in New Orleans, of course, but his specific placing of both the metaphor itself and its construction through narrative in the voice of one thus specifically identified makes clear and vital the importance of perspective. The piece retreads an old cliché, but at the same time points to its doing so. As such, it serves both to capture and restate the image but also to renew it, by bringing it back into the dialogue that has inevitably shaped it up until now; the piece forces us to reflect on both the impulses behind and the consequences of such cultural fashioning. As many later Faulkner texts do in more intensive ways, this piece—and by extension the whole series of portraits for the *Double Dealer*—constructs narratives and also the conditions in which those narratives are constructed. A wealth of suggested dialogue between voices opens up here, in the Bakhtinian sense, and each voice in this New Orleanian heteroglossia is itself shown to be stratified, complex, the product of multiple dialogues. Without suggesting that this heteroglossia reaches later Yoknapatawphan heights, we might note that Faulkner's early published experiments with prose nevertheless figure New Orleans as both the site and the product of continual dialogue, in which every participant, including the writer and reader, must bring their own perspective to bear and consider its effects.[10]

The pieces written for the *Times-Picayune* are longer and are more obviously intended as stories: if plots of sorts are implied in the *Double Dealer* sketches, then they are rather followed here, albeit in fairly limited fashion. A couple of the longer pieces—"The Cobbler" and "The Kid Learns"—are direct developments of portraits in the "New Orleans" series, and elsewhere the plots rarely develop much beyond this—the sketch, indeed. Here, too, we get a parade of aliens and misfits: tramps, touts, jealous Italian lovers. Some of the sketches are better than others, but overall their greatest value is cumulative, highlighting the ways in which they work, or don't work, with each other, to construct a shifting dialogic web of the city. Though the characters of the stories rarely directly interact, their narrative threads weave together in the collection as a whole. If this takes place primarily at the point of reception, of our readership, this in no way diminishes its effectiveness—far from it, indeed. Wolfgang Iser points out that it is precisely in the reader's intense engagement with textual "gaps" that narrative comes most fully to life: "one text is potentially capable of several different realizations, and no reading can ever exhaust the full potential, for each individual reader will fill in the gaps in his own way, thereby excluding the various other possibilities; as he reads, he will make his own decision as to how the gap is to be filled. In this very act the dynamics of reading are revealed. By making his decision he implicitly acknowledges the inexhaustibility of the text; at the same time it is this inexhaustibility that forces him to make his decision."[11] In this way, the New Orleans of Faulkner's early work takes shape in some perhaps unexpectedly similar ways to the great Yoknapatawphan reading challenges to come: we are required to become fundamentally involved in the construction of this rendered place, and the dynamics of the particular text(s) at hand exploit this fully.

Furthermore, there are some recurring motifs that reflect this narrative process at the same time as they enable consideration of New Orleans's place in wider contexts, both personal and geographical. Time and again in the *Sketches*, the night sky above New Orleans, and at times elsewhere, is used to site the individual and the city and to mirror the narrative trajectories of the characters. The stars are used to signify various things and appropriately mean different things to different people, though there is a common sense in which their observation usually marks the observer as from elsewhere, as a representative of one of New Orleans's many diaspora. Sometimes the image is simply juxtaposed with thoughts of "Home," as when Jean-Baptiste, in the sketch of that title, watches "the quiet rooftops cutting the sky, watching the stars like cast roses arrested above an open coffin," while "thinking of the dark corners which men's destinies turn," these destinies—or his, at any rate—implictly mapped out on the night sky above the city.[12] In "The Cobbler," developed from the shorter, earlier piece of the same title, the stars are used to denote more explicitly a nostalgic sense of better times and more loved places: the Tuscan cobbler, in Faulkner's reworked sketch, remembers walking hand in hand with his lost love, "while the stars came out so big, so near—it is not like that in your America, signor."[13] This version of "The Cobbler" is ostensibly a tale of Tuscany, but this assertion of the inferiority of New Orleanian stars reinforces his story as part of the narrative fabric of New Orleans, as is his evident alienation in America: indeed, the distance that he feels from these American stars echoes the distance he feels from his youth, his love. Elsewhere, however, the stars are a binding link between New Orleans and places of origin: a jealous husband stares "at the starred sky stretching like taut silk above the walled well of the alley, watching the same stars at which he had gazed in far-away Sicily, in his youth, when he had been a boy and life was clear and fine and simple; and that lads would stare wondering upon long after he and his dream and his problem were quiet underground." These are "the heedless, flying stars among which his problem had got so interwoven and tangled"; they care nothing for the narrative that he ascribes to them.[14] This sense of personal and geographical insignificance as denoted by the stars is starker still at the conclusion of "Sunset," where they register the failure of the protagonist to travel to Africa as he is tricked and then mown down by a machine gun: his dead face is "turned up to the sky and the cold, cold stars. Africa or Louisiana: what care they?"[15] His quest to reverse the journey of his forebears and use New Orleans to leave America in search of Africa, signifies, it seems, nothing.

Except, of course, that this narrative, all these narratives, these stars, and so on *are* used to signify in various ways. We might look at one further use of the New Orleanian night sky, here in relation to the observation of a vagrant on Chartres Street: "Later, from a railed balcony—Mendelssohn impervious in iron—I saw him for the last time. The moon had crawled up the sky like a fat spider and planes of light and shadow were despair for the Vorticist schools. (Even those who carved those strange flat-handed creatures on the Temple of Rameses must have dreamed New Orleans by moonlight.)"[16] This, of course, is a use of the night-sky image and of New Orleans in explicitly artful and artistic terms, and it is used by a figure we meet in several of the *Sketches* and whom we might cautiously identify as "William Faulkner." However autobiographical some of these pieces may seem, though, the "I" of the narrative is always a literary construct, a "voice." The "Faulkner" character, if so we may call him for convenience, is generally an observer, relating the activities and speech of New Orleanians, telling their stories. At times, their stories interact with his own, and on these occasions this figures him as conduit: a listener or observer of the tale or action, and transmitter of it to us, the reader. None of this makes him any less important a narrative presence in the city in his own right, of course, as he becomes part of the projected and self-projected bohemian Vieux Carré scene of the 1920s—itself a text of New Orleans and turned into a literal text by Faulkner in the form of *Mosquitoes* (which also makes repeated use of the image of the night sky). This figure is very consciously an artist who is there to render the city and its texts in creative form and to work with and on the people he finds and the stories they tell—and if they won't tell their stories, he will construct some for them, as we see in possibly the finest of the *New Orleans Sketches*, "Episode."

In this initially slight-seeming account of William Spratling's sketching of an elderly couple, we are given one of the most revealing depictions in the collection of Faulkner's own engagement with New Orleans. It both describes his circumstances there and his narrative construction of the city and its inhabitants. Faulkner specifically uses his own outsider's perspective, a strategy bringing to mind "The Tourist" and his observations regarding the courtesan and the courtesan city. But he gets more specific even than this, right from the start, and in the process nudges towards the great cultural encounters we see in *Absalom, Absalom!* "Every day at noon they pass. He in a brushed suit and a gray hat, never collarless nor tieless, she in a neat cotton print dress and a sunbonnet. I have seen her any number of times, sitting and rocking upon wooden porches before the crude, shabby cottages among my own hills in Mississippi."[17] In this opening observation, the young writer (or his narrative stand-in, at any rate) brings northern Mississippi into New Orleans; in effect, he imposes his rural narrative upon this urban environment, at once asserting the simultaneity of these two worlds and the perhaps inevitable connections between them, and the otherness of this couple coming to beg at the St. Louis Cathedral. Subjects and artists then come into direct contact when "Spratling from the balcony called to her." This call specifically places the scene outside the house in what is now Pirate's Alley where Faulkner and Spratling lived and worked. Lives and texts merge here: readers of the *Times-Picayune* in 1925 may not have known the specific house, but they would surely have known the scene; latter-day Faulknerians, or indeed any visitor to Faulkner House Books, can of course picture it exactly. Just as Faulkner's own biography comes into play in the opening of this sketch (and throughout it) so then, surely, does the reader's, given the specificity of the detail offered and the knowledge we can now have of Faulkner's living circumstances in New Orleans. We might say that this is always the case (a reading of Jefferson and Yoknapatawpha will inevitably take on new dimensions if the reader visits Oxford and Lafayette County, for instance), but this is a key point here because perception and perspective, and the ways in which they impinge on a sense of place, are central concerns of the sketch.

When the couple are bidden to pose for a sketch by Spratling, the layers of narrative deepen further. The old woman takes the lead, guiding her blind husband into the pose that "one knew immediately they had been photographed [in] on their wedding day": "She was a bride again; with that ability for fine fabling which death alone can rob us of, she was once more dressed in silk (or its equivalent) and jewels, a wreath and a veil, and probably a bouquet. She was a bride again, young and fair, with her trembling hand on young Joe's shoulder; Joe beside her was once more something to shake her heart with dread and adoration and vanity—something to be a little frightened of" (188). Joe, too, assumes "that fixed and impossible attitude of the male and his bride being photographed in the year 1880" (189). They exist, in the narrator's perception at least, as a young nuptial couple as well as a pair of beggars. The proximity of the cathedral adds poignancy to both these now concurrent images. There could well be a great deal of accuracy in this narrative of their youth, of course, and "Faulkner" as carefully positions and dresses them (especially her) in the past as he has in the present-day scene before him—the invocation of portrait poses of the 1880s is powerful. However, the assertion that "one knew immediately" that this is how they appeared in 1880 paradoxically highlights necessary uncertainty in the account, in a similar way, perhaps, to the repeated use of "doubtless" to introduce doubt in *Absalom, Absalom!* There is conscious artistic creation on "Faulkner's" part here, emphasised by the consciously artistic setup of the scene: this is a pose for a sketch, onto which is imposed the further visual representation of the wedding photograph, all in the present context of one of New Orleans's most picturesque and well-known settings. Between the vibrancy, not to mention the apparent wealth, of the imagined wedding day now effectively reenacted at the cathedral, and the destitution and infirmity that now blights them, there is a lifetime of narrative possibility, a network of stories stretching between these two points. Again, notwithstanding, or possibly even because of, the professed confidence in his depiction, both narrative endpoints are couched in supposition: lest we forget, "Faulkner" has "seen" these people many times "among my own hills in Mississippi"—itself an imposition in the present, but which must surely suggest the possibility that theirs was a rural wedding, in not much greater finery than they now sport. My point is that "Faulkner's" insistence upon a very particular narrative image here must surely bring forth any number of possible alternatives, not explicitly there in the prose, but running in the gaps. We might think again of Iser's "inexhaustible text," or of Norman N. Holland's suggestion that readers determine texts in much the same way as they do identities: furthermore, every person to read a text or person does so according to his own individual "identity theme," and "each will have different ways of making the text into an experience with a coherence and significance that satisfies."[18] This principle is dramatized within "Episode," as the contingent relationship between writer, reader, and text is mirrored within the scene itself: the writer of the scene is pointedly also a reader within it, creating the "text," the identity of the old lady, to address his own interpretive needs. However, the old lady herself is apparently very keen to take narrative control here—it is she, not "Faulkner," who strikes this pose with her husband, and "Faulkner" himself recognizes her own creative power, the "ability for fine fabling" that runs through this whole fiction, however based in fact it may or may not be. In effect, we have two assertive writer figures unwittingly struggling for narrative control over this particular text of New Orleans.

At a stroke, however, this web of narrative potential is dismissed, as Spratling is unsatisfied with their pose: "No, no," he directs, "not like that." Spratling then seeks to become the dominant creative force, telling her to "Turn toward him, look at him," brushing aside the old lady's (writerly) complaint that he will then not be able to see or sketch her face with a promise to draw it in later. As "Faulkner" then reads this new pose, whole new dynamics enter the old folks' relationship: while the husband's "arrogance dissolve[s]," she "at once became maternal. She was no longer a bride; she had been married long enough to know that Joe was not anything to be either loved or feared very passionately, but on the contrary he was something to be a little disparaging of" (189). But though she seems to have lost any narrative control at this point, she claims it back at the last (or at least in "Faulkner's" interpretation she does), by reminding Spratling that he still needs to sketch her face: "And now there was something in her face that was not her face. It partook of something in time, in the race, ambiguous, enigmatic. Was she posing? I wondered, watching her. She was facing Spratling, but I don't believe her eyes saw him, nor the wall behind him. Her eyes were contemplative, yet personal—it was as if someone had whispered a sublime and colossal joke in the ear of an idol" (190). There is a feeling here that "Faulkner," the narrator, is sensing that the old lady herself has more power over her representation than he'd previously recognized; indeed, that his previously confident—overconfident, perhaps? —creative power over her is failing in the face of some indefinable mystery. Even the nature or site of this mystery remains mysterious: is it hers to "pose," or is it imparted by the teller of the "sublime and colossal joke"? All of this is now suggested by an increasingly desparate "Faulkner," all narrative certainty now dissipated, as he is left, somewhat like Robert Frost peering into wells in "For Once, Then, Something," "wondering what I had seen in her face—or had I seen anything at all."

In this very brief piece, we have seen an apparently simple episode of New Orleanian "local color," sketched in confident directorial strokes

by both Faulkner and Spratling, both build and dissolve into something infinitely richer and more complex. Trite closing references to the
Mona Lisa and the "eternal age" of women notwithstanding, this sketch
both gives notice of the complexity of Faulkner's dialogic and identifies
New Orleans as a vital heteroglot site in his work. A simple portrait in
Faulkner's Orleans Alley, today's Pirate's Alley, is actually the catalyst for
an exploration of a site of potentially inexhaustible stories.

2. New Orleans as City-Text: *Mosquitoes*, *Pylon*, and *Absalom, Absalom!*

The levels of narrative complexity that can be discerned in the *Sketches*
collection are present in varying ways and to varying degrees throughout
Faulkner's New Orleans texts, in large part because they are necessarily
there in the "texts" of New Orleans that the fiction engages with, as "Episode" has demonstrated. *Absalom, Absalom!* offers the richest portrayal
of the city in Faulkner's mature career, but before turning to this mas-
terpiece it is worth looking at two New Orleanian rooms, and their narration, in earlier books. Although *Mosquitoes*, to begin with, is primarily
interested in portraying the artistic set of the 1920s and in discussing
the significance of art and artists, it still allows reflection on the creative
processes of the city itself. In the first chapter, an authorial voice that tells
us that outside the sculptor Gordon's window, "New Orleans, the vieux
carré, brooded in a faintly tarnished languor like an aging yet still beautiful courtesan in a smokefilled room, avid yet weary too of ardent ways."
This image seems a little too ready to propound uncritically the romantic
vision of "The Tourist," but we need to recognize that the narrative is,
at this point, following Mr. Talliaferro, who swallows it hook, line, and
sinker.[19] This does not wholly vindicate it, however. I suggest that this
novel is less successful—or at least less interesting—than *Sketches* in its
handling of dialogic voices. But, even Mr. Talliaferro's banality, or the
author's willingness to indulge a little too readily in the city's romantic
cover art, does not prevent an alertness to the more intricate narratives
enshrined in this room: "What troubled this room was something eternal
in the race, something immortal. . . . This unevenly boarded floor, these
rough stained walls broken by high small practically useless windows
beautifully set, these crouching lintels cutting the immaculate ruined
pitch of walls which had housed slaves long ago, slaves long dead and
dust with the age that had produced them and which they had served
with a kind and gracious dignity—shades of servants and masters now in
a more gracious region, lending dignity to eternity" (10). Mr. Talliaferro,

and maybe the narrator, longs to paint the earlier occupants with the same romantic gloss that he imparts to the artist's studio itself, casing them in historical aspic—not for him, Quentin Compson's realizations of the never-ending presence of the past in the present. But the room still contains the "shades" of the lives of the slaves who previously occupied it, who maybe built it. Little is done with this here, but the slaves are registered as part of the narrative fabric of the city: the vieux carré may have an aching beauty, but its buildings are also testament to its particular modes of the "peculiar institution" of slavery often predating its status as part of the U.S. South, as such. These buildings contain, perhaps, what Barbara Ladd has called the "traces" of "the impact of colonial experience in the Deep South."[20]

By the time of *Pylon*, published in 1935, such romanticized views of New Orleans (or the "New Valois" that stands in for it) have been largely expunged: the city here largely stands for the asserted soulless horrors of modernity, as several critics have discussed most effectively, such romantic baton as there is being passed on instead to the flyers that serve as paradoxical counterpoint.[21] Much has been made of the peculiar place of this book in the Faulkner canon, particularly given its contemporaneousness with the writing of *Absalom, Absalom!*, with regard to its apparent lack of engagement with the past, New Orleanian, Southern, or otherwise.[22] However, the figure that many identify as the novel's protagonist, the unnamed reporter, does serve as a focus for the crisis of identity in the modern world. His apparently boundless obsession with the flyers, and especially with Laverne, is counterposed with the description of his Vieux Carré room, a "gaunt cavern roofed like a barn," "which the reporter called bohemian": "It was filled with objects whose dessicated and fragile inutility bore a kinship to their owner's own physical being as though he and they were all conceived in one womb and spawned in one litter—objects which possessed that quality of veteran prostitutes, of being overlaid by the ghosts of so many anonymous proprietors that even the present titleholder held merely rights but no actual possession—a room apparently exhumed from a theatrical morgue and rented intact from one month to the next."[23] As one might expect from a novel written alongside *Absalom, Absalom!*, this wonderfully rich and problematic description manages to squeeze the implicit dialogic possibilities between the various *New Orleans Sketches* into the kind of cramped narrative space tentatively charted in that room in *Mosquitoes*. As with the Tuscan cobbler, the reporter and his room are here deemed of a piece; the crucial difference is his own agency in this construct. Whereas the Cobbler was imprisoned by a house that enveloped his whole life and history, the reporter has painstakingly created this space, "with the

eager and deluded absorption of a child hunting coloured easter eggs"
(66). His, in effect, is the womb that has spawned both man and room: it
is a studied, contrived attempt at bohemian New Orleanian/New Valoi-
sian living, which is not to say that it can't achieve that goal. We have a
version, yet again, of the courtesan image, but the effect here is much
more myriad: rather than the whole city reduced to a single image (however plural that image may end up being when studied closely) here it is
the constituent objects of a place within that city that bear the "veteran
prostitute's" seductive, commanding yet claimed qualities. Each one of
these objects is "overlaid" with the ghosts of past "proprietors," whose
anonymity further emphasizes the plural nature of the construct. Each
object has stood in other rooms, served similar or perhaps entirely dissimilar functions; some are completely *without* apparent function and
seem included purely to signify a bohemian life in the Vieux Carré. The
reporter, therefore, has actively constructed a place with a certain project
in mind; he has written a text of New Orleans (New Valois) that is itself
constructed of myriad other texts. If the room represents his life, so it
also invokes the countless other lives that "overlay" its creation. And if
its "exhumation" from a "theatrical morgue" summons up intertwined
notions of creation and death, its evident rented temporariness stands in
awkward dialogue with its self-conscious participation in and representation of the ancient cumulative cultural identities of the city. If *Pylon* as
a whole is comparable with its near neighbor *Absalom, Absalom!* chiefly
through its desperation, its bleakness, this brief evocation of a particular
New Orleanian place works as a primer both for that novel's narrative
complexity and its realization of New Orleans as an endlessly contested,
narrativized site, a city text constantly subject to the machinations of
those who regard it from within and without.

    In her contribution to Suzanne W. Jones and Sharon Monteith's col-
lection *South to a New Place* (2002), Barbara Ladd considers the relations between "place" and "regionalism": "More and more, place needs
to be constructed not as a stable site of tradition and history within a progressive nation but as something more provisional, more fleeting, more
subversive, and likewise more creative . . . a site of memory and meaning
both for the past and the future. Places, like memories, are always in
transition, always redefined, resituated, by experience over time" (56).
Ladd writes about the need to view Southern places transnationally, to
liberate them from the strictures of a falsely imposed U.S. nationalistic
historiography. New Orleans, it seems to me, has *always* required this
flexibility of perspective, given its perpetual fluidity of identity, not to
mention ownership, as Ladd's own incisive work on George Washington
Cable, elsewhere, vividly illustrates.[24] If New Orleans can be considered

Faulkner's second apocryphal site, then *Absalom, Absalom!* is the most important of Faulkner's New Orleans books; the fact that very little of it is actually set there does little to diminish that status, but makes it all the more crucial to the textual construction of the city. One might say, indeed, that in this text the relations that we might construe between Yoknapatawpha and New Orleans in Faulkner's work are brought to bear in the fabric of the fiction itself. But if the relationship is made explicit in some ways, at the level of the writer and reader of *Absalom* itself, then it is scarcely so for the characters within the novel. Indeed, if this is a book in large part concerned with the processes of narrative construction, then we may say that its "setting," as such, is a series of yet more story-filled rooms (well, one is a porch) in Jefferson and at Harvard in 1909–10. Everything else, whether personal memory or historical interpretation, whether of Yoknapatawpha, New Orleans, Virginia, or Haiti, is a projection, or to be more precise, a projection of other projections. In this way, Yoknapatawphan projections of New Orleans are an inextricable and crucial part of the narratives of the county itself, while at the same time serving both to enact further and to interrogate the kinds of narrative creations of the city we have seen thus far in other texts.

As it goes, for all the professed foreignness, the two places are "just one night's hard ride" and a steamboat journey apart;[25] more importantly, though, they are linked through perception throughout, even if these are perceptions of difference. If *Absalom* is one of Faulkner's texts most motivated by absent centers and presences—Sutpen, most obviously, but also Bon and indeed Henry—then New Orleans is surely one of them. Regarding Thomas Sutpen's arrival on the Yoknapatawpha scene, the city is not named in the early stages: he is rumoured to have "apparently come into town from the south," a "south" that we come to realize takes in New Orleans, at least in passing, and places to *its* south, a Caribbean world of which the city is a part—as is, to follow Edouard Glissant's model, Yoknapatawpha itself. More prominently, however, the city is figured as the distant site of quests for enlightenment. Trips to the city by Bon, Sutpen, Clytie, and, of course, by Henry and Bon together are always couched in mystery, lack of knowledge, as vague and shady as the "truth" being sought, here and in the entire quest to understand the Sutpen phenomenon overall. For instance, we are told of "the summer in which Sutpen himself went away, on business, Ellen said, doubtless unaware, such was her existence then, that she did not know where her husband had gone and not even conscious that she was not curious. No one but your grandfather and perhaps Clytie was ever to know that Sutpen had gone to New Orleans too" (70). New Orleans is here a liminal place, existing (or not?) on a scarcely even subconscious level at the extreme

edges of narrative, but where "truth" is supposed to lie. New Orleans
is, insofar as we can tell from these accounts, where pivotal stuff is actually happening, or at least might be, but it is almost without narrative
presence whereas the Yoknapatawpha we *do* see lives in ignorance and
wonderment as to Sutpen and his doings. We learn just enough about
what we and Jefferson don't know to register that there are probably
things to know in this crucial place that we are not, at this stage, seeing
in any way. As with Sutpen, as with Bon, the apparent unknowability of
New Orleans, at each of the novel's narrative levels, makes it one of the
key concerns.

So, a good deal of the interchange between Yoknapatawpha and New
Orleans is founded—or unfounded—on distance. But there is, of course,
the personal encounter as represented by Bon himself, or at least the
representative quality that he is attributed by everyone who regards him.
Bon is not really allowed human individuality by anyone, but is always
required to fulfil some function, the variations between these themselves
signifying the malleable quality of the city he is deemed synonomous
with. Often, as "Charles Bon of New Orleans," he has the "worldly elegance" that the city is also said to have, in stark contrast to rural Jefferson
and Sutpen's Hundred (74). At other times, the "worldly" city and the
man are more specifically othered, as when New Orleans is refered to as
"a French city" (195) and Bon, in Wash Jones's memorable words, "that
durn French feller" (133). But most intense and dialogic of all is the
relationship between Bon and Henry, particularly when it is taken further
and reimagined by Mr. Compson and then by Quentin and Shreve.

In chapter 4, when Quentin Compson listens to his father describing Henry Sutpen's first encounter with New Orleans, Mr. Compson
allows himself to extemporize here as he generally does throughout:
"I can imagine him, with his puritan heritage—that heritage peculiarly
Anglo-Saxon—of fierce proud mysticism and that ability to be ashamed
of ignorance and inexperience, in that city foreign and paradoxical, with
its atmosphere at once fatal and langorous, at once feminine and steel-
hard—this grim humorless yokel out of a granite heritage where even the
houses, let alone clothing and conduct, are built in the image of a jealous
and sadistic Jehovah, put suddenly down in a place whose denizens had
created their All-Powerful and His supporting hierarchy chorus of beautiful saints and handsome angels in the image of their houses and personal ornaments and voluptuous lives" (108–9). This is the first extended
consideration of New Orleans itself, though it has, as I have suggested,
been an absent presence throughout. Mr. Compson himself notes his
own "imagining," his conscious fictionalizing of a place not unlike that
depicted by "The Tourist," in the earlier *Sketches*, "fatal and langorous,

at once feminine and steel-hard"; he also notes the city's self-creation, its spiritual life and sense of itself apparently constructed according to the model followed by *Pylon*'s reporter in the construction of his New Orleanian simulacra through the "personal objects" in his house (though the reporter does not quite manage the "voluptuous life" himself, perhaps). Mr. Compson offers this city effectively as the product of his own vision and his understanding of Henry's vision, itself founded upon his projection of Henry and Henry's sense of his own life and its great difference from Charles Bon's. Given that Henry's own "granite heritage" is shown in this novel to have foundations no less swampy, literally and conceptually, than those of New Orleans itself, things are even less sure. He is one of the human products of Thomas Sutpen's design, itself an "artist's impression" of plantation aristocracy; Henry is a character in his father's narrative, the product of a reading and reconstruction of a model itself surely suggested to be the result of conscious and pointed self-fashioning. This plantation model is, of course, the world from which Mr. Compson and Quentin themselves come, whose demise they witness and participate in. Despite Mr. Compson's suggestion here of fearful piety, surely the life that Henry lives and represents is as much a conscious creation as the more "beautiful," "voluptuous" one he "imagines" in New Orleans.

In a sense then, what we have here is a clash and interaction of narratives as well as of cultures. In *Absalom*'s model, the two are inextricable: this is New Orleans's otherness to Henry, or vice versa, but also to Mr. Compson—the "foreignness" and "paradox" operates at every level. Mr. Compson goes on to "imagine" a sequence of events in New Orleans in which Henry is very pointedly "an American," an outsider as denoted, in French, by Bon (113), who in turn gradually constructs a "text" of New Orleans for his foreign guest: "So I can imagine him, the way he did it: the way in which he took the innocent and negative plate of Henry's provincial soul and intellect and exposed it by slow degrees to this esoteric milieu, building gradually toward the picture which he desired it to retain, accept. I can see him corrupting Henry gradually into the purlieus of elegance, with no foreword, no warning, the postulation to come after the fact, exposing Henry slowly to the surface aspect—the architecture a little curious, a little femininely flamboyant and therefore to Henry opulent, sensuous, sinful; the inference of great and easy wealth measured by steamboat loads in place of a tedious inching of sweating human figures across cotton fields" (110). And so it continues; Bon patiently and painstakingly creates a series of pictures to build his New Orleans world for Henry, through a "dialogue without words, speech, which would fix and then remove without obliterating one line of the picture, this background, leaving the background, the plate prepared innocent again" (111). All this lays the ground for the meeting with Bon's octoroon mistress and their son, when Bon attempts to induct Henry into the particular racial and sexual codes of the city. On the one hand, he suggests that "Henry Sutpen of Sutpen's Hundred in Mississippi" should realize that the ceremony, the *placage*, that Bon has undertaken is meaningless because "this woman, this child, are niggers" (118). But on the other, he is at pains to make Henry understand systems of slavery, of racial gradations, of sexual politics that are unlike anything he has ever come across: indeed, he perhaps takes a position to an extent anologous to Quentin's in relation to Shreve. And along with the creation of New Orleans that he has attempted with Henry, he also suggests that New Orleanian white men "created" the city's octoroons by declaring that "one eighth of a specified kind of blood shall outweigh seven eighths of another kind," and they also save individual members of that created class from slavery by entering into this arrangement so alien and inexplicable to Henry (115). If the *New Orleans Sketches*, for instance, have something of the local-color air of George Washington Cable's tales of the city, then *Absalom, Absalom!* takes Cable's most compelling and powerful concern and makes it the business of everybody involved, joining all voices in the New Orleanian web of narrative. All are complicit, all are cocreators of this New Orleans text.

To conclude, I should like to look at one last New Orleanian textual room from *Absalom, Absalom!*, a room to complement those in *Mosquitoes* and *Pylon*. Bon's son, Charles Etienne de Saint Velery Bon, according to General Compson via his son Mr. Compson (and possibly also via Quentin and Shreve), "could neither have heard yet nor recognized the term 'nigger,' who even had no word for it in the tongue he knew who had been born and grown up in a padded silken vacuum cell which might have been suspended on a cable a thousand fathoms in the sea, where pigmentation had no more moral value than silk walls and the scent and the rose-colored candle shades, where the very abstractions which he might have observed—monogamy and fidelity and decorum and gentleness and affection—were as purely rooted in the flesh's offices as the digestive processes" (199). This child, who might be said to represent the full complexity of the colonial and racial history and politics of the vast region of the slaveholding Americas of which the U.S. South is the northern province, lives in a room that at once epitomises the "fatal, langorous" decadence of the city of his childhood, but also maintains his isolation from it. With its occupant at once uniquely New Orleanian and kept ignorant and immune from the codes that have led to his being, this room, more than Gordon's studio, even more than the reporter's theatrical morgue, is a repository of New Orleans stories, a monument to its particular and peculiar place in the narrative of the entire region. It is one further example of how "that city foreign and paradoxical" is a vital narrative in Faulkner's fictions, Yoknapatawphan and otherwise, and of how Faulkner's narratives are themselves so richly attuned to its beguiling, myriad dialogues.

NOTES

I wish to thank Don Kartiganer for the invitation to speak at the Faulkner and Yoknapatawpha Conference in 2008 and conference delegates for their comments and questions; thanks are also due to Annette Trefzer and Ann Abadie for their very helpful comments and guidance in preparing the essay for publication. I am grateful to the British Academy for the award of an Overseas Conference Grant, which greatly assisted me in my attendance and the preparation of this essay. I also thank the Arts and Humanities Research Council for their continued support of my work on the project "American Tropics: Towards a Literary Geography," of which this forms a part.

1. Owen Robinson, *Creating Yoknapatawpha: Readers and Writers in Faulkner's Fiction* (New York: Routledge, 2006).

2. Carvel Collins, "About the Sketches," in William Faulkner, *New Orleans Sketches*, ed. Carvel Collins (London: Sidgwick & Jackson, 1959), 27. A good deal of the relatively scarce (for Faulkner) criticism on *Sketches* concurs broadly with Cleanth Brooks's verdict that they are "generally speaking . . . flat and banal," but that "however limited, however perfunctory, the works of a man of genius are rarely completely unrewarding. After all, they are the product of the same mind, even if it is running at only half-throttle, that produced the masterpieces." (*William Faulkner: Toward Yoknapatawpha and Beyond* [New Haven: Yale University Press, 1978], 100-1.) Even Collins, in his introduction to the volume, accounts for the literary value of *Sketches* mostly through charting their presaging of themes and techniques that were to come to fruition in the years and writing to come, rather than through any great inherent worth of their own, a general line taken by much of the subsequent scholarship.

3. Mikhail Bakhtin, "Discourse in the Novel," in *The Dialogic Imagination: Four Essays*, ed. Michael Holquist, trans. Caryl Emerson & Michael Holquist (Austin: University of Texas Press, 1981), 272.

4. Daniel J. Singal, *William Faulkner: The Making of a Modernist* (Chapel Hill: University of North Carolina Press, 1997), 59.

5. William Faulkner, "Wealthy Jew," in *New Orleans Sketches*, 37–38.

6. William Faulkner, "The Sailor," in *New Orleans Sketches*, 42.

7. William Faulkner, "The Beggar," in *New Orleans Sketches*, 46–47.

8. William Faulkner, "The Cobbler," in *New Orleans Sketches*, 42.

9. William Faulkner, "Magdalen," in *New Orleans Sketches*, 48–49.

10. William Faulkner, "The Tourist," in *New Orleans Sketches*, 48–49.

11. Wolfgang Iser, "The Reading Process: A Phenomenological Approach," in Jane P. Tompkins, ed., *Reader-Response Criticism: From Formalism to Post-Structuralism* (Baltimore: Johns Hopkins University Press, 1980), 55.

12. William Faulkner, "Home," in *New Orleans Sketches*, 73.

13. William Faulkner, "The Cobbler," in *New Orleans Sketches*, 133.

14. William Faulkner, "Jealousy," in *New Orleans Sketches*, 88–89.

15. William Faulkner, "Sunset," in *New Orleans Sketches*, 157.

16. William Faulkner, "Mirrors of Chartres Street," in *New Orleans Sketches*, 54.

17. William Faulkner, "Episode," in *New Orleans Sketches*, 187. Subsequent references in parentheses are to this edition.

18. Norman N. Holland, "Unity Identity Text Self," in Tompkins, 123.

19. William Faulkner, *Mosquitoes* (New York: Dell Publishing, 1965), 10. Subsequent references in parentheses are to this edition.

20. Barbara Ladd, "Dismantling the Monolith: Southern Places—Past, Present, and Future," in Suzanne W. Jones and Sharon Monteith, eds., *South to a New Place: Region, Literature, Culture* (Baton Rouge: Louisiana State University Press, 2002), 53–54. Subsequent references in parentheses are to this edition.

21. See, for example, Joshua Gaylord, "The Radiance of the Fake: *Pylon's* Postmodern Narrative of Disease," in *Faulkner Journal*, 20:1 (Fall 2004): 177–94; Richard Gray, *William Faulkner: A Critical Biography* (Oxford: Blackwell, 1994), 197–98; Gary Harrington, *Faulkner's Fables of Creativity: The Non-Yoknapatawpha Novels* (Houndmills: Macmillan, 1990), 55–56; Taylor Hagood, "Media, Ideology, and the Role of Literature in *Pylon*," in *Faulkner Journal*, 21:1 (Fall, 2005): 107–19; Axel Knönagel, "Modernity and Mechanization: Faulkner's *Pylon* and the Novels of John Dos Passos," *Amerikastudien/ American Studies*, 42:4 (1997): 591–600; Olga W. Vickery, *The Novels of William Faulkner: A Critical Interpretation* (Baton Rouge: Louisiana State University Press, 1964), 145–54.

22. As Richard Gray has discussed, Faulkner claimed to have written *Pylon* because "I'd got in trouble with *Absalom, Absalom!* and I had to get away from it" (Gray, 203), though the unremittingly bleak novel he turned to might be considered a strange sort of relief. Its apparent lack of regard for history and the related narrative complexities that so drive its more celebrated near neighbor render the two novels interestingly odd bedfellows. Faulkner's visit to the opening of New Orleans's Shushan Airport and his work on screenplays for Hollywood flying movies are clear influences on the rather underrated novel he published in 1935, before returning to work on *Absalom, Absalom!*, which he began early in 1934 and eventually published in 1936.

23. William Faulkner, *Pylon* (Chatto & Windus, 1954), 66–67. Subsequent references in parentheses are to this edition.

24. Barbara Ladd, *Nationalism and the Color Line in George W. Cable, Mark Twain, and William Faulkner* (Baton Rouge: Louisiana State University Press, 1996).

25. William Faulkner, *Absalom, Absalom!* (1936; London: Chatto & Windus, 1969), 17. Subsequent references in parentheses are to this edition.

Sanctuary's Reversible Bodies

James Harding

The title of my paper, "*Sanctuary*'s Reversible Bodies," may, at first, appear something of a conceit. As it will become clear, the majority of the following arguments focus less on physical bodies than on what might be termed "textual" ones. Yet the conceit within my title aims to bring what I shall characterize as an implicit relation between textual and physical form into focus. Put differently, this work seeks to assign a musculature to Faulkner's textual practices and, by so doing, highlight the vital, and often difficult, intersections of text and body that occur in Faulkner's work. Readers and critics of Faulkner's texts are surely familiar with the prominence afforded to the body. The list is legion: Addie Bundren, Joe Christmas, Caddy Compson, and Temple Drake are all, through burial, castration, pregnancy, and rape respectively, made painfully aware of their own bodies. Recent critical work has widely considered these various anatomical crises. Indeed, much of this work has, quite ably, characterized Faulkner's bodies as sites of historical, sexual, or psychological stress.[1] Consequently—and with no small amount of irony given the body's tendency toward opacity—the Faulknerian body has become familiar ground, a "known place" upon which critical discussions can be easily—often *too easily*—reaffirmed.

Less familiar to us, and less commented on, are the ways in which this physicality is made manifest at the level of Faulkner's *text*. The current paper concentrates upon a text that famously bears the marks of such physicality: Faulkner's 1931 novel, *Sanctuary*.[2] In particular, I shall seek to give a precise textual location to the novel's problematic materiality by exploring the workings of the third person singular neuter pronoun "it." Through an extended close reading, I shall contend that the pronoun "it" is the preeminent place of semantic conflict in the novel and, more, that the novel's employment of this specific type of pronoun characterizes Faulkner's grammar as a place of violence.

The *grammatical* violence that I investigate in this essay stems, of course, from a conspicuously *material* violation. As Diane Roberts asserts, "*Sanctuary* is about rape."[3] Specifically it is about the rape of Temple Drake, a seventeen-year-old virgin, with a corncob, in a disused barn. While rape is the novel's central preoccupation, it also constitutes the novel's central silence. Providing the novel with its *ur-scene* and with its dirty secret, rape is the elephant in the room, both the event from which the novel grew and the one that it refuses to sufficiently address. As John T. Matthews notes, "vague diction, vacancies in syntax, breakages in thought and utterance, and violations of place, time, and character conspire to blur the presentation of the novel's crucial event."[4] That Temple's rape remains un- (or, better, *under-*) articulated is significant and will provide a point of departure for the coming arguments.

Temple's rape occurs at the end of chapter 13, yet passes with the barest of mention. The reader *is* notified that "something is happening" to Temple, although the nature of this "something" is ultimately withheld, rendered mute. As Temple remarks, "it was as though sound and silence had become inverted" (*S*, 250). The violence of this "something" stuns the next five chapters into a "bright silence." In fact, between chapters 14 and 18 Temple, whom one presumes is attempting to recover from the brutality of her attack, remains silent. This period of remission reaches a terminus in chapter 18. Here, Faulkner's narrative rejoins Temple and provides the first material traces of her violation. Slumped in Popeye's Ford awaiting imprisonment in a Memphis whorehouse, "Temple gazed dully forward as the road she had traversed yesterday began to flee backward under the wheels as onto a spool, feeling her blood seeping slowly inside her loins. She sat limp in the corner of the seat, watching the steady backward rush of the land—pines in opening vistas splashed with fading dogwood; sedge; fields green with new cotton and empty of any movement, peaceful, as though Sunday were a quality of atmosphere, of light and shade—sitting with her legs close together, listening to the hot minute seeping of her blood, saying dully to herself, I'm still bleeding. I'm still bleeding" (273–74). The "minute seeping" of Temple's blood is a metonym for the novel's wider tendency to muffle or offset the brutality of its central act. Despite the modest scale of the bleeding, its significance is far from slight. Not only does this passage provide the first material evidence of Temple's penetration but it also sets up an antagonistic correspondence between going forward with going back. This antagonism, I will argue below, conditions the formal strategies of the novel.

It is not until chapter 23 (ten chapters after its occurring) that Temple commits to a narration of her ordeal. In Temple's narration, the tension between backward and forward motion again proves a prominent feature. Sitting in a Memphis whorehouse with local lawyer Horace Benbow, Temple gradually begins to find the words through which she can recount the moments leading up to her violation. In anticipation of a close reading, I have numbered my pronouns for the sake of clarity:

I thought if he'd just go on and get it [1] over with, I could go to sleep. So I'd say You're a coward if you dont! and I could feel my mouth getting fixed to scream, and that little hot ball inside you that screams. Then it [2] touched me, that nasty little cold hand, fiddling around inside the coat where I was naked. It [3] was like alive ice and my skin started jumping away from it [4] like those little flying fish in front of a boat. It [5] was like my skin knew which way it [6] was going to go before it [7] started moving, and my skin would keep on jerking just ahead of it [8] like there wouldn't be anything there when the hand got there.

Then it [9] got down to where my insides began, and I hadn't eaten since yesterday at dinner and my insides started bubbling and going on and the shucks began to make so much noise it [10] was like laughing. I'd think they were laughing at me because all the time his hand was going inside the top of my knickers and I hadn't changed into a boy yet. (330)

In this relatively short extract "it" is the dominant term, featuring ten times.[5] The density with which Temple applies the pronoun is noteworthy. Nowhere else in the novel do so many third-person pronouns mean so many different things within such a short space of time. Yet it is less the *frequency* of the pronoun than the *rhythms of its movement* that concern me here. By listing the referents of Temple's pronoun in quick succession, one can begin to decipher the logic behind such rhythms. Temple's chain of pronouns runs as follows: "it" [1] refers to a sex act, (which, as I will discuss below, culminates in Temple's rape); "it" [2], [3], and [4] refer—in different stages of realization—to Popeye's offending hand; "it" [5] appears, at least on first impressions, to be an inert or "dummy" signifier (in other words, the reader is not really sure what this one might mean); "it" [6] and "it" [7] are seemingly interchangeable, both of them referring either to Temple's skin or to Popeye's hand; "it" [8] and "it" [9] return to the hand; "it" [10] refers to the noise of "the shucks," which Temple likens to a kind of "laughing." A series of ten "its," then, move to the following pattern: rape (or, more exactly, the threat of rape), hand, hand, hand, blank, skin or hand, skin or hand, hand, hand, laughter.

Isolating Temple's pronouns and locating them in this chain of signification clearly shows that the term "it" functions as an indeterminate and highly volatile lexical unit. Neither stable nor singular in its meaning, Temple's pronoun constantly threatens to vacate one meaning and take up occupancy in another. Of course, "it" remains the same word all the way through, but as the above compression demonstrates, "it"—while under Temple's jurisdiction at least—provides a forum for semantic ambiguity. Temple's linguistic varieties and contortions of the pronoun "it," beginning as the threat of rape and finishing as "laughter," cover considerable semantic ground. The linguist Valentin Volosinov, a contemporary of Faulkner, would have cited this tendency to move as evidence of the "fundamental polysemanticity of the word." Volosinov contends that semantic "contexts do not stand side by side in a row, as if unaware of each other, but are in a state of constant tension, or interaction and conflict."[6] That language is essentially "multivocal" (and in the present context the assertion surely holds) does not mean that its various semantic possibilities are arrived at arbitrarily. Nor does it mean that the pronoun operates solely as a textual event; on the contrary, Temple's "it" has a specific material imperative. In an attempt to classify the nature of this imperative, I will pull apart the chain of pronouns and ponder each one in greater detail.

"It" [1] refers to the novel's generative event: Temple's rape by Popeye in the Old Frenchman barn. Yet the meaning of this first pronoun is communicated by inference rather than by direct address. Temple does not say "my rape," yet the context within which Temple speaks the pronoun confirms such meaning as irrefutable. (The prospect of Temple suffering a rape has been one of the text's only constant features; in fact, Temple's penetration has seemed likely ever since she made her first foray into the Old Frenchman barn, at chapter 6.) Temple's inaugural "it" constitutes what linguists refer to as a "deictic" pronoun. The term "deixis," as John Lyons suggests, "comes from a Greek word meaning 'pointing' or 'indicating' [and] is now used in linguistics to refer to the function of personal and demonstrative pronouns, of tense and of a variety of other grammatical and lexical features which relate utterances to the spatio-temporal co-ordinates of the act of utterance."[7] Put simply, the deictic pronoun indicates the meaning of a thing or an object that the text fails to directly name. As a condition of its working, the deictic pronoun requires contextual support if its meaning is to be fully understood. Such context is provided by a glut of surrounding terms: a "he" is doing something that Temple hopes might pass quickly (Temple implores Popeye to "go on and get it over with");[8] more, the "it" involves a "fiddling," "it" happens late at night ("I could go to sleep"), and Temple is "naked" whilst "it" is taking place. Providing context, these terms clearly inform the reader that the "it" is sexual in kind and that Temple has not invited, nor is enjoying, such attention.

Temple's deictic first pronoun is employed to absorb the shock of literal meaning. Through the rape a corporeal barrier has been breached. Through the telling, another rupture threatens. This rupture must come (or we have no novel) yet Temple fears a direct retelling and so defers it—with "it" [1]. Simply, the pronoun provides Temple with a means of referring to her rape without actually reprising it. As an "it" rather than a concrete event, "my rape" effectively becomes "that thing"; as such, the rape is easier to cope with. This verbal strategy, Temple hopes, will impose a fictitious distance between her "insides" and Popeye's "cob." Figuratively speaking the deictic "it" [1] reverses Temple's body back into virginity. However, Temple's effort to dematerialize her body into text, her attempt to become "a printed object,"⁹ proves impossible.

As the chain of pronouns progresses, the restorative ambition of 'it' [1] is ruined by the sheer physicality of "it" [2]. Grammatically speaking, Temple's second pronoun shifts out of the deictic form and into the anaphoric, our second means of pronominal reference. Unlike the deictic pronoun, which cannot be understood without recourse to contextual information, the anaphoric pronoun stands in for that object or thing that has already appeared (or in some cases is *about* to appear) in the text. Problematically, Temple's second pronoun undermines "it" [1]'s attempt to eke out a neutral zone between her body and its traumatic history. That this second pronoun, a forward-looking anaphoric pronoun, seems to acquire an impossible physical agency ("it touched me" Temple claims) only compounds the sense of dread with which "it" [2] nominates a part of Popeye's body: specifically, his "nasty little cold hand." If "it" [1] is the reinstatement of the hymen, then, "it" [2] is the "hand" that ultimately breaks it (one recalls that because of Popeye's impotence he uses his *hand* to rape Temple).

The semantic value of this second pronoun (its value as "hand") is not immediately available to the reader, however, but is subject to a deferral. This deferral complicates the rhythms of the first two pronouns. At the precise moment of "it" [2]'s reading, the pronoun is lacking concrete semantic affiliation. Gazing "dully forward" (*S* 273), this second pronoun is, as Lear's fool might contend, "an o without a figure."¹⁰ Soon, however, the seemingly "empty" second pronoun is drawn to its meaning. Feeding into a qualifying clause ("that nasty little cold hand") the epistemological impasse appears resolved. Having discovered meaning further down the line, the reader feels subsequently obliged to revisit, or move backward, and inscribe this retrospectively acquired meaning onto what was a previously empty signifier. Having passed through and then reversed back into "it" [2], "it" [2] clearly nominates a physical part of Popeye's body: "hand."

Before considering the remaining pronouns in the series, it is useful to recap the movement of Temple's first two pronouns. Beginning at "it" [1] (an inferred threat of penetration), Temple's speech progressed to "it" [2], which was a temporarily empty pronoun; on the eventual discovery of meaning the reader was sent back, by Popeye's hand, to a newly meaningful "it" [2]. In this early exchange, the semantic traffic clearly does not flow in one, but in two directions. With this new knowledge of "hand" (a knowledge that was prohibited when we first encountered "it" [2]) we are associatively taken—or slapped—back a further remove, to "it" [1]. At the mercy of Temple's erratic pronoun, the reader has been bounced back between a rape and a hand. Such semantic backtracking (which, if we are to continue reading, necessarily infers a returning move forward) implicates the rhythms of reading with the rhythms of rape. These rhythms are duly complicated by the remaining pronouns.

From "it" [3] to "it" [10], Temple's pronouns appear to follow a more sedate course. Certainly, the coming "its" repeat neither the semantic nor the material gyrations that were enacted by "its" [1] and [2]. In fact, "it" [3] reverses (out of) the unusual "forward-looking" anaphoric tendency of "it" [2] and thus sets in motion a more traditional means of lexical reference. "It" [3] is a "backward-looking" anaphoric pronoun, in that it follows rather than anticipates the object to which it is semantically anchored. Not only does "it" [3] follow its referent—and by doing satisfy the rules of a traditional grammar—but it also recycles the *meaning* of the previous pronoun. In short, "it" [3] uses "it" [2] as a preestablished reference and by doing so endorses "it" [2]'s meaning. "It" [3], then, means what "it" [2] (eventually) meant: "that nasty little cold hand."

"It" [4] continues the pattern established by "it" [3], and recalls Popeye's "hand." That the fourth pronoun grows out of the third (which grew, in turn, out of the second) is significant. By reaffirming—rather than *redirecting*—meaning, "it" [3] and "it" [4] bring a greater fluidity to Temple's syntax. These two pronouns do not need contextual support (as did "it" [1]), nor do they need to reach forward for meaning (as did "it" [2]). By moving incrementally rather than in staccato fashion, "its" [3] and [4] fulfill the demands of a useable grammar. More, the rhythms of rape that materialize as a result of this semantic back and forth appear to have abated. Temple, then, seems to have wrested some kind of control of her language by "its" [3] and [4]. Certainly, these two pronouns suggest a more instantaneous, and perhaps more effective, semantic transmission. However, this is not to say that their rhythms pose no threat to Temple. In fact, "it" [3] and "it" [4], by repeating the mention of Popeye's hand, bracket off a period of intense trauma. Temple's use of the pronoun may have afforded her syntax a greater fluidity, but by so doing the pronoun has simultaneously reinscribed the presence of the "hand" that raped her. As if chanting "his hand, his hand" in a concussive series, Temple's third and fourth pronouns demonstrate an inability to remove herself from the terrifying memory of Popeye's hand.

As Temple's fourth pronoun slides into a fifth, however, the impetus is suddenly halted. "It" [5] is what linguists refer to as a dummy, or "neuter" pronoun. The dummy pronoun, linguists maintain, does not have a referential duty but is transparent and essentially passive; its only function is to make the sentence *grammatical*. On one level, this claim holds. Temple's fifth "it" works like the *it* in the declarative phrase *it's raining*; one knows fully what this utterance means without needing to ask, perhaps, *what* is raining. In addition to satisfying the demands of a generative grammar, this particular pronoun, I suggest, possesses a more radical intent. Specifically—and uniquely, given the inclinations of the pronoun so far—"it" [5] generates meaning through its *resistance* toward meaning. Given the problematic semantic inflections of the previous pronouns, the fact that this pronoun *doesn't* mean—specifically, it doesn't mean "hand" or "rape"—is a pertinent detail. Up to this point in the pronominal sequence, the term "it" has carried terrifying implications for Temple, referring each time to a moment of violence. This particular pronoun, however, is different, and suggests a kind of semantic clearout. "It" [5] does not enact a process of *"avoiding"* (as was the case with Temple's previous four pronouns) but of *"voiding."* Specifically, the fifth pronoun begins Temple's campaign of "voiding the words like hot silent bubbles" (*S* 250) or, in our terms, of emptying them of traumatic literal meaning. "It" [5] carries what Marx might have referred to as a "practical consciousness" in that it offers Temple some necessary respite from the attendant trauma of previous "its." "It" [5] is important, then, not as a presence but *as a silence*, an empty space. "It" [5] may be immune to linguistic affiliation, but it is not free from semantic meaning. Rather "it" [5] means by *not* meaning, which is not the same as being "meaningless."

Countering "it" [5]'s resilience to the absorption of literal meaning, "it" [6] symbolizes a return to "positive" meaning, that is, meaning that comes through materialization rather than erasure, addition rather than subtraction. In fact, "it" [6] symbolizes a return to *multiple* meaning. Demonstrating what Mikhail Bakhtin would have called the "internal dialogism of the word,"[11] "it" [6] is "double voiced" by providing a housing for a number of competing semantic inflections: "it" [6] refers simultaneously to Popeye's hand *and* to Temple's skin. The conflation of these two meanings is intentional: "it" [6] warns of a penetration involving a hand. The two competing referents here—"hand" being perhaps the dominant and "skin" perhaps the marginal—are the two body parts that will shortly come into distressing congress. Two meanings, then, operate in macabre tension within a single word. If we could not state it already we surely cannot fail to now: the pronoun, as used by Temple, is a place of violence, a place in which semantic clash translates into material clash.

"It" [7] reiterates the ambivalence of "it" [6], and thus replicates the kind of relation brokered by "it" [3] and [4]. The reader is ultimately unsure as to whether "it" [7] means "skin" or "hand." Given the doubling of the previous pronouns (notably [3] and [4]; and then [6]), and given the associative logic that has, since "it" [4], bound "skin" to "hand," one could claim quite sensibly that "it" [7], in fact, indicates *both*. "It" [8] and "it" [9] provide grim syncopation for the countdown to Temple's fantasy penetration. Like "it" [6] and "it" [7]—which replicated each other's meaning— "it" [8] and "it" [9] are semantically "twinned." Yet both "it" [8] and "it" [9] refer to a *singular* source: hand. That Temple might concentrate on this particular body part comes as no surprise: as the pronominal series has unfolded, the admission of rape is getting closer. By "it" [9] Popeye's "hand" has forced its way back into the foreground of Temple's mind. "Hand" seems the only thing about which Temple can think.

The eighth pronoun displays Temple's panic that the borders of her body are essentially indefensible. As a last-ditch attempt to avoid the telling of the rape, "it" [8] prefaces what seems an amazing vanishing trick: "my skin would keep on jerking just ahead of 'it' [8] like there wouldn't be anything there when the hand got there." The implied dematerialization of Temple's cringing body is short-lived: "it" [9] realizes full contact with Temple's "insides"—a euphemism for vagina—and, in one fell swoop ruins the defensive work of the previous pronouns, which attempted alternatively to freeze (see "alive ice"), or cramp (see "jerking") the movement of Popeye's hand. Instead of arresting the motion of Popeye's "hand," Temple appears by "it" [9] to be responding favorably to the touch that it provides. Temple, following the conjunction given by "it" [9], reports a "bubbling," presumably resulting from the stimulation of Popeye's "hand" making contact with Temple's "insides."[12] The "bubbling" that issued from Temple's remembering of "it" [9] finds a sonic counterpart in "it" [10], which Temple likens to the "laughter" of the shucks. Acting as a coda or summation, this tenth pronoun closes off Temple's intense, fraught, and troubled narrative dependency upon the pronoun.

In a passage that follows only one page later, Temple attempts to reconstruct the rape in a second narrative phase. Here, Temple's employment of the pronoun undergoes a substantial revision. Instead of using the word "it" as a means of indirectly referring to an act that she finds unspeakable, Temple now uses the term as lexical material out of which she will form a material defence to her rape. Temple's "it" now aims not only to repel or defend from Popeye's advances but to directly punish him:

I'd lie there with the shucks laughing at me and me jerking away in front of his hand and I'd think what I'd say to him. I'd talk to him like the teacher in school, and then I was a teacher in school and it was a little black thing like a nigger boy, kind of, and I was the teacher . . . I was telling it what I'd do, and it kind of drawing up and drawing up like it could already see the switch.

Then I said That wont do. I ought to be a man. So I was an old man, with a long white beard, and then the little black man got littler and littler and I was saying Now. You see now. I'm a man now. Then I thought about being a man, and as soon as I thought it, *it happened. It made a kind of plopping sound, like blowing a little rubber tube wrong-side outward.* It felt cold, like the inside of your mouth when you hold it open. I could feel it, and I lay right still to keep from laughing about how surprised he was going to be. I could feel the jerking going on inside my knickers ahead of his hand and me lying there trying not to laugh about how surprised he was going to be in about a minute. (330–31, italics added.)

Temple's "it" no longer works to deaden or blunt the memory of her recently traumatic past but to match Popeye's violence with one of her own. This "intersecting of making and telling,"[13] in Grace Elizabeth Hale's formulation, allows Temple to reappropriate the pronoun as a weapon to attack Popeye. Newly configured, the term "it" refers not to Popeye's but to *Temple's* penis (here "it" means "a little rubber tube").[14] Put simply, Temple's "it" is the thing that will facilitate what Dawn Trouard and Edwin T. Arnold call the "reverse rape" of Popeye.[15] Reoriented as such, the ambition of Temple's pronoun is twofold: first, it allows Temple to deflect, or redirect unwanted attention away from her own body; second, it allows her to sample the benefits of inhabiting *other*—and indeed "othered"—bodies. By "occupying" or "trying out" such bodies, Temple can make an informed judgment upon which one is most likely to deter Popeye's "cob." The "switch," as Temple calls it, allows her not only a way of opting out of her own problematic body, but provides her with the (rubbery) equipment with which she is able to mount a counterattack: she can fabricate a proxy body and rape Popeye back. Temple, of course, does not have a "cob" of her own with which she might enforce this punitive reversal; subsequently she must "borrow" one from elsewhere.

In an attempt to find the most effective repellent, Temple reverses into—and subsequently reverses out the other side of—a weighty folio of "undesirable" bodies: working-class teachers, rural blacks, bearded old men. After rejecting the pedagogical austerity of the female "teacher" (presumably on grounds of practicality), Temple moves into the body of a "nigger boy," but swiftly refuses its "it," its "little black thing" (interestingly, for its *lack* of size). On one level, Temple's phrase "little black thing" mobilizes a phallic *reduction* and, by implication, disables a prevailing racist stereotype: that a black man has a larger penis than a white man.

Yet the preliminary diminishment of black sexual prominence offered by *"little* black thing" is immediately problematized by the paternalistic inflection within Temple's term "boy." Born out of a heritage of paternalism and white-black racism, this "demeaning designation"[16] initializes a return to stereotype and thus cancels the good work of the diminutive "little black thing." Temple's phrase is a site of contradiction, liberating the body of the black from a racist stereotype only as it shrinks, or be*littles* black presence at the level of the text.

Practically speaking, the "little black thing" ultimately proves insufficient in fending off the advances of the "black man" who is threatening rape. Blackness, Temple asserts, "wont do. I ought to be a *man*": an "old man, with a long white beard" (emphasis added). It is in this (white) incarnation, Temple hopes, that she will really "surpris[e]" Popeye, will really "Pop" his "eyes." Yet the "old white "man" maintains only a brief supremacy over the recently dismissed black "boy." For Temple, the "switch" (in which corn is exchanged for rubber)[17] is immediate: "as soon as I thought it, it happened. It made a kind of plopping sound like blowing a little rubber tube wrong-side outward." Temple's declarative clause refers to the emergence of a rubbery penis, one that is inflated from a reversal of Temple's clitoris, or, as Temple euphemistically calls it, that "little hot ball that screams." Clearly, the "plopping sound" notifies us of an *outward* move, an emergence that aims to land a preemptive penetration of Popeye and thus thwart his planned rape of Temple. Yet this move out disguises an additional move *in*. Given the resonances of Temple's earlier "its," which denote both the act of rape itself and the "hand" that committed the rape, it is a reasonable assertion that the phrase "Then it happened" describes the moment of Temple's rape. Immediately following the *happening* is the sound of her penetration: "It made a kind of plopping sound." The "plopping," then, like the "little black thing of the nigger boy," moves in *two directions*. Likening Popeye's "cob" (that which goes *in*) to Temple's "knob" (that which comes *out*), rubber thus materializes as a phallus that Temple then "blow[s]" "wrong-side out" to greet Popeye's invading "cob." The emergence of the tube returns Temple to the fantasy of miscegenation that was interrupted by her move out of the body of the "nigger boy" and into the body of the "old white man." By way of the rubber image, Temple has moved back to black. The racial inflections of the rubber tube are worth pondering. Clearly, the reference to a "little rubber tube" is analogous, in the first instance, to a condom. In the 1920s condoms were fashioned from dark brown latex. The coloration of the condom attests to a visual link between sex and blackness and, by extension, reinforces traditional stereotypes about black sexuality. Complicating the resemblance between the "little rubber tube" and the darkly colored condom is a racist trope that spans much of Faulkner: that of the "balloon face of the nigger." From Thomas Sutpen to Quentin Compson to Temple Drake, the sighting of the black often conjures a sighting of the balloon.[18] Here, Temple does not pump up a balloon *face*, of course, but a balloon *penis*, yet the affinity between the (imagined) "rubber tube" and the (imagined) black penis surely holds. Racialized by Temple's narrative, rubber "flashes up at [this] moment of danger,"[19] signalling the difficult emergence of black through white. Like a hideous hourglass turned on its head, Temple is an inverted Bovary; "that black stuff that ran out of Bovary's mouth" (184), as Benbow terms it, is reversed as black matter emerges from Temple's vagina.

Temple, then, a white Southern "belle," becomes black in order to prevent her penetration at the hands of what Faulkner's text frequently refers to as a "black man."[20] Such a dependence upon the workings of the black body should not, however, be read as an ahistorical mutation. Rather, Temple's frequent shifting between white and black localizes a system of racial dependency that was being worked out at the level of Southern history. Specifically, this relation of dependency, coming in the wake of Emancipation, delivered what was a shattering psychological realization: that white and black were essentially two parts of a conjoined body. Temple's problematic blackness speaks of wider problems, then, at the level of the *political body* of the South. As Joel Williamson has written, the splitting of black from white traumatized the psychological character of the South. "In order for an individual white person to let black people go," Williamson argues, "the white person, in a sense, had to die, had to cease to be in an important way what he or she had been."[21] Through her rape, Temple, for sure, has ceased to be what she was, or "had been," yet it is at the level of her traumatized body that the nightmare of Southern history can be made visible. The reversibility of Temple's body, an act that places at its center a (reversible) black penis, demonstrates the problematic (often silently erotic) intersections of black and white that permeated the fabric of the American South from Reconstruction through the struggle for black civil rights. If *Sanctuary* is about rape, it is also about race. To consider the rape of a white woman, in the 1920s, in the South, without considering the black body (if only as a racist, "balloon-face" or "black beast" stereotype) is inconceivable.[22]

So far in this paper I have considered how the movement of the pronoun might inform or mobilize the movement of Temple Drake's body. Broadly speaking, I have argued that Temple's use of the pronoun offers her a means through which she can distort and reconfigure the violence of her terrifying past. More specifically, I have considered how Temple's pronoun attempts to swerve and evade the potency of literal meaning. More, I have examined how a modification at the level of Temple's pronoun provides a means of enacting a modification at the level of her physical body. I have hinted, albeit briefly, that Temple's retaliation is made possible by a coopting of the black body. I shall seek to shore up these inflections with a look to a final passage. Here, Temple's language betrays a similar predilection for the pronoun, and, I would venture, suggests a similar trauma at the level of (black) history.

Chapter 23 is not, then, the only point in the novel at which the pronoun and the body enter into congress. Providing an early indication of the extraordinary plasticity of Temple Drake's body comes an extract from chapter 8. As if it were a signpost for the grim contortions of chapter 23,

> Temple's head began to move. It turned slowly, as if she were following the passage of someone beyond the wall. It turned on to an excruciating degree, though no other muscle moved, like one of those papier-mâché Easter toys filled with candy, and became motionless in that reverted position. Then it turned back, slowly, as though pacing invisible feet beyond the wall, back to the chair against the door and became motionless there for a moment. Then she faced forward and Tommy watched her take a tiny watch from the top of her stocking and look at it. With the watch in her hand she lifted her head and looked directly at him, her eyes calm and empty as two holes. After a while she looked down at the watch again and returned it to her stocking. (226)

Moving one way, pausing, and then reversing in the direction from which it came, Temple's head performs an "excruciating" regime of move and countermove, of turn and return. Inspired by the terrifying "masculine sounds" (S 216) from "beyond the wall" (226) this appalling—almost superhuman—show of dexterity sees Temple's head (or more accurately her "it") rotate whilst her body stays still. The regressive turn of Temple's head/"it" embodies that most Faulknerian of tensions and situates Temple in an unliveable place between rigidity and mobilization.[23] As William Rossky has written, "Temple seems almost constantly in motion [but] yet remains terrifyingly fixed."[24] At the literal level, this contradiction is understandable, given the context: Temple is quite literally scared stiff (pun intended), yet at the same time is determined to get a better view of the threats that surround her, even though they remain "beyond the wall." Temple's body, to borrow a term from *Absalom, Absalom!* (1936), is a place of "fierce dynamic rigidity."[25] Yet the regressive turn of Temple's head does more than just highlight an antagonism between movement and stasis.

The striking turn of Temple's head indicates, then, an immediate fear of rape. Metaphorically, however, this tortured act does more than just highlight a personal threat. I would like to conclude with the suggestion that the turn, and return, of Temple's head speaks silently of wider historical anxieties, concerns with looking back. Throughout this paper I have traced some of these efforts to return or to revise, yet a final example should solidify my point. The threat of rape forces Temple's head to turn, forces her to look back. As her head returns forward, her appearance seems somewhat altered. Her eyes, "calm and empty as two holes," have witnessed a trauma outside of the "walls" of her room. This trauma "beyond the walls" testifies, I would venture, to the South's problematic relationship to its (black) history. Temple carries this traumatic historical sediment with her throughout the novel, so much so that the anxiety of backwardness provided by Faulkner subsequently (dis)colors Temple's attempt to move forward, to forget her history, and, ultimately, to split whiteness from blackness. Yet these operations ultimately prove fruitless. However reversible the novel's bodies might be, they ultimately prove unable to fully expunge the traces of a violence that permeates the grammar of Temple Drake and the grammar of the South.

NOTES

1. A raft of scholarship attests to the problematic materiality that often weighs down Faulkner's prose. A selection of the leading accounts will suffice to give some kind of context to this previous effort. See André Bleikasten, *The Ink of Melancholy: Faulkner's Novels from "The Sound and the Fury" to "Light in August"* (Bloomington: Indiana University Press, 1990); Patricia Yaeger, *Dirt and Desire: Reconstructing Southern Women's Writing, 1930–1990* (Chicago: University of Chicago Press, 2000); Doreen Fowler, *Faulkner: The Return of the Repressed* (Charlottesville: University Press of Virginia, 1997).

2. William Faulkner, *Sanctuary* (1931) in Noel Polk, ed., *Faulkner: Novels, 1930–1935* (New York: Library of America, 1985). All citations will refer to this edition.

3. Diane Roberts, *Faulkner and Southern Womanhood* (Athens: University of Georgia Press, 1994), 123. Roberts is correct in her assertion that rape is the novel's primary thematic concern. Yet *Sanctuary* is not a story of one but of *two* rapes. Drawn to the rape of Temple Drake (which occurs at the end of chapter 13) is the rape of Lee Goodwin (which occurs at the end of chapter 29). The circumstances surrounding Goodwin's rape are, like those surrounding Temple's, shrouded in ambiguity. The text gives no more than a darkly cryptic indication of the details of this rape: "we never used a cob. We made him wish we used a cob." The ambiguity of these lines provokes the reader into questioning what exactly *was* used in the novel's second rape. I would venture a speculative claim: that—as an additional punitive measure—Goodwin is castrated and subsequently raped with his own (severed) penis. As Joel Williamson has written, "The way of death in a lynching generally bore a direct relation to the crime." In fact, rapists, he continues, "ordinarily suffered the loss of sexual organs: in the act of lynching" (Joel Williamson, *The Crucible of*

Race: Black White Relations in the American South since Emancipation [New York: Oxford University Press, 1984], 188).

4. John T. Matthews, "The Elliptical Nature of *Sanctuary*," in *Novel: A Forum on Fiction*, 17:3 (Spring, 1984): 246–65 [246].

5. *Sanctuary* is saturated with the impersonal pronoun "it." The term features 1,129 times in 217 pages.

6. V. N. Volosinov, *Marxism and the Philosophy of Language*, trans. Ladislav Matejka and I. R. Titunik (Cambridge: Harvard University Press, 1973), 80. Volosinov's term is part of a wider argument that aims to emphasize the material and, by extension, the social character of the verbal sign. For him, the (generative) crisis at the center of language is a marker of the inherently social nature of discourse.

7. John Lyons, *Semantics, Vol. 2* (Cambridge: Cambridge University Press, 1977), 636.

8. As we discover, the attack is a prolonged one, beginning with the "fiddling" on a Saturday night and ending with full penetration on a Sunday morning.

9. In his 1932 introduction to the Modern Library Edition of *Sanctuary*, Faulkner proposed a similar transformation from body into text: "I began to think of myself again as a printed object." See James B. Meriwether, ed., *Essays, Speeches, and Public Letters by William Faulkner* (London: Chatto and Windus, 1967), 177.

10. William Shakespeare, *King Lear*, Act 1, Scene 4, ll. 188–89 (London: Penguin Classics, 1972), 84.

11. Michael Holquist, ed., Mikhail Mikhailovich Bakhtin, *The Dialogic Imagination* (Austin: University of Texas Press, 2002), 282.

12. Keen to deflect any suggestion that the rape might have been a source of pleasure, Temple pretends that this "bubbling" sensation is emanating not from her clitoris but from her stomach. For Horace, the story of Temple Drake has its own erotic charge. Temple is not blind to this fact and seems to be playing up to the fantasy that Horace has come for. Indeed, as the narrative progresses, Temple seems more and more to be acting up to her (intimate) audience. The language of Temple's telling is essentially that of an act of solicitation. Horace, we remember, "told her what he wanted" before the narrative took place (326). Temple is acting under instruction, however: "Will you do what he wants you to?" (327) Miss Reba inquires. In the context of a brothel room, the sexual undertones of Temple's telling are unmistakeable.

13. Grace Elizabeth Hale, *Making Whiteness: The Culture of Segregation in the South, 1890–1940* (New York: Random House, 1999), 11.

14. I use the term "penis" advisedly, in the knowledge that both Temple's and Popeye's penises are fabricated.

15. Edwin T. Arnold and Dawn Trouard, *Reading Faulkner: "Sanctuary"* (Jackson: University Press of Mississippi, 1996), 177.

16. John N. Duvall, "A Strange Nigger? Faulkner and the Minstrel Performance of Whiteness," *Faulkner Journal* 22 (Fall 2006/Spring 2007): 106–19 [209].

17. Owing in part to the growing production of illicit bootleg whiskey during prohibition, corn was a principal export crop from the American South during the 1920s. The corncob, then, on top of its structural resemblance to a penis, acquires additional currency as a metonymic figure of the violence implicit within Southern labor regimes, specifically as it related to the cultivation of corn crops. Seen in this light, we might be able to make a case that the rape of Temple by the cob bleeds into a larger raping: that which saw the exploitation of the sharecropper or tenant who worked the land.

18. See *Absalom, Absalom!* (66, 191, 192). The racist epithet does not contain itself to *Absalom, Absalom!* In *The Sound and the Fury* Jason Compson is especially fond of the balloon image, if only to refer to *his own* head. Specifically, Jason's metaphor relates to the terrifying *head*aches (referred to as *"black*outs") that threaten to reassign his whiteness.

Jason commits to localized variations upon this central rubbery metaphor—one that nominates a *bursting*: "bang" (1057), "blow" (1051), "blowing . . . blowing . . . blowing" (1063), "burst" (1063), "explode" (1058 1062), "pump" (1063), "pump . . . "pump" (1064).

19. See Walter Benjamin, "Theses on the Philosophy of History" (1940), in *Illuminations* (London: Fontana Press, 1992), 245–55: "To articulate the past historically does not mean to recognize it 'the way it really was' (Ranke). It means to seize hold of a memory as it flashes up at a moment of danger" (247).

20. See *Sanctuary*, 207, 212, 255.

21. Williamson, 499.

22. Much historiography has cogently argued that rape is inextricably tied in with racist assumptions of black bestiality. As Susan Estrich has attested, "Between 1930 and 1967, 89% of the men executed for rape in [the United States] were black" ("Rape," *Yale Law Journal* 95:6 (May 1986): 1087–1184 [1089, n2]. As Eugene D. Genovese has written, rape was even racialized at the level of the victim: "Rape meant, by definition, rape of a white woman, for no such crime as rape of a black woman existed at law" (Genovese, *Roll, Jordan, Roll: The World the Slaves Made* [New York: Vintage, 1976], 33.) For other pertinent discussions of the racialization of rape, see Williamson, *Crucible*, 111–34; bell hooks, *Black Looks: Race and Representation* (London: Turnaround Books, 1992), 97–113.

23. Additionally, of course, the rotation of Temple's head carries Orphean overtones and gives a mythological context to Temple's subsequent descent into the "underworld" of Memphis.

24. William Rossky, "The Pattern of Nightmare in *Sanctuary*; or, Miss Reba's Dogs," in *Twentieth Century Interpretations of "Sanctuary": A Collection of Critical Essays* (New Jersey: Prentice Hall), 70–78 [71].

25. William Faulkner, *Absalom, Absalom!* (1936), in Joseph Blotner and Noel Polk, eds., *Faulkner: Novels, 1936–1940* (New York: Library of America, 1990), 131.

The Secret Machinery of Textuality, Or, What Is Benjy Compson Really Thinking?

TAYLOR HAGOOD

I would like to return to a text that is one of the sacred cows of William Faulkner's canon—the first section of *The Sound and the Fury* "narrated" by Benjamin "Benjy" Compson.[1] It has received a great deal of strong textual analysis, and yet there are certain questions that have not been asked regarding it. I want to ask some of those questions—questions about just what it means that Faulkner employs a mentally challenged narrator, about what exactly this narrative does, what its functions are, and, most importantly, what Benjy may be up to in his narrative and in the action of the novel. Following these questions leads to some unorthodox answers: specifically that this text, so long celebrated as a radical experiment, is surprisingly conservative in its essential form as well as in its sociopolitical assertions and assumptions, and that Benjy Compson, Faulkner's most famous disabled person, is not only much more intellectually complex but also more prescient, conscious, and skillful as a narrativist than Faulkner scholarship has conventionally thought. Ultimately, in Benjy Compson Faulkner finds a vehicle through whom he can normalize the attitudes of the white Southern aristocracy while simultaneously—and perhaps unintentionally—creating a character who has his own inner thoughts and attitudes that are ironically and not a little problematically beyond Faulkner's control.

My reexamination of Benjy is in part a response to Maria Truchan-Tataryn's 2005 article "Textual Abuse: Faulkner's Benjy." Truchan-Tataryn lowers the boom on Faulkner and Faulkner critics alike for their treatment of Benjy, opining that the "critical cliché" that "the first section of *The Sound and the Fury* is applauded as Faulkner's most remarkable achievement" has "resisted notice" (159).[2] Faulkner criticism, she writes, "manifests not only an overwhelming admiration for the unparalleled skill with which Faulkner produced such a plausible idiot in the character of Benjamin Compson but also an ignorance of changing concepts of disability" (163).[3] "Despite the growth of a global disability rights movement and the development of the discipline of disability studies in the humanities," she continues, "the figure of Benjy's mindless, voiceless subhumanity continues to resonate through Faulknerian scholarship as a believable portrait of disability" (160). Scholars thus need to take another look at Faulkner's famous "idiot," for "reinterpreting Benjy, problematizing the idea of absence of thought in a conscious individual as a realistic possibility, invites a deeper consideration of the need to engage with diversity in human experience and its textual representation" (172). Above all else, she explains, Benjy "illuminates not the (lack of) subjectivity of a cognitively impaired individual in lived experience but rather imaginings projected upon a population denied agency and voice by authors of public policy as well as narrative texts" (163).[4]

Although not all scholars have been so insensitive in their views of Benjy, Truchan-Tataryn's point is well taken.[5] The field of disability studies *does* permit us ways of thinking more fully about the specific nature of Benjy's marginalization. As Rosemarie Garland Thomson has particularly shown, literary texts well exhibit the nuances of the specific modes of marginalization of individuals marked by human variation: she and others have convincingly argued that constructions of abnormality lie in the nexus of cultural, economic, and political forces much as do those of race, class, ethnicity, and gender.[6] And since Faulkner scholarship has indeed not fully considered this particular dynamic in regard to Benjy, it *is* important to heed Truchan-Tataryn's call. Unfortunately, for all of her criticism of Faulkner studies and insistence on focusing on "projected imaginings" in literary texts, Truchan-Tataryn does not herself roll up her sleeves and undertake this messy textual exploration.

In executing this task myself, I first want to point out that although disability studies was not a discourse available to Faulkner as it is now, he nevertheless realizes Benjy's marginalization on several levels and hinges that marginalization on the recognition of his disability. When Benjy's name is changed from Maury to Benjamin, Versh explains that he has been turned into a "bluegum," which is something that in this novel happens to black people. The fact that Benjy crosses over into African American spaces on Easter Sunday testifies to the fact that he "belongs" in the marginal space of the other. It is precisely his disability that signals the name change, the transformation into "bluegum," and his being placed among African Americans, making him less white, perhaps even nonwhite, in the sense that lower-class white people are raced as well as classed as "poor white trash." A case could also be made that he is marginalized as *too white*: with "dead looking and hairless" skin, "pale and fine" hair, and eyes "of the pale sweet blue of cornflowers," Benjy seems conspicuous for his paleness (1088). His silence, broken only by animal-like moans, mixes with his conspicuous whiteness to render him a figure of horror as it has for other writers, such as Melville and Poe.[7]

Finally, his disability emasculates him practically (he does not possess the power of other white men) and literally (by way of his castration), so that he is further marginalized in terms of gender.[8] Whether figured as nonwhite, too white, feminine, or even an animal (compared as he is to a horse and a "trained bear"), Benjy is a figure of inaccessible otherness in the novel.

Which is, of course, what makes Benjy's section so radically daring— Faulkner invades the inviolate and lets us come with him. The chiaroscuro effect of juxtaposing what is "inside" Benjy's head with what his "outside" looks like is what allows Faulkner to up the ante in his own game. Almost as if he were writing his own review, Faulkner wants his readers to know just how good he is when he gives us an image of Benjy later in the text designed to shock the reader. Like a good magician, Faulkner has enhanced the contrast between the possible and the impossible, the expected and unexpected, the concealed and unconcealed. He gives us the "secret" world of Benjy Compson's consciousness—life as seen by the inscrutable other. But what is perhaps *most* shocking about that world is not its strangeness but its recognizability. Leslie Fiedler argues that what is so shocking about the "freak" is the possibility that the self resides in the other marked by human variation, that ultimately the freak is "one of us."[9] Likewise, the surprise of Benjy's monologue is that we can understand him at all, that he is so *normal*. Not just normal, in fact, but more . . . an accomplished architect of narrative.

In order to delineate the specific beams and braces of Benjy's narrative, I want to revisit the text of the first section of *The Sound and the Fury* as if it is the first time I am reading it. Recapturing the experiences of reading any text is as difficult and perhaps as impossible as new historical critics have taught us that the attempt to peer through the lens of the present into the past is. But however problematic doing so may be, I would like to try and (re)create as best I can an initial engagement with the book and try to ponder the questions that could arise in an uninitiated reader's mind. At the very least, the questions I want to raise in such a process will hopefully help illuminate aspects of the text that years of lauding it have tended to obscure, one of the foremost of which is just how wrought this text actually is. In many ways, it is a skillfully constructed narrative masquerading as a mess.

As with any text, the opening paragraphs of Benjy's section establish the rules of reading peculiar to this specific text. These paragraphs present the reader with certain clues. Immediately, the reader can see that there is a first person narrator whose sense of identity is consolidated enough for that person to offer up utterance from the position of the self. The person is an "I." Also from the first sentence, we can see that the narrator is capable of presenting a somewhat sophisticatedly modi-fied lexical unit: "the curling flower spaces."[10] The image is strikingly visual, strikingly poetic, arguably reminiscent of a line from a Wallace Stevens poem. Another thing that happens beginning in the first sen-tence and continuing throughout the first paragraph is that the reader is bombarded with a series of pronouns without antecedents and verbs with no direct objects. "They" who are being watched through the "flower spaces" of the "flower tree" are "hitting" while "Luster" is "hunting." Who are "they" and what are they "hitting"? Who is "Luster" and what is he "hunting"? We are not kept in suspense long: already we know that "they" are approaching a "flag," and when we find out that "they" "took the flag out," then we can pretty safely assume that they are golfing. Indeed, we quickly hear one of the "hitters" say, "Here, caddie," and we can now set our minds at ease that this initial mystery is solved. It is a little strange that the narrator should call the golf course a pasture, but it is early in the text and the reader is probably in a hurry to get to the bottom of the mystery of the narrator and of the story the narrator has to tell.

But what effect has been established at this point on the reader? Accepted knowledge says that Faulkner presented all of these awkward lexical items to show that the narrator lacks the sophistication to present facilitative engaging prose. Faulkner teachers as well as Faulkner schol-ars have often promoted the notion that these linguistic codes are to be interpreted as signs of mental limitation. It may be, however, that schol-arly understanding of this text's implied reader has been overdetermined, for it could just as well be argued that the text's refusal to be engaging and facilitative actually makes it highly engaging precisely because of that refusal. There is not necessarily any reason to think, after the first two paragraphs of *The Sound and the Fury*, that we are not in the hands of a capable, if unreliable, narrator. Moreover, the first eight paragraphs give us what is, in terms of formatting, a very traditional narrative. The paragraphs are organized logically and organically. The dialogue is prop-erly set apart in quotes. No words are misspelled. There is no reason to think there is anything unusual about this text beyond the fact that the language is odd. Most of all, it does not necessarily follow, based on the text's style, that the narrator is cognitively disabled.

However, the third paragraph alerts us to the fact that something is indeed not quite "normal." Luster speaks, letting the cat out of the bag in his usual trickster way, saying, "Listen at you, now. . . . Aint you some-thing, thirty three years old, going on that way. After I done went all the way to town to buy you that cake. Hush up that moaning. Aint you going to help me find that quarter so I can go to the show tonight" (879).

Now we are confronted with a triangulated Lacanian moment, learning something about who the "I" of the text is from another character that clashes with what our sense of that "I" (or even its sense of itself) may be. We now know that the narrator is thirty-three and moaning and that this person Luster has enough authority to tell the person to "hush up" and order the narrator around to help find the quarter (which Luster apparently is hunting). Arguably, the first shock might come to the first-time reader *now* and not in section four. The juxtaposition of the age of thirty-three and the action of moaning are clues that immediately signal the narrator as disabled, and this revelation presumably causes the reader to review what she already knows about the narrator. The credibility of the text now changes because the narrator's reliability is brought into serious doubt, which forces the reader to look to other characters for help in negotiating what is "really going on" in the text.

Without Luster's comments (and those of other characters that follow), there are a number of reasons why this text would not necessarily be seen as being generated by a person with a cognitive disability. First, stream of consciousness as a style in itself does not automatically signify mental disability—certainly it does not do so later in Quentin's monologue. Second, if Luster does not drop these hints here in the third paragraph, not only is there no reason for the reader to make the assumption of mental limitation but the reader may well be impressed with the deftness of the narrative. Third, there is a strong possibility that if the other characters do not inform us of Benjy's condition, the entire first section of the novel could seem not only that of a "normal" person but also a text that is extremely contrived: the reader is supposed to buy the idea that a person over the course of an hour or two is going to think about his entire life in a way that presents a narrative that is both discernable and meaningful, that the person's mind is going to jump *involuntarily* from point to point in a way that will add up to a story full of metaphorical and narrative significance.

In fact, the text *is* contrived in a way that has a somewhat conventional precedent, for its strategies of plot construction, radical as they seem, actually replicate in principle the forms of plotting found in classic detective fiction. Peter Hühn discusses the layers of narrative and secrecy in this kind of plotting, writing that "the basic internal tension in a classic-formula [mystery/detective] novel can be conceptualized as a contest between . . . *writing* stories and *reading* stories. The criminal devises or *writes* the story of his criminal act, at the same time, however, protecting it against reading, composing it as an unreadable secret story" while the "detective attempts to decipher its traces and interpret their meaning, and in the end he succeeds in *reading* it."[11] What Faulkner gives us in

Benjy's section is a chronological narrative that is scrambled and hence a variation on the same kinds of plots that appear in Arthur Conan Doyle stories or Agatha Christie novels. In this regard, the text is essentially nothing new but rather an established form skillfully repackaged. What makes this repackaging different is that where classic detective fiction features a sleuth who puts the mixed up pieces of the criminal's narrative together, Faulkner forces his readers to be the sleuths.

But an important question to raise at this point is who exactly is supposed to have forged this narrative—Benjy or Faulkner? Stated another way, to what extent does the suspension of disbelief apply in the case of the first section of *The Sound and the Fury*? Robert Dale Parker's answer is that Faulkner is the architect and that we can and must believe in his speaking for Benjy. He writes that in "the first section of *The Sound and the Fury* we get not Benjy's language, although we might sometimes call it that as a convenient shorthand, but instead we get what he *would* say, if he *could* say, *which he can't*" (28). Parker further asserts that "Benjy uses no language at all. In the absence of language, the more unusual words are no more radical a distortion or illusion than the use of any language to render a state of no language—what he *would* say, if he *could* say, *which he can't*. Faulkner has it both ways, forging an impossible compromise that evokes a lack of language and a minimum of intellectual complexity while also maximizing the representation of those incapacities through language" (29). The "impossible compromise" Parker recognizes sounds something akin to Spivak's doomed subaltern who cannot speak because she is caught between the language of the center and that of the margin.[12] But Parker does not permit Benjy even Spivak's "subaltern" status, for he is simply unable to speak. For Parker, the narrative is Faulkner's, and Parker is certainly not alone in his reading. Readers generally seem to cut Faulkner some slack: after all, they would well argue, he is "approximating" what may be in Benjy's mind.

If we choose to read the monologue as Faulkner's "speaking for" Benjy, then we must confront a rather thorny issue. By the light of this perspective, Faulkner does not come off very well in making the decision to colonize the body and mind of a disabled person. Indeed, read this way Faulkner appears as the precocious and even reckless person we know he could be, a show-off using a clever gimmick. In such a reading, Benjy and his thoughts become the very instance of "projected imaginings" of a normate upon a nonnormate body that Truchan-Tataryn complains about. Although Faulkner gives us what Benjy is allegedly thinking, he also uses Benjy as a ventriloquist dummy, a figure set up not necessarily to explore his own thoughts and feelings but rather to tell the puppeteer's story. In fact, moving plot along takes precedence over exploring Benjy's feelings, for Faulkner uses only those memories that serve to propel the narrative, creating a very lean story that has none of the kind of subterfuge and excess that could have come closer to realizing the true inner workings of a mind, whether a disabled one or not. One can imagine James Joyce, for example, writing this book and throwing in passages entirely unconnected to the storyline; but even Benjy's red herrings serve to propel the narrative, however obscurely.[13]

If we read Faulkner as the architect of Benjy's section, then, as Truchan-Tataryn suggests, we can learn much more about Faulkner and what he thinks and what he thinks Benjy thinks than we do about what the person born Maury Compson thinks. The specific thing we can learn about Faulkner is that his radical experiment is in yet another way tempered by a *conservative* design, for he employs a narrative tactic that uses Benjy as the other only to confirm and normalize the rhetoric of the self. Benjy stands in as a counterfeit other constructed for the express purpose of further marginalizing true others and reifying the narrative of the empowered, which is in this case the white Southern aristocratic patriarchy. One of the most curious things about the critical reception of his monologue is that scholars have not considered other ways Faulkner might have represented Benjy's thoughts. Ben Wasson might have tried to "normalize" Benjy's time jumps (which Faulkner promptly reversed), but these days we rarely question Faulkner's representational approach, despite the fact that he could well have shown disability in the text through misspelling, odd arrangement of text on the page, poor punctuation, and so on. Yet, as noted before, Benjy's style is impeccable. He does not misspell words, he puts quotes in the proper places, and however limited his vocabulary may be, he speaks the language of the other Compsons, which is to say that he speaks in the "invisible" dialect of the center, the white aristocratic patriarchy. This language stands in marked contrast to the way that the speech of African Americans is represented: they speak in dialect, with Versh worrying about Benjy "holding onto that ahun gate" (881) and Luster telling Quentin's boyfriend from the show that he does not "ricklick" seeing him before (915). Indeed, although Luster chastises Benjy for not playing "in the branch like folks" and complains that "folks dont like to look at a looney" (891), Benjy is, on the inside at least, much more one of the folks than is Luster.

The effect of Faulkner's endowing Benjy with the speech of the aristocracy is that the focus of the novel's tragedy remains securely focused on the Compson family. I do not mean to imply that Faulkner entirely excludes the African Americans in the novel from the weighty tragedy that pervades it, although I am not sure that Faulkner was as thoroughly aware of the extent of their role in it when he first wrote and published the novel as he was when he wrote the Compson appendix. But instead of realizing a way that Benjy as a hybrid figure who is both a white Compson and a black bluegum (as well as a poor white aristocrat and feminized man) can articulate a hybrid poetics, Faulkner makes him a spokesperson for empowered whiteness, whose narrative style confirms rather than subverts traditional Southern race and class hierarchy.

There was ample precedent for Faulkner of white Southern writers performing this maneuver of creating an othered figure who stands in to speak the narrative of the self, most notably in the early frame narratives of Thomas Nelson Page. Collected in his volume, *In Ole Virginia, Or, Marse Chan and Other Stories*, these stories use African American narrators to confirm the proslavery image of the Old South as a nostalgic place of peaceful race relations. For example, Sam, the ex-slave who tells the story of Master Channing in "Marse Chan," says to the white auditor who is the narrator of the frame, that the years of slavery before the Civil War "wuz good ole times . . . the bes' Sam ever see! . . . Dyar warn' no trouble nor nothin'."[14] The logic of the story is that if this slave says that the old days were good old days then they really must have been good old days. The black narrators of Page's fiction are white aristocratic Southerners masquerading as black ex-slaves, and their function is to normalize slavery and the slave owners' propagated image of race relations as harmonious. Page's ultimate goal is to present an effective reconciliation romance, which envisions a reunion of Northern and Southern *whites* after the Civil War. As Karen A. Keely explains, in order to bring about these narrative visions of reconciliation, writers such as Page "deliberately ignored . . . the exploited and devastated black bodies on which such romance is built" (643).[15]

There is a problem, however, with such a depiction of the other—the problem of authenticity. I am not referring to a naïve notion of authenticity but rather the crisis of authenticity, or the need to instill and distill as much authority and believability in a character as possible. The crisis is that when a fictional other is employed in the furtherance of the desires of the self, the other must be endowed with the aura of authenticity in order for that figure's arguments to be convincing. The counterfeit other cannot be seen as being too obviously fake, else the entire project implodes because it is seen as the ventriloquism it is. Of course, in some ways this problem is easily solved by using marginal figures about whom the center knows very little anyway. The level of knowledge white readers actually had about black people beyond minstrel stereotypes was generally limited enough for Page to pull off a believable act of puppeteering—not only does Ralph Ellison's *Invisible Man* retroactively attest to the "projected imaginings" of white people on black bodies, but this phenomenon is also confirmed in the fact that when Charles Chesnutt wrote stories designed to beat Page at his own game his white readers simply thought he was writing Page all over again.[16] Turning to Faulkner, Truchan-Tataryn's very point is that he and his readers had such little understanding of disability that Benjy could be a convincing figure. Certainly Faulkner has stacked the deck, speaking for someone who cannot speak, and among scholars the matter of authenticity is rarely considered regarding Benjy as it is when discussing Faulkner's women or African American characters.[17]

This crisis of authenticity, however, also has the peculiar effect of endowing these authors' counterfeit others with their own secret thoughts that can run counter to and escape the authors' control. It is as if, because these writers do not "know" what in actuality black or disabled people are thinking, they take extra measures to negotiate the authenticity of those characters. In Page's frame narratives, this crisis of authenticity emerges in the fact that his black narrators occasionally let slip their secret modus operandi, revealing the possibility that their narratives of joyous ex-slave days may not be entirely truthful. These black people engage in a game of what they call "prodjickin'," which is essentially a form of lying, a type of Signifying that is, as I have elsewhere argued, "a rhetorical strategy of harmless subversion the harmless nature of which is suspect yet convincing enough for the listener to overlook its threat."[18] Thus Sam first appears talking to his former master's dog, saying "Yo' so sp'ilt yo' kyahn hardly walk. Jes' ez able to git over [the fence] as I is! Jes' like white folks—think cuz you's white and I's black, I got to wait on yo' all de time" (2). When Sam realizes that the white frame narrator has heard him talking to the dog that way, he assures the white man that the dog "know I don' mean nothin' by what I sez. . . . He know I'se jes' prodjickin' wid 'im" (3). This strategy of double-speak is ostensibly contained in the benign situation of Sam's talking to the dog, but the fact that Sam admits to lying, to "prodjickin'," has the effect of throwing everything else he says into a dubious light. Any thinking reader must wonder if his claims about how wonderful it is to be a slave are just more of his "prodjickin'."

The perplexing thing about this "prodjickin'" in Page's stories is that one might wonder why he decided to include it as a performative strategy at all when he could have just had his narrators tell their proslavery narratives; again, the answer lies in the problem of authenticity. In his effort to create a convincing character who uses language and performative strategies that bear some verisimilitude to whatever it is that Page thinks of as authentic behavior of an African American man, he somehow felt the need to include the man's conversation with the dog. Perhaps a late nineteenth-century white Southern aristocratic mentality—long accustomed to relegating African Americans and their perspectives—simply could not imagine a black person being subtle enough actually to lie to a white person about such a thing as a prewar race relations. Or maybe the paternal attitude of the aristocracy was so deeply invested in its notion of the slave and master relationship in the United States South being pseudofamilial that it could not think that an ex-slave would betray that. Certainly in Page's writing there is a sharp distinction between "good" black people (ex-slaves who are "one of us" aristocratic whites—although not too much so) and "bad" black people who seek various types of independence. Whatever the case, the fact is that this prodjickin' opens a window not only upon these African Americans' "true" ideas but also on the secret machinery of the visible texts they generate for whites to consume.

What might we learn if we consider how this same dynamic applies to the case of Benjamin Compson? If we read the first section of *The Sound and the Fury* from this standpoint, then we find that Faulkner takes the opposite route of Page to achieve what is nevertheless the same effect. Specifically, the monologue of the first section is marked by a conspicuous antiauthenticity in that it breaks its own rules of authentification. This dynamic appears in what Gene Fant Jr. has referred to as "the novel's most famous linguistic pun": the confusion of the signifier "caddie" with the phonetically identical signifier "Caddy."[19] From the standpoint of authenticity, this device simply does not hold up: "caddie" just simply cannot be "caddie" in Benjy's mind. It must always be "Caddy," and a much more accurate rendering of that phoneme from Benjy's perspective is simply "Caddy," whether referring to golfing or to his sister. The whole point of the text and the device itself is that he cannot distinguish the difference between a "caddie" and "Caddy," or the monologue ceases to function according to its assumed rules.

Unless, of course, Benjamin Compson *does* know the difference between the two. In sacrificing rather than overworking authenticity, Faulkner either intentionally or unintentionally introduces the possibility of Benjy's also operating within his own secret machinery of textuality in a way that subverts the dynamics and assumptions embedded in Faulkner's use of him as a puppet. Intentionally or not, Faulkner gives us the possibility that Benjy is more prescient than he has been seen as being by other characters as well as by readers. And this possibility leads the way to the further possibility that the great tragedy of Maury/Benjamin Compson is not that he is sadly and ironically confused by anything that sounds like the name of his sister but rather that the signifier itself (and the phoneme which he knows refers to the signifier) carries a much more complex set of meanings that are equally and just as deeply troubling and sad to him. Seen in this way, the signifier "Caddy" emerges as a very different kind of symbolic repository, the site wherein is focused Maury's frustration at his inability to articulate what is in fact a complex inner self.

Consider, for example, just what sorts of dynamics are associated with the name "Caddy" beyond just its sound: toward the end of the monologue, Benjy remembers his mother talking to Caddy when they are children. "'Candace.' Mother said. 'I told you not to call him [Benjy]. It was bad enough when your father insisted on calling you by that silly nickname, and I will not have him called by one. Nicknames are vulgar. Only common people use them. Benjamin.' She said" (926). Added to the other ways Benjy's name-change has marginalized him is this moral-tinged-with-class marginalization coming with Caddy's nicknaming him. Now he is "common." More importantly, so is Caddy, and Mrs. Compson's implying that Candace is herself "common," or vulgar, for having a nickname anticipates and highlights the labels of vulgarity applied to her later in life (and carries interesting implications about Mr. Compson). The word "Caddy" contains the very aspersions cast upon Candace by her family, and there is every reason to believe that Benjy well understands exactly what his mother has said and its implications. In short, the signifier "Caddy" evokes not just Benjy's love for his sister but his awareness of her marginalization, and even his own marginalization as a nicknamed person as well as a person called by perjorative names such as "looney." Benjy, in other words, is well aware of the power of a name, having experienced the limiting and marginalization of such labeling.

If we rethink Benjy's section by reexamining the text in terms of its complexity and considering how Benjy himself engages that complexity, then we find that he is "abnormal" in a very different sense than readers have generally thought. Scholars have long understood that Benjy's text is complex, and not a few first-time readers have abandoned it in disgust and frustration. But the consensus has generally been that the complexity is unconscious, arising from Benjy's impairments as represented rather than from any conscious complexity in Benjy's thought.[20] I am suggesting, however, that no matter how physically impaired he may be he is nevertheless consciously complex and is actually similar to another Faulkner character who faces the threat of being sent to Jackson: Darl Bundren. Part of Darl's abnormality is his uncanny ability to narrate with such power. The fact that he actually narrates his mother's death scene from miles away highlights the other extraordinary thing about him—that he can see things that others cannot. Although he is punished for his abnormality, it is a dramatic irony of *As I Lay Dying* that Darl's threat is essentially his greater *ability*.[21] He knows too much, and he can present what he knows in devastating ways. If we think of Benjy in the same way, then he becomes abnormal not in the sense of being "lesser" than but "greater" than the norm—a skillful architect of a complex associative narrative. And our decoding of his text transforms into a much different sort of an enterprise that is in fact much truer to the actual functioning of the text: rather than decoders of a mess, we become assemblers of an elaborate and intentional puzzle.

To some extent, this possibility of intentionality resituates the locus of narrative control on Benjy rather than Faulkner, and such reorientation carries certain implications. Arguably, all the deeply embedded white aristocratic attitudes become Benjy's own, and he now seems the dangerous figure many other characters perceive him to be, although not necessarily for the same reasons. Indeed, he now stands in as the "criminal" of the detective story, and this repositioning changes the status of certain characters, for where Faulkner gives us no sleuths for his skillfully constructed secretive text, Benjy does. One is Caddy herself, who "more than anyone actively attempts to interpret Benjy's cries" (Roggenbuck 583). The other is Luster, an unreliable sleuth for an unreliable narrator. Hühn writes that added to the two layers of narrative in classic detective fiction is yet another secret layer of narrative, which is that "the *story* of his interpretation and reading process is also hidden from its readers" (41). Although Luster tells the man with the red tie that Benjy "cant tell what you saying. . . . He deef and dumb" (914), the fact is that Luster is well aware that Benjy can hear and understand when he says, "Beller. . . . Beller. You want something to beller about. All right, then. Caddy." he whispered. "Caddy. Beller now. Caddy" (919). It may be just too much coincidence that Dilsey promptly calls the two over and queries Luster as to what he has done, asking him, "Is you been projeckin with his graveyard" (920). Luster, the trickster, with his own secret story in the tradition of the prodjickers of Thomas Nelson Page, well understands the quiet life of desperation led by his charge.

In the end, it is difficult to discern between what of the text is supposed to be Faulkner and what is Benjy, bringing us to its fundamental problem—that it is a jumble. In trying to make an authentic character through whom to tell a story that maintains white aristocratic cultural assumptions, Faulkner simply takes on too much. Benjy emerges as simultaneously a projected imagining and a real character behind the functioning mask. This have-cake-eat-it-too dynamic makes it difficult to make a final judgment as to just how Benjy is to be read. Nevertheless, although the effect seems unintentional, it renders a text even richer than it has already been understood to be. Indeed, although I may also fall into the trap of lauding Faulkner's achievement, I wish to acknowledge the author's perceptual shortcoming in his ambition to give Benjy a voice, however problematically. In so doing, Faulkner presents a character who is by his own linguistic performance more than a functioning unit for his author. In the end, Benjy not only lays bare the hidden scaffolding of Faulkner's architecture, but he is also a character we are just beginning to know.

NOTES

1. I am indebted to much excellent feedback at the Faulkner and Yoknapatawpha Conference, especially Mary Carruth, Dustin Morrow, Theresa Towner, and Jay Watson. Thank you to Donald M. Kartiganer for the invitation to the conference, and to Annette Trefzer and Ann J. Abadie for their thought-provoking questions and excellent editing.

2. Maria Truchan-Tataryn, "Textual Abuse: Faulkner's Benjy," *Journal of Medical Humanities*, 26.2–3 (2005): 159.

3. Truchan-Tataryn is not alone. David T. Mitchell and Sharon L. Snyder point out that "nearly all of the criticism of the novel 'promotes' Benjy to the status of a symbolic representative of human tragedy" despite the fact that "on closer reading the chapter provides an important sustained reading of the social circumstances surrounding the reception of cognitive disability" (David T. Mitchell and Sharon L. Snyder, *Narrative Prosthesis: Disability and the Dependencies of Discourse* [Ann Arbor: University of Michigan Press, 2000], 167).

4. Truchan-Tataryn goes on to explain that her "intent is not to add yet another variation to the established themes of explication of Benjy but to demonstrate how unquestioning acceptance of him as a successful representation of intellectual disability reveals an underlying ableism in the literary critical endeavor and an academic acquiescence to date socio-cultural constructions of disability" (159–60).

5. Important treatments of Benjy include the following: Ineke Bockting, "Mind Style as an Interdisciplinary Approach to Characterisation in Faulkner," *Language and Literature* 3 (1994): 157–74; Cleanth Brooks, *William Faulkner: The Yoknapatawpha Country* (Baton Rouge: Louisiana State University Press, 1990); L. Moffitt Cecil, "A Rhetoric for Benjy," *Southern Literary Journal* 3 (1970): 32–46; Carvel Collins, "The Interior Monologues of *The Sound and the Fury*," *English Institute Essay*, 1952, ed. Alan S. Downer (New York: Columbia University Press, 1954), 29–56; Arthur F. Kinney, *Faulkner's Narrative Poetics: Style as Vision* (Amherst: University of Massachusetts Press, 1978); Robert Dale Parker, "'Through the Fence, between the Curling Flower Spaces': Teaching the First Section of *The Sound and the Fury*," *Approaches to Teaching Faulkner's "The Sound and the Fury*," ed. Stephen Hahn and Arthur F. Kinney, Approaches to Teaching World Literature Series, ed. Joseph Gibaldi (New York: Modern Language Association of America, 1996), 27–37; Ted Roggenbuck, "'The way he looked said Hush': Benjy's Mental Atrophy in *The Sound and the Fury*," *Mississippi Quarterly: The Journal of Southern Cultures* 58 (2005): 581–93; Stephen M. Ross, *Fiction's Inexhaustible Voice: Speech and Writing in Faulkner* (Athens: University of Georgia Press, 1989); and Seiji Sasamoto, "The First Section of *The Sound and the Fury*: Benjy and His Expressions," *William Faulkner: Materials, Studies, and Criticism*, 4.2 (1982): 19–36.

6. See Thomson's *Extraordinary Bodies: Figuring Physical Disability in American Culture and Literature* (New York: Columbia University Press, 1997). See also Mitchell

and Snyder as well as the essays in *Freakery: Cultural Spectacles of the Extraordinary Body* (New York: New York University Press, 1996), ed. Thomson, and Gary L. Albrecht, Katherine D. Seelman, and Michael Bury, *Handbook of Disability Studies* (Thousand Oaks, Calif.: Sage, 2001).

7. See Herman Melville, *Moby Dick* (New York: Norton, 2002) and Edgar Allan Poe, *The Narrative of Arthur Gordon Pym. The Essential Tales and Poems of Edgar Allan Poe*, ed. Benjamin F. Fisher (New York: Barnes and Noble, 2004), 443–606.

8. Thomson asserts that "the nonnormate status accorded disability feminizes all disabled figures" (*Extraordinary Bodies*, 9).

9. Leslie Fiedler, *Freaks: Myths and Images of the Secret Self* (New York: Touchstone, 1978).

10. William Faulkner, *The Sound and the Fury* (1929), in *William Faulkner: Novels 1926–1929* (New York: Library of America, 2006), 877.

11. Peter Hühn, "The Politics of Secrecy and Publicity: The Functions of Hidden Stories in Some recent British Mystery Fiction," in *Theory and Practice of Classic Detective Fiction*, ed. Jerome H. Delamater and Ruth Prigozy (Westport, CT: Greenwood Press, 1997), 40–41.

12. Gayatri Chakravorty Spivak, "Can the Subaltern Speak?," in *Colonial Discourse and Post-Colonial Theory: A Reader*, ed. Patrick Williams and Laura Chrisman (New York: Columbia University Press, 1994), 66–111.

13. The soundness of the narrative is well shown in the hypertext version of *The Sound and the Fury*, ed. by R. P. Stoicheff, Joel Deshaye, et al., "The Sound and the Fury": *A Hypertext Edition*, updated July 2004, University of Saskatchewan, accessed 8 Sep. 2008, http://www.usask.ca/english/faulkner. The text offers the option of being rearranged chronologically, demonstrating the fact that the text represents a logical narrative that is scrambled rather than a text with little or no narrative thread. The editors of this project, incidentally, include Truchan-Tataryn.

14. Thomas Nelson Page, *In Ole Virginia, Or Marse Chan and Other Stories* (Nashville, J. S. Sanders, 1991), 10.

15. 14. Karen A. Keely, "Marriage Plots and National Reunion: The Trope of Romantic Reconciliation in Postbellum Literature," *Mississippi Quarterly: The Journal of Southern Culture* 51 (1998): 643.

16. Ralph Ellison, *Invisible Man* (New York: Vintage, 1980) and Charles W. Chesnutt, *The Conjure Woman, and Other Tales* (Durham: Duke University Press, 1993). On Chesnutt's too-identical mimicry, see Keith Byerman, "Black Voices, White Stories: An Intertextual Analysis of Thomas Nelson Page and Charles Waddell Chesnutt," *North Carolina Literary Review* 8 (1999): 98–105.

17. On authenticity and Faulkner, see Jeff Karem, *The Romance of Authenticity: The Cultural Politics of Regional and Ethnic Literatures* (Charlottesville: University of Virginia Press, 2004).

18. Taylor Hagood, "Prodjickin', or mekin' a present to yo' fam'ly: Rereading Empowerment in Thomas Nelson Page's Frame Narratives," *Mississippi Quarterly: The Journal of Southern Cultures* 57 (2004): 431.

19. Gene Fant Jr., "Faulkner's *The Sound and the Fury*," *Explicator* 52.2 (1994): 104. Fant goes on to argue that Benjy also confuses Caddy's given name "Candace" with the phoneme "candles."

20. Roggenbuck's recent article is a notable exception in which he argues that "as a child Benjy demonstrates greater intellectual ability than most critics give him credit for" (581). Roggenbuck cites such scholars as Kinney and Brooks as seeing ways that Benjy does have will, but they locate that will in Benjy's unconscious—certainly they do not see

him as a conscious and skillful forger of narrative. Ultimately, even Roggenbuck modifies his claim for Benjy's intellectual ability, writing that "by 1928 [Benjy] has so withdrawn both mentally and emotionally from the world and the people around him that he no longer possesses enough emotional investment in it to attempt to interpret much of what transpires" (581).

21. William Faulkner, *As I Lay Dying* (1930), in *William Faulkner: Novels 1930–1935* (New York: Library of America, 1985), 1–178.

Visualizing *Light in August*: Text, Author, Textuality, Authority

THADIOUS M. DAVIS

The opening scenes of the animated Disney film *WALL-E* (2008) with its abandoned canyons of debris and rusty skyscrapers of molded trash reminded me not so much of some futuristic sci-fi film world, but rather ironically of William Faulkner's several descriptions of the waste left behind at abandoned lumber-clearing sites, such as that projected of Doane's Mill's future in *Light in August* (1932).[1] The description Faulkner provides there is arresting, especially in the context of the futuristic deserted landscape in 2700, resulting from the "Buy and Large" mentality touted in the film *WALL-E*, where, for instance, the humans have long ago abandoned the earth as a result of the overwhelming waste; they leave the cleanup to robots who collect and smash the piles into manageable square blocks that can be stacked high into imitations of the earth's former building model, the skyscraper. WALL-E (Waste Allocation Load Lifter Earth-Class) spends his time on the uninhabited planet clearing trash but also collecting souvenirs from the life that once existed on earth. The scenes are in monochromatic sepia color and rendered in virtual silence with a clear aim to secure focused attention on the spectacle. While the robot is charming, cute, and engaging, his surroundings and his work make the reality of overconsumption and waste a nightmarish reality.

It is that landscape of the deserted debris-filled earth that reminded me of the visual representation of environmental concerns that Faulkner writes into texts such as *Light in August* and *Go Down, Moses*. In the opening pages of the Depression-era *Light in August*, Faulkner envisions a futuristic Doane's Mill seven years after the timber has been exhausted and the mill operation has moved on to a new location: "Then some of the machinery and most of the men who ran it and existed because of and for it would be loaded onto freight cars and moved away. But some of the machinery would be left, since new pieces could always be bought on the installment plan—gaunt, staring, motionless wheels rising from mounds of brick rubble and ragged weeds with a quality profoundly astonishing, and gutted boilers lifting their rusting and unsmoking stacks with an air stubborn, baffled, and bemused upon a stumppocked scene of profound and peaceful desolation, unplowed, untilled, gutting slowly into red and choked ravines located beneath the long quiet rains of autumn and the galloping fury of vernal equinoxes."[2] Without exaggeration, I found that this cinematic description made it easy to grasp the heterotopic in Faulkner's construction of space and to configure its social geography not merely in terms of those characters with direct connections to Doane's Mill but also in relation to those for whom specific textual renderings in language place them within the linguistic order of the mill. The language describing the "scene of profound and peaceful desolation" foreshadows that representing Joe Christmas's death; "galloping fury of venal equinoxes" evokes Gail Hightower's dream; and "a quality profoundly astonishing" links to the "quiet astonishment" with which Byron Bunch imagines Lena Grove telling herself: "'My, my. Here I have come clean from Alabama, and now I am in Jefferson at last, sure enough.'"[3] From the outset, then, the visualization of Doane's Mill as a wasted environment prefigures the representation of the major characters.

1.

These initial textual references allow for a connection between seeing the environment, the landscape as denuded and ravished by the rapacious owners of the mills and lumber operations, and seeing Faulkner's human subjects, people who are also stripped bare by the processes of consumption and categories, by dehumanizing operations and social categorization that classify and contain human beings and cast out or scapegoat those who do not fit or refuse to fit into the classifications. At a glance, sight and seeing, watching and observing partly determine the place and positioning of people as refuse in *Light in August*. The waste initially represented in the text as industrial becomes human waste, not excrement, but abject human bodies themselves cast into the place of waste. This waste is embodied ultimately perhaps in the abjection of Joe Christmas, but it is also evident in all of the central figures.[4]

The easily replaceable parts of the whole mill operation and its exchangeable workers are signposts of the text's social and economic landscape as much as of the deserted Doane's Mill, the focal point of affective value in my reading. At the very outset of the narrative, Faulkner represents the procession of wagons as replaceable, one substituting for another without any disruption to the flow of Lena's movement across space and time. Joe Christmas's arrival at the planning mill in Jefferson speaks to the ever-shifting replaceable mill workers who show up or fade out, though Joe's own negated appearance—absent work clothing and lack of a lunch pail, for instance—also inserts economics into a discourse on exchangeable workers. Replaceability linked to the idea of the disposable is also embedded in Faulkner's description and concomitantly in his representation of subjectivity. Disposability, for example, is very much evident in Lucas Burch's treatment of Lena, in Hightower's treatment of his wife, in Joe's of various women in his life, but ultimately also in the location of Joe himself in the orphanage with the McEacherns, on the road, in Jefferson, in death, and in the symbolic melding with the baby Lena delivers. In terms of human ecology, the text takes on how some individuals, such as a Joe or Lena, attempt to resist, passively or actively, being used up and discarded. It takes its impetus perhaps from Gandhi's Salt March in India and its protocol of resistance, which was contemporary with Faulkner's composition. It recounts in visual terms how the seen can undermine the hidden essence or substance of human beings, and how for some that very essence is so distorted that it cannot be adequately recognized or accessed. *Light in August* takes on the difficult question of how some humans attempt to dispose of others, those othered because they are seen, perceived, and understood as inconsequential (Lena) or different (Joe).

The opening of *Light in August* combines "watching" and seeing a panorama and a person: "Sitting beside the road, watching the wagon mount the hill toward her, Lena thinks, 'I have come from Alabama: a fur piece. All the way from Alabama a-walking. A fur piece.' Thinking *although I have not been quite a month on the road I am already in Mississippi, further from home than I have ever been before. I am now further from Doane's Mill than I have been since I was twelve years old*" (3). The scene involves image, movement, a camera pan across a wide expanse of road and over the figure of the girl Lena. It also evokes imagined views of Alabama and Mississippi, a sense of seeing both states as distinct and yet contiguous and coextensive, an early indication of spatial construction figured in human geography. Lena watches the wagon mounting the hill, but she also reflects on the perspective of where she had been and what she has witnessed. At the same time, it depends upon unfolding Lena's interior. The direction of interiority here, however, functions as a road map to the movement of the external body across space and through time: "not quite a month on the road"; "in Mississippi"; "further from home"; "from Doane's Mill"; "since I was twelve years old." The emphasis is on measuring distances and time simultaneously as part of Lena's interior world and constructing her subjectivity. These are the simplest means of accessing what lies within and melding it with what lies without, with the image of Lena, a girl pregnant carrying her shoes and her bundle on the road.

The focus on distance in the external world matches the idea of distance in the internal order during Lena's four-week journey that opens the novel: "the evocation of *far* is a peaceful corridor paved with unflagging and tranquil faith and peopled with kind and nameless faces and voices" (7). While the snatches of conversations from those voices do appear in the text in italics so that they are in fact given stress and emphasized, the main point of the narrative revelations is perhaps the visualizing of the scene and Lena's movement though time-space: "backrolling now behind her a long monotonous succession of peaceful and undeviating changes from day to dark and dark to day again, through which she advanced in identical and anonymous and deliberate wagons as through a succession of creakwheeled and limpeared avatars, like something moving forever and without progress across an urn" (7). Much critical attention has been paid to the "urn" as a recurrent symbol in Faulkner's ideology, but added to that classical symbolism may also be the way landscape vistas and outdoor panoramas appeared repetitiously in early film, not necessarily slow given the technology, but undeviating and monotonous with actors moving across a still background.

To see Lena is to visualize her condition and her situation, her place and her class: "She carried a palm leaf fan and a small bundle tied neatly in a bandanna handkerchief. It contained among other things thirtyfive cents in nickels and dimes. Her shoes were but slightly worn, since in the summer neither of them wore shoes at all. When she felt the dust of the road beneath her feet she removed the shoes and carried them in her hand" (7). The description appears several times in the opening chapter, and with slight variations. For example, the second instance: "Neither of them had seen her so much as glance at them when she passed in a shapeless garment of faded blue, carrying a palm leaf fan and a small cloth bundle" (9). Or the third instance: "Beneath the faded garment of that same weathered blue her body is shapeless and immobile. The fan and the bundle lie on her lap. She wears no stockings. Her bare feet rest side by side in the shallow ditch. The pair of dusty, heavy, manlooking shoes beside them are not more inert" (11). And yet another, "She holds the shoes, the bundle, the fan awkwardly in one hand, the other free to help her down" (14); and "The woman sits back, though she still holds the fan, the bundle, the shoes" (14). And finally, "Then sitting on the top step, the fan and the bundle upon her lap, Lena tells her story again, with that patient and transparent recapitulation of a lying child, the squatting overalled men listening quietly" (25). Cumulatively, the repetitions ingrain the picture, the pictorial image with moving and manipulated parts, observable from multiple angles and against an unmoving backdrop.

Lena, projected onto a screen, is visually a displaced person, out of sync with what was to have been her place in society, and yet not fully occupying a new space. Readers come to know Lena by means of the descriptions of her being seen by strangers on the road, and in a move of reciprocity unexpected in particular kinds of portraiture, Lena's seeing provides access to all those she meets on the road. The gaze is not operating in one direction and is not bound by gender. For instance, in the representation of Lena in the opening sequence, as the wagon moves toward her, mounting the hill, Faulkner interjects a sequence of verbs related to movement and sight: "She *passed* it about a mile back down the road. . . . She *saw* it and she *saw* the two men squatting beside a barn beyond the fence. She *looked* at the wagon and the men once: a single glance allrembracing, swift, innocent and profound. She did not stop; very likely the men beyond the fence had not *seen* her even *look* at the wagon or at them. Neither did she *look* back. She went on out of sight, walking slowly, the shoes unlaced about her ankles, until she reached the top of the hill a mile beyond" (my emphasis, 7).

As a witness and an actor, Lena is both observer and participant; she provides the moviegoer perspective and the moviemaking perspective, this latter not to be missed. Both she and Joe Christmas will find themselves situated at the crossroads of being and doing, of watching and being watched, of making and being made by the processes of sight. The visual link to Joe Christmas is not so much in appearance—after all they contrast in gender and age, clothing and condition—but rather the link is in their seeing and being seen, in their visible stance on the road, in their appearance as a moving transition within a place and time. Joe even recognizes the price of being seen: "That is why I am different from the others: because he [Doc Hines] is watching me all the time" (138). Yet, the reality is that Joe becomes a watcher, the inescapable positionality of all inhabiting this text.

Lena and Joe are obviously not the only participants in these aspects of visuality. Importantly, too, without literally being on the road, Gail Hightower, who only imagines the road and the charges into battle, completes the triad regarding the moving picture aspect, the tropes of seeing and being seen: "From his study window, he can see the street. It is not far away, since the lawn is not deep. It is a small lawn, containing a half dozen lowgrowing maples. The house, the brown, unpainted and unobtrusive bungalow is small too and by bushing crepe myrtle and syringa and althea almost hidden save for the gap through which from his study window he watches the street" (57). The opening of chapter 3, introducing Hightower, repeats "seeing" and "watching" as the operative activities, and it incorporates the street, though unlike Joe or Lena, Hightower is removed from its expanse even within the small town.

One significant object within Hightower's line of vision is the sign, "which he calls his monument," though for the reader it may be read as a

tombstone. The sign is visible from the street while Hightower only sees
the back of it, but since he fashioned it himself, he knows what is written
there:

> Hence the sign, carpentered neatly by himself and by himself lettered, with
> bits of broken glass contrived cunningly into the paint, so that at night, when
> the corner street lamps shone upon it, the letters glittered with an effect as of
> Christmas:
>
>
>
> REV. GAIL HIGHTOWER, D.D.
>
> Art Lessons
>
> Handpainted Xmas & Anniversary Card
>
> Photographs Developed (58)
>
>

The sign signifies the making of visual art, referencing images, painting, and photography; it signs the artist/author as one and the same. In
emphasizing the production of the visual within the spatial purview of
an individual who is engaged in the process of seeing and watching, the
sign becomes necessarily a reflection of the making visible various kinds
of effects, "as of Christmas" in Faulkner's narrative rendering. The reference to "Christmas" in the context of photography ("Photographs Developed") anticipates the moment when Faulkner describes a naked Joe
Christmas standing next to the road: "He watched his body, grow white
out of the darkness like a Kodak print emerging from the liquid" (108).
Emerging as well in this photographic reference is an imbricated allusion
to birth, to the body becoming material.

Visualizing *Light in August* leads to reading its concern with ways of
seeing, with what I call an epistemology of the visual and perspectives
on visuality—its use, abuse, and potential for personal transformation
or societal reformation of the eye, the visual apparatus, which may be a
nod to Dos Passos whose optical USA Trilogy, including *The Big Money*,
appeared while Faulkner was writing *Light in August*. Included in the
potential is the "I," the person, the subject, the personal. The epistemology of the visual can become a way of reading in Byron Bunch's avoidance of translating the seen into the felt, of reconciling his knowing by
sight with the range of feeling, an affective range blocked in his conduct
or meticulous, rote doing. Or an epistemology of the visual might be put
to use reading Lena's seeing but not admitting the strategies of sight she
deploys and how these enable her, define her wit and ability to negotiate
the perils of a lone pregnant woman on the road. Or a way of thinking about how Joe Christmas suffered damage that was a consequence
of overreliance on the visual as a determinant of character and place
marker of identity. Or, an access route to reading Gail Hightower as an
overdetermined candidate for a place in Walker Percy's *Moviegoer* and

as undeniably kin to *Star Wars* fanatics, or simply someone who watches one film way too many times. However, *Light in August* is not a text emphasizing the primacy of the visual or the superiority of sight as an arbiter of social justice or communal morality. Faulkner writes in *Light in August*, for instance, "watching . . . the eye loses it as sight and sense drowsily merge and bend" (8). In effect, in this text Faulkner challenges ways of interpreting people, places, and events based on sight, yet he uses the protocols of the moving picture to magnify and intensify the effects of specularity and the possibilities it produces in print art and in literary art.

In writing Doane's Mill into existence, for example, Faulkner insists upon our seeing it as small (five families) and as insignificant: "There was a track and a station, and once a day a mixed train fled shrieking through it. The train could be stopped with a red flag, but by ordinary it appeared out of the devastated hills with apparitionlike suddenness and wailing like a banshee, athwart and past that little less-than-village like a forgotten bead from a broken string" (5). The imagery demands figuration not as a still painting but as a moving picture. Movement characterizes the way of looking and seeing and envisioning the not-quite village of Doane's Mill. The fast-moving train contrasts with the slow-moving wagon, transportation vehicles signifying the simultaneity of the present/future and the present/past, and in a calculated analogy, Faulkner uses a similar bead image in making the wagon visible:

> After a while she began to hear the wagon. . . . Then it came into sight, mounting the hill. The sharp and brittle crack and clatter of its weathered and ungreased wood and metal is low and terrific: a series of dry sluggish reports carrying for a half mile across the hot still pinewiney silence of the August afternoon. Though the mules plod in a steady and unflagging hypnosis, *the vehicle does not seem to progress. It seems to hang suspended in the middle distance forever and forever, so infinitesimal is its progress, like a shabby bead upon the mild red string of road. So much so is this that in the watching of it the eye loses it as sight and sense drowsily merge and blend, like the road itself, with all the peaceful and monotonous changes between darkness and day, like already measured thread being rewound onto a spool.* So that at last, as though out of some trivial and unimportant region beyond even distance, the sound of it seems to come slow and terrific and without meaning, as though it were a ghost traveling a half mile ahead of its own shape. 'That far within my hearing before my seeing,' Lena thinks. (8, my emphasis)

In the epistemology of the visual, the bead in this instance is "shabby" and on a "mild red string of road," whereas previously Doane's Mill sat "like a forgotten bead on a broken string." In both instances, the image is designed for seeing, although also with a surrounding context of hearing. (The train roaring "like a banshee," and the wagon's "crack and clatter" heard as "sluggish reports carrying for a half mile.") The primacy, nevertheless, is given to sight, for its configuration of narrative action that moves forward in time but with a progression either in its rapid repetition or its steady slowness evokes a grounded timelessness unfolding in the very character of Lena Grove who, for all the stated smallness and hence insignificance of Doane's Mill, emerges as a very large presence in the text. Sound also is reduced to sight as "a ghost traveling a half mile ahead of its own shape." This image of the ghost suggests, of course, Joe Christmas, who is described "like a phantom, a spirit, strayed out of its own world, and lost." The ghost image, in its dual transparency and opacity, begs to be imagined visually and takes its shape from the mental imaginary of the reader-viewer. Here the perspective on visuality may as well be a nod toward the visualization associated with the new field of film animation, and the slow process of hand drawing the images to create the motion that on the flat drawing plane or table carries only the slightest sense of motion. Textuality in this case takes in a wider range, so that not merely the literary productions of the past or of the contemporary moment make their marks as presence within *Light in August*, but also modern cinematic productions from Hollywood, which Faulkner actively and optimistically pursued during this period.

2.

In the 1930s the animated Mickey Mouse films, much like *WALL-E* today, took on the world in disguised terms. With the emphasis on visualizing the mouse or the robot WALL-E, the viewer watches and learns from the seen with little attention to talk and sound. With its title a parody of *Steamboat Bill Jr.*, a Buster Keaton film, *Steamboat Willie* was released in November 1928, the third of the Mickey Mouse cartoons, following *Plane Crazy* (August 1928) and *The Gallopin' Gaucho* (August 1928), all forerunners of a long list of new Mickey Mouse animated films to appear throughout the 1930s.[5]

The formal properties of producing animation attracted Faulkner, who absorbed all new techniques for experimenting with the construction of a prose fiction text. (Recall, for example, his several references to the "carpentry" of writing or building the novel.) Faulkner's familiarity with Mickey Mouse is evident from several of his letters written during the composition and publication of *Light in August*. He wrote to Ben Wasson in September of 1932 while reading the galleys for *Light in*

August: "About Light in August, Marx asked me about it before I left. I told him I didn't think they could use it. It would make a good Mickey Mouse picture, though Popeye is the part for Mickey Mouse. The frog could play Clarence Snopes. I hope to hell Paramount does take Sanctuary."[6] Although Paramount Pictures did in fact buy *Sanctuary* and made the film *The Story of Temple Drake* (released 12 May 12 1933), it did not option *Light in August*. The point that Faulkner makes in this casual reference to Mickey Mouse may speak directly to the outsized visibility, big screen–ready characters in his novel as much as to the textual possibilities such as Disney's adoption of familiar texts, film or print, for Mickey's film. At the same time, it also points to Faulkner's familiarity with the animated films. Sam Marx of Metro-Goldwyn-Mayer had sought Faulkner out to write in Hollywood, which was an industry relatively unaffected by the Depression. Although clearly ironic, his rationale for thinking that MGM could not use *Light in August* may also have to do with the pornographic nature of much of the sex scenes: not romance, but raw sex as in Joe's rape of Joanna Burden, his games of sexual intercourse with her, his masturbating while standing outside in his underwear, and so on.

Faulkner's use of Mickey Mouse in seriousness or in jest occurred several times in his references to arriving to work for Marx in May of 1932. Faulkner announced that he had "some bright ideas for Mickey Mouse cartoons. Failing to get the joke Marx explained to him matter-of-factly that the great mouse worked for Walt Disney, not MGM."[7] Faulkner's awareness of the Mickey Mouse films, as well as their popularity, underscores his attention to popular culture outside of printed materials or ephemera. However, both cartoons and films constituted cultural production for him in the 1930s.

Before starting to type *Light in August* to send to Ben Wasson, Faulkner had the movies on his mind as a way of making $500 to $750 a week, the sum that he mentioned while in NYC in 1931: "I cant send you Light in August because none of it is typed yet. I had not intended typing at all until I finished it. It is going too well to break the thread and cast back, unless absolutely necessary. But I may strike a stale spell. Then I will type some. I will be better off here until this novel is finished. Maybe then I can try the movies later on."[8] Faulkner typed the manuscript of *Light in August* during a concentrated period during which he also entertained thoughts of Hollywood and the movies. His handwritten copy was in good shape, and several observers have noticed that unlike *The Sound and the Fury* or *Sanctuary*, *Light in August* seemingly was not written in great haste or with a great rush of creative energy. As Hugh Ruppersburg posits, "Perhaps because of his confidence as a writer, his increased emphasis on narrative, Faulkner felt little need to inflate *Light in August* with gratuitous literary and mythological allusions (as he had done in his earliest work)."[9] Indeed, the long novel bears the marks of deliberation and control. The multiple plot lines, multiple central figures, multiple locations and time periods, all suggest a careful balancing of a great many details in the process of writing. The observable, clinical psychological descriptions of Joe Christmas and Gail Hightower, and lesser characters such as Percy Grimm or the furniture maker who make their way into central positions toward the end of the narrative, all suggest the care with which Faulkner unfolded his plot and characters.

Juxtaposed to Faulkner's lighthearted linking of *Light in August* and Mickey Mouse is his own estimation of his seventh novel. In a letter to Ben Wasson about both his contract with MGM and the sale of "Turn About" to Howard Hawks, Faulkner comments: "I have just finished reading the galley of LIGHT IN AUGUST. I don't see anything wrong with it. I want it to stand as it is. This one is a novel: not an anecdote; that's why it seems topheavy, perhaps."[10] In several references to *Light in August*, Faulkner situates it as an important novel. The weight that he gives to it comes after his experiments in style in *The Sound and the Fury* and *As I Lay Dying*. By 1932 he seems to link both of these novels to anecdotal writing or writing based on a single anecdote rather than to what he distinguishes as a novel. Although much of Faulkner's attention was on the writing and the publication of his short story collection *These Thirteen* during the period when he was writing *Light in August*, the novel differs from the stories and the novels preceding it in length, intricacy, and detail.

Considered one of the "major" Faulkner novels, *Light in August* receives its share of critical attention routinely given to Faulkner's amazingly creative period between 1929 and 1936.[11] While all of the novels produced along with short stories during this period bear the marks of Faulkner's vision, *Light in August* suggests a melding of many of the previous concerns and a foreshadowing of future concerns. Faulkner considered this novel to be a major book, a big book, one the author wrote with authority. This point of the author as authority is evident not just in his deft and certain handling of complex psychologies and pathologies, but also in the authorial insistence that the text of *Light in August* not be changed. He wrote, for example, to Wasson: "I have not finished the typing yet. That's why you have not heard from me. I am still making changes, and for that reason I do not send you what I have typed. I see that I shall not know until I have typed it all, whether what I have done already will stands as it is. I should finish it in about two weeks more. I will not want to take less than $5000.00 for it, and not a word to be changed. This may sound not only hard, but a little swell-headed. But I

can get along somehow if it is not serialized. But I will take five thousand
and no editing."[12] In a second letter, Faulkner reiterates the terms for
Light in August: "The manuscript goes to you today by express. If you
can get $5000.00 with no changes, take it. If not, and the movie offer is
still open, that should tide me along. If you cant get $5000.00, I reckon
I'll just turn it over to Hal [Harrison Smith]. . . . I hope you will like it.
I believe it will stand up."[13] Two points stand out in these letters: first,
Faulkner's sense of the value of *Light in August*, its artistic achievement
that "will stand up" and thus his insistence on "no changes"; and second,
his estimation of the monetary value of the novel, $5000.00 reiterated
without deviation.

In his two-pronged commentary on *Light in August* while it was in
negotiation and production, Faulkner is not tentative. There is no acqui-
escing to money as a driving force, though he clearly is thinking about
money and managing his finances and his placement of his products commercially. There is instead a repeated insistence on leaving the text as
is: "no changes," "no editing." While this aspect of Faulkner, the author,
does exist early on (and here we are only looking at his initial career of
at best six years in length), with the publishing of *Light in August* he
voices his authority over the text in very strong and assertive terms. He
sees himself as the engine in charge. His invitation to the Conference of
Southern Writers, 23–24 October 1931, in Charlottesville, Virginia, may
have played a part in his confidence as a major writer linked to the most
prestigious authors in the South and at the university founded by Thomas
Jefferson. His self-assertiveness gave him control over his production at
this juncture; he himself noted, just after the conference, that he was
now "famous."

The invitation to and participation in the Conference of Southern
Writers should not be underestimated in terms of situating Faulkner in
a position of authority over his work. On the recommendation of Ellen
Glasgow, James Southall Wilson, a professor at the University of Virginia, organized the conference and invited Faulkner to attend along
with both luminaries and rising stars: James Branch Cabell, Paul Green,
Stark Young, Thomas Wolfe, Donald Davidson, Allen Tate, Sherwood
Anderson, and Ellen Glasgow.[14] Faulkner's invitation gave him greater
visibility among his fellow Southern writers and placed him in the higher
pantheon of major Southern writers. The visibility and the sense of place
among the famous Southern writers may have contributed to his emphasis on *Light in August* as a *novel*, not an "anecdote." This newly found
sense of his importance as a Southern writer translated into his sense of
Light in August as an important novel, and that estimation was further
compounded by the success of *Sanctuary*, which was optioned for the

movies. The sensational South of *Sanctuary* and Faulkner's anecdote regarding its genesis give way to a more multilayered, complex, and mobile South—mobile in terms of affect, emotions, and feeling, as well as of the material body in *Light in August*. Both kinds of mobility, emotional and material, translate well in fiction and in film.

3.

With this understanding of Faulkner's authority over *Light in August*, I situate this text as a self-consciously global, aesthetic work drawing not simply upon the ideas of the visual experimentation from animation as I have suggested, but also drawing from a diverse world of the historical present that was increasingly presented in images in the news media. Most often we read *Light in August* in black and white against the background of the racially segregated world of the American South and Oxford, Mississippi, in particular the Nelse Patton case of a brutal murder and horrific lynching that occurred during Faulkner's youth. If we visualize the text as cinematic and not merely in black and white but "colorized" with shades and tints added in for high definition, we may return the text to more of the situational complexity and heightened "mystery" that *Light in August* most likely would have produced among readers in 1932. Beginning with the catastrophic Stock Market Crash in 1929 and continuing through the Great Depression, the twentieth-century U.S. experienced dramatic changes in its ideology and its actual landscape. The economic devolution would have registered with Faulkner because of the economic vulnerability of Mississippi in relation to the rest of the nation and the larger world, particularly given its continuing dependency on international markets for cotton crops. There is such an evident effort on Faulkner's part to make *Light in August* problematical in regard to past and present, unresolvable and unresolved in connection with the future, and to undergird its narrative with traces of the "big" issues emerging in the 1930s cultural moment, including deprivation, fanaticism, domination, and uprootedness. Calling attention to this aspect of Faulkner's text shows that an artist like Faulkner who consciously, though not always admittedly, kept abreast of the larger world along side the rural South around him would not in 1931–1932 be stuck back within the aesthetic paradigms or dominant thematics of the post–World War I era.

One way of concretizing this way of seeing Faulkner's *Light in August* is to deploy Roland Barthes's concept of the "agent of blindness." Barthes suggested that a travel guide is "an agent of blindness" because it directs the traveler to look only at a narrow range of landscape features, and as a result it creates an illusion of cultural continuity and stability.[15] Just as Barthes calls attention to the illusory aspect inherent in the work of limiting what is seen, so too may we perform ritualized blinding in overemphasizing and reading *Light in August* in terms surrounding Joe Christmas's material body. In so doing we narrow our field of vision and deny the text an expansiveness and a changing system of valuation. Reading strategies for this text have often functioned much like the travel guides in focusing attention on some aspects of the text to the exclusion of others. Think for a moment of *Light in August* and its prophetic rendering of Doane's Mill as a prediction of what 1936 or 1938 might look like as the nation sank deeper into economic depression and rallied in programs of public works. Think of how the Tennessee Valley Authority, for instance, reshaped parts of Virginia, North Carolina, Georgia, Tennessee, Alabama, and Mississippi by not only enabling soil conservation, flood control, and reforestation, but also bringing electricity and new futures to rural people living in isolated communities. In "The New Deal Return to the Land," Phoebe Cutler observes the extent to which during "a brief time—1933–1942—government merged with artist, craftsman, and conservationist in common purpose and vision": "From this conflation of disparate elements materialized many objects and places of enduring value and appeal. The parks, towers, walls, gardens, lakes, walks, and woods of the Depression are the artifacts of hard times."[16]

All of the undertakings under Roosevelt were intended to revitalize the nation's resources and core infrastructures through renewal and development. Part of the development was the removal and dislocation of hardscrabble farmers from eight hundred square miles of the southern Appalachian Mountains for the making of the Great Smoky Mountain National Park. Here we may also think about "eminent domain" and its effects and consequences for individuals and states. Faulkner certainly railed against Roosevelt and the concept of eminent domain, especially in *Go Down, Moses*. To accomplish the work of revitalization, the administration to its credit, however, did not overlook the place of art and artists. Landscape architecture, for example, emerged as a profession for those who designed "outdoor spaces for human use and enjoyment" and who arranged both the grounds themselves and the objects upon them. Like landscape architects, the practitioners combining beauty and utility in a new type of art became indispensable to reshaping, revitalizing, and domesticating the land, so too writers were central to the social well being of the people inhabiting that landscape. The domestication of the American landscape is similar to the integration of the writing profession by similar processes of creating new institutional spaces and "public works" that were also intellectual activities. Combined, these socially engineered spaces created a new public sphere concerned with social and economic well being. During this period, according to Cutler, "the *purpose* of place" was romanticized rather than *place* itself: "A cohesive, integrated society was sought, in which land patterns could promote a wholesome combination of work, play, and education. In the 1930s, Americans still viewed the landscape, along with church and family, as a force in character formation," so that "the chain of events triggered by Depression-era public works . . . shaped the nation's topography," and our thinking about the intersections of human ecology, social geography, and landscape.[17]

The more familiar projects of the Works Progress Administration were obviously public works that changed the look of the United States by transforming visually the nation's topography and modernizing the lives of the citizenry. In Faulkner's fiction written in the 1930s and 1940s, there is a noticeable concern with visualizing the landscape that his characters inhabit. In *Light in August*, in particular, there is representation of the devastated land left by "progress," mechanization, and commercialization, all of which connect to visualizing human devastation.

There are several other relationships between current world events and Faulkner's *Light in August* that seem pertinent to the concept of visuality here. Foremost is the rise of Hitler and the Nazi Party. In statements well after the publication of *Light in August*, Faulkner insisted that when he created Percy Grimm in 1931 he was unaware of Hitler: "I didn't realize until after Hitler got into the newspapers that I had created a Nazi before he did."[18] Nonetheless, with the increased worldwide tensions around differences of race and religion, attention to whiteness as a superior race (following the reduction of the "races" of Europe to one), Faulkner's Percy Grimm follows the line of both the Nazi Party and its martial component and the eugenics advocates and white supremacists whose rise through the 1920s reached an alarming height in the 1930s.[19]

At odds with the scientific efforts to reduce people of color to subservient and negated positions were both the transformative emergence of Gandhi and the power of civil disobedience. With the March 1930 Salt March in India, Gandhi challenged the British monopoly of salt and with it control over the people. In a two hundred mile protest march to the sea, Gandhi not only disobeyed a ban on non-British making of salt, but developed a mode of overcoming an oppressive power. Gandhi's method of civil disobedience as resistance to oppression became known. Resisting a superior social power and winning against the prevailing social structure seemed almost miraculous and quite unimaginable. Both Lena Grove and Joe Christmas resist, with varying failure and success, the tenacious hold of the powerful hegemonic social structures and conventions. In a sense we can visualize them in motion as characters who are consciously disobedient, active practitioners of civil disobedience without a larger social cohort or objective. Faulkner represents the personal aspect of their civil resistance by means of their conduct and behavior.

Joe's personality, however, recalls another aspect of popular 1930s filmmaking that seems related to Faulkner's vision of character in *Light in August*. In addition to the advent of Mickey Mouse and animated films already discussed, Faulkner was aware during his stint in Hollywood of the success of a specific genre of films known today as horror films. *Frankenstein, Dr. Jekyll and Mr. Hyde*, and *Dracula*, all of which won academy awards for actors in roles showcasing divided selves, allowed film audiences to see the transformations of the psyche within the physical body on screen. Boris Karloff in *Frankenstein*, Frederick March in *Dr. Jekyll and Mr. Hyde*, and Bela Lugosi in *Dracula* all engage the new psychological theories in the "temple of the imagination"—the movie theater. The attention to the psychological dimension of character, particularly the division of self into parts such as the observer and the observed, is a hallmark of Faulkner's characters in *Light in August*. Faulkner produced the text during a period in which he was star struck, consciously courted the movie industry, and happily planned to write a script for Tallulah Bankhead and earn $10,000 doing so.

One of the more significant contemporary visualizations of the concepts of race, ethics, and difference that are at the center of *Light in August* occurred with the arrest in March of 1931 of nine African American boys on charges of rape in Alabama. The Scottsboro Boys, as they became known, were riding the Southern Railroad from Chattanooga to Memphis when they were arrested for allegedly raping two white girls who were also riding the rails in the Depression. The worlds of impoverished black and white people riding the rails collided in the strictly segregated South and within the social mores of Alabama. The rape charges were added after the initial arrests and appeared to stem from the hegemonic view of black sexuality and criminality. The subsequent recanting of the testimony by one of the girls did not halt the trials, which emphasized the continuing racial clash of blacks and whites and the ever-present danger black males faced in the South. The Scottsboro trials with convictions, appeals, overturns, retrials, and so on lasted from 1932 to 1938 and reached the United States Supreme Court as well as news outlets and political activists across the nation.

What is seen in the representation of Joe Christmas, unlike in the case of the Scottsboro boys, is his "guilt." He does kill Joanna Burden, and he repeatedly had sexual intercourse with her. Consensual sex between a black man and a white woman, according to the code of the segregated South, was an impossibility; it did not and could not exist. Importantly, Scottsboro functioned as a rallying point for activists in the 1930s and achieved notoriety as a "watched" spectacle of the injustice of the South and as a panorama of the victimization of blacks in the South. The public show that Scottsboro became is evoked in the final authorial narrative following Joe's death: "He just lay there, with his eyes open and empty of everything save consciousness, and with something, a shadow, about his mouth. For a long moment, he looked up at them with peaceful and unfathomable and unbearable eyes. Then his face, body, all, seemed to collapse, to fall in upon itself . . . then he seemed to rise roaring into their memories forever and ever. . . . It will be there, musing, quiet, steadfast, not fading and not particularly threatful, but of itself alone serene, of itself alone triumphant" (*Light in August*, 465).

Faulkner positions the impact of this death on the community as a watched and observable spectacle. All along his path in life Joe is both spectacle and specular; he is the watched, and he knows that seeing eyes are always upon him so that he performs for his audience, even unwittingly. He may desire to escape the gaze that challenges his actions and his being, but he succumbs at every juncture to a complicity with the specular controlling, or desiring to control his life. As an adult, he dresses for the visual play of his situation; he plays to being seen. In his role as the silent stranger, outfitted in black and white, he is ready for his screen appearance. Not coincidently, in *WALL-E*, the little robot entertains himself by projecting an old black-and-white film saved from the junk of an abandoned civilization, and in the process of repeatedly screening a romance, he relieves his loneliness and isolation in an abject world from which humans have defected. In *Light in August*, that screen, projected outward and Joe's movement across it, is intricately connected to screen memories. Joe's hidden and concealed memories relate to Freud's theories and reveal a more complicated psychological ground than I have indicated thus far.

4.

Faulkner's representations of Joe Christmas, Gail Hightower, Joanna Burden, and Lena Grove all depend on screening and screen memories. "Screen Memory" is Freud's term for the early childhood memories that while seemingly ordinary are vividly remembered. This discrepancy between the event and the memory exists because "the relevant screen may perhaps have been incompletely retained in memory, and that may be why it seems so unenlightening."[20] Freud maintains that "screen memories will . . . be formed from residues of memories relation to later life" and "owe their importance to a connection with experiences in early youth which have remained suppressed." According to Freud in "Screen Memories,": "it may indeed be questioned whether we have any memories at all from our childhood: memories relating to our childhood may be all that we possess. Our childhood memories show us our earliest years not as they were but as they appeared at later periods when these (early) memories were (again) aroused. In these later periods of arousal, the childhood memories did not, as people are accustomed to say, emerge; they were formed at that time. And a number of motives, with no concern for historical accuracy, had a part in forming them, as well as in the selection of the memories themselves."

The explanation is that the forgotten though emotionally important experience has been repressed. What has been forgotten contains the material that made the experience significant. By condensing and displacing the experience, the screen memory becomes the conscious memory created out of the repressed experience. The highly unresolved experience is not what is remembered, but instead some other psychical element that has close association with the charged, objectionable experience. The conflict produced by the original experience is responded to by a displacement of its psychological meanings onto an indifferent image or memory. While Faulkner represents Joe's childhood more expansively and specifically in terms of memory and screens, he also renders the unresolved screened elements in the psychic lives of the other main subjects. In Freud's speculations, the ideas of screening and screen memory develop into much more complicated psychological ground in his later work.[21]

Screening of the self can occur behind other bodies, solid objects, or ideologies. While the verb "to screen" means to conceal, protect, or shelter from something dangerous or unpleasant, it also carries the connotation of both presence and absence. "Screen" as absence and presence may be read in relation to the twoness of a black body in the systems of slavery and Jim Crow. The "peculiar institution" and its aftermath in segregation constituted black bodies as both visible and complete within what could be seen or viewed. That constitution denoted presence and visible property, transparently legible. However, when the unseen (that which is screened from view) is taken into account, then the absence may be read as a space in which a twinned existence resides; this existence is ever shape-shifting and necessarily invisible under the definitions of black bodies as object and property. It may follow, then, that in the arena of will so prominently constitutive of the master-slave relationship, what may seem invisible may not be nonexistent. Instead, it may also obtain as a space of absent presence in the narrative, as a screen to hide in plain sight the extent of desire to be constituted differently in body and to deflect attention away from the embodied anger at both law and government for their failure to protect and emancipate entrapped individuals.

But what of Joanna Burden and the visual image of her as a twin to Joe, or a psychological double? There is another aspect of "screening" that emerges out of a different system of practices and beliefs. It is the residue of a legal notion of the coverture of married women and their location in a legal space not dissimilar to that of children and slaves. The remnants of legal coverture functioned well into the twentieth century as social residue of the past. On the more transparent level regarding the screening of Lena under coverture, the idea is straightforward. Were she to marry, she would be subsumed into the identity of her husband. However, less apparent is an application of coverture to Joe. He is depicted in a taunt and curiously queered relation to the man-hard Joanna. His fear may not simply be read as being forced to bend to the will of a religious fanaticism, which of course echoes that of Doc Hines, but it can be interpreted as a fear of being subsumed into the masculinized Joanna's desires for him. His own complex desires would become feminized under her identity. Joe's identity is race-based, but it also carries with it a residue of coverture and with it screening as in the hiding of oneself and the loss of integrity of self.

According to Patricia Williams, "At the root of integrity is an Aristotelian notion of being oneself. Much like our understanding of an integer in math, it conveys a sense of being undivided, not split into fractious parts. To have integrity is to be whole."[22] The issue of wholeness is operating within *Light in August* in conjunction with visibility. In the realm of law, Williams reminds us of the complexity of integrity: "law also serves to protect certain regions of truth from public scrutiny, as when the knowledge is too private, too personal, too close to the heart; or when the extraction of information would require undue state of violence."[23] She concludes, "All such rules are designed to make sure that citizens can remain 'true' to themselves—or whole within themselves—particularly against the power of the state. Having such protection ensures that the government cannot 'dismember' you or your family or designated surrogates, literally or figuratively, an interest that outweighs even the pursuit of certain justice interests. It is, after all, a primal challenge to the notion of liberty: the tension between the security of the citizenry as a collective body and the security (or integrity) of the individual citizen's body."[24]

The sense of being undivided and the ability to have bodily integrity protected by law are precisely what could not and did not happen to either Joe Christmas or Lena Grove in Faulkner's text. Given the divisive nature of property itself, as moveables and as real estate, Faulkner fathoms the categories of black and woman as both individual and collective, but only one, if disassociated from the other, can demand legal protection. Patricia Williams remembers pretending that she and her sister were twins: "I was fascinated by the ease with which I believed twins could trade places. I thought of them as being a single person, I suppose. Two whole halves and thus able to be in two places at the same time. One twin could witness an event, clandestinely yet openly, while people thought it was the other to whom they were speaking. To me it seemed as though the real you could huddle up and hide while someone else took over. It was simultaneously a rest from oneself, an excuse for oneself, an eavesdropping on oneself."[25] Her recollection suggests a related aspect of Faulkner's narrative and his "authority" over the text.

Although Faulkner can project a distinct and individual subjectivity for Joe, he cannot disengage Joe's body from the classes defining it, leaving it vulnerable and exposed. Yet, if Faulkner is placed not within his character Joe, but outside, alongside, but joined to him in a process of twinning, then the separate entities have more power, more force, and ultimately more control not only over one body, but two, and authority over the text as well. As Williams put it, this twinning is a process by which the single person is at once multiple, and to reiterate her explanation: "Two who halves and thus able to be in two places at the same time. *One twin could witness an event, clandestinely yet openly, while people thought it was the other to whom they were speaking.* To me it seemed as thought *the real you could huddle up and hide while someone else took over. It was simultaneously a rest from oneself, an excuse for oneself, an eavesdropping on oneself*" (my emphasis).

Because screen denotes both presence and absence both in the Freudian sense and in the material sense, it leads me back to my focus on Lena. While Joe's constitution denotes presence, visible property, transparently legible, his screen Lena (not Joanna as twin) resides in shape shifting definition, self-definition. Perhaps what makes it possible for Lena to move on, to resist the forces that would contain, shape, and determine her fate, is that as she is represented there are no childhood memories. Think back to the opening segment of the text and its representation of her life. The erasure (or the unseen) in her past ultimately is not a failing or a negative to be overcome but rather a positive escape from the oppressive nature of memory and the ways in which Freud suggests we make memories, especially the screen memories that are so much a part of the personality development of Joe Christmas. Lena can escape memory, perhaps also because of the more obvious very bovinelike traits of stubborn determination in the face of and against the odds that Faulkner inserts into his narrative of her movement over roads and through spaces that otherwise should provoke more than a sense of being on the road, her "My, my, A body does get around." We see her "getting around," and as a result getting through and beyond the social circumstances that should break and recalibrate her quality of life by confining her movement and confirming her social position. But Lena escapes the overdetermination of memory because she is future directed in her vision and present oriented in her reflection. Think of her asking even as she delivers her child without having caught Lucas Burch: "'Is he [Hightower] enough of a minister to still marry folks?'" Lena escapes Doane's Mill, and the negatively envisioned future projected for the town, by going out the window. Although she does not have to squeeze her very pregnant body through that space, she does so as a matter of fact. Here I would suggest that the window frames a past that is not a memory of childhood influencing the present moment, but the spatial separation between being contained and being free. The window frames a view, a way of seeing, that allows access both into and out of; moreover, the window reasserts the specular quality, the viewing that goes on necessarily and by design as the text is constructed. That window, like an open viewer box, makes the watching, the seeing, and the viewing of Lena within set boundaries that force undivided attention to her and in particular to her pregnant body. It functions like a frame in a movie picture and institutes the visualization for screening a landscape and people.

With the very specific and peculiarly opaque window in a reading of visuality, I end by conflating screen memories and screen projectors—psychological and cinematic—both conjoined in visualizing *Light in August*, both envisioning Faulkner's future. With *Light in August*, Faulkner constructed not only a visual challenge to rigid social conventions, but also an experimental preface to the scenic eruptions of *Absalom, Absalom!* across space-time and to the projected images of Hollywood screen writing for moving pictures.

NOTES

1. *WALL-E*, directed by Andre Stanton (Walt Disney Pictures, 27 June 2008), computer animation, 98 minutes.

2. William Faulkner, *Light in August* (1932; New York: Vintage International, 1990) 4–5.

3. Ibid, 101.

4. See Eric Gary Anderson, "Environed Blood: Ecology and Violence in *The Sound and the Fury* and *Sanctuary*," in *Faulkner and the Ecology of the South: Faulkner and*

Yoknapatawpha, 2003, ed. Joseph R. Urgo and Ann J. Abadie (Jackson: University Press of Mississippi, 2005) 30–46. Anderson uses Gail Hightower and the phrase "his own environed blood" from *Light in August* as the key to his essay on ecology and violence in *The Sound and the Fury* and *Sanctuary*, but without linking Hightower to waste (30–32). Hightower's "environed blood" spews out in a form of abjection from his body and may thus be connected specifically to both environmental waste and the human waste it references in the text.

5. *Steamboat Willie*, directed by Walt Disney and Ub Iwerks (Walt Disney Pictures, silent: 27 July 1928, sound: 18 November 1928), animation, 7 minutes.

6. See *Selected Letters of William Faulkner*, ed. Joseph Blotner (New York: Vintage Books, 1978), 65.

7. Jay Parini, *One Matchless Time: A Life of William Faulkner* (New York: Harper Perennial, 2004), 172.

8. Letter to Ben Wasson, received 26 January 1932, *Selected Letters*, 39.

9. Hugh Ruppersburg, *Reading Faulkner's "Light in August": Glossary and Commentary* (Jackson: University Press of Mississippi, 1994), xii.

10. Selected *Letters*, 66.

11. See for instance, David Minter, ed. *Twentieth Century Interpretations of "Light in August": A Collection of Critical Essays* (Englewood Cliffs, N.J.: Prentice-Hall, 1969) and François Pitavy's *Faulkner's "Light in August"* (1970), trans. Gillian E. Cook (Bloomington: Indiana University Press, 1973).

12. *Selected Letters*, 61.

13. Ibid., 62.

14. Joseph Blotner, *Faulkner: A Biography*, 1-vol. ed. (New York: Random House, 1984), 282–83. See also Parini, 165.

15. See Roland Barthes, "The Blue Guide," in *Mythologies* (1957; New York: Hill and Wang, 1986), 74–77.

16. Phoebe Cutler, *The Public Landscape of the New Deal* (Princeton: Princeton University Press, 1986), 4.

17. Cutler, 4.

18. Letter to Malcolm Cowley, September 1945.

19. For example, F. Scott Fitzgerald's use of Lothrop Stoddard in *The Great Gatsby*, when the boorish Tom Buchannan expresses his hostility toward and concern about the rise of people of color. Stoddard's 1920 book, *The Rising Tide of Color against White World-Supremacy*, was the best known of his many books asserting that all of Western civilization would be destroyed if the white race was absorbed by the increasing numbers of people of the colored races and their revolt against colonialism, and arguing for the preservation of whites by eugenics and the unity of whites (Nordic, Alpine, and Mediterranean) through assimilation. Stoddard was concerned with all of the ways in which people of color posed threats to whites. Taking on the differences in religion and the non-Christian belief systems of people of color, he wrote of the modern-day threat of Islamic religious fanaticism in *The New World of Islam* (1921). Taking his impetus directly from Stoddard, Fitzgerald has Tom cite a fictional author named Goddard and his book *The Rise of the Color Races*. Scientific race studies from Stoddard and others such as Madison Grant, based on sight, or optical observation as hard data, fanned the supposed threat posed by people of color and their values, beliefs, and religions. Patricia McKee's chapter, "Playing White Men in *Light in August*," in her book *Producing American Races: Henry James, William Faulkner, Toni Morrison* (Durham: Duke University Press, 1999) examines the issue of race formation and scientific racism.

20. Sigmund Freud, "Screen Memories," 1899, 3:306–7, 320, 322. In *The Standard Edition of the Complete Psychological Works of Sigmund Freud*, 24 vols., trans. under the

general editorship of James Strachey, with Anna Freud (London: Hogarth Press, 1953–1974): 15:200–202.

21. Sigmund Freud uses the term "screen memory" to apply to a memory that is associatively displaced onto another. See Freud, "Introductory Lectures on Psychoanalysis," in *The Standard Edition of the Complete Psychological Works of Sigmund Freud*, 15:200–202.

22. Patricia J. Williams, *Open Houses: Of Family, Friends, Food, Piano Lessons, and the Search for a Room of My Own* (New York: Farrar, Straus and Giroux, 2004), 14.

23. Ibid., 14.

24. Ibid., 15.

25. Ibid., 11.

The Impenetrable Lightness of Being: Miscegenation Imagery and the Anxiety of Whiteness in *Go Down, Moses*

TED ATKINSON

At one point in William Faulkner's *Go Down, Moses*, Ike McCaslin engages in a lengthy and intense dialogue with his older cousin Cass Edmonds over the familial history contained in the ledgers kept by the family patriarch, Lucius Quintus Carothers McCaslin. Ike tries to justify his intention to repudiate his inheritance of the McCaslin estate on the grounds that "this land is, indubitably, of and by itself cursed." Cass responds not with words but with a simple gesture: lifting one hand in defiance of Ike's claim. The narrator goes on to explain that "as the stereopticon condenses into one instantaneous field the myriad minutia of its scope, so did that slight and rapid gesture establish in the small cramped and cluttered twilit room not only the ledgers but the whole plantation in its mazed and intricate entirety."[1] The imagery is striking for many reasons. First, it underscores the "blood guilt" thesis, as numerous scholars have noted, that shapes Faulkner's representation of the South's tragic history of racial oppression in *Go Down, Moses* and other works. Clearly, Ike is prepared to accept this thesis and to respond to its implications in a material way, while his cousin prefers a willful denial of reality. On one level, this disagreement between kinsmen represents two ways for Southerners like the McCaslin-Edmondses to respond to the legacy of the past in the present. As suggested by the atmosphere of twilight, though, these alternatives are not as starkly defined as they might initially seem, for the lines between them become increasingly obscure the more the matter is held up to scrutiny. On another level, there is a more elemental issue raised by Faulkner's imagery in depicting this impasse: the desire to shape racial strife, one of the most complicated issues in the history of the U.S. South and the nation at large, into a microcosmic and thus more manageable form. The narrator's strained attempt to compound the significance of Cass's gesture—to make it mean more than it possibly can—is indicative of this desire and of the frustration that arises from the impossibility of satisfying it. No matter what Cass intends—or what the narrator intends for him—a full and mutual understanding of the "curse" in relation to racial oppression remains elusive. Consequently, the dialogue, the flow of words, must continue.

The simile of the stereopticon, a device dubbed the "magic lantern" in the nineteenth century, is a useful starting point for tracing a motif that yields fuller understanding of how Faulkner represents race in *Go Down, Moses*—in particular, the highly charged issue of miscegenation that has concerned scholars and general readers alike since the novel's publication. A stereopticon was a projection device used for educational and recreational purposes before the dawn of motion pictures; its popularity and novelty derived from the use of dual lenses to fuse images, yielding the effect of depth perception—or viewing in stereo, as the name of the device indicates. Arguably, the optical illusion brought visual pleasure because it was able to render the vastness of the natural world in a manipulated image, lending viewers the sense of power afforded by a privileged perspective. This process is, in many respects, similar to the white gaze that Faulkner depicts in *Go Down, Moses*, most often through imagery associated with miscegenation. Employed by major characters and often framed by the narrator, this way of looking betrays a need to capture the mixed-race subject through the powers of visual perception so as to reduce the complexity of racial identity into a comprehensible essence. However, as Faulkner repeatedly demonstrates through his deft control of imagery, the white gaze, like Cass's inadequate hand gesture, invariably fails in this endeavor, resulting in a perpetual cycle of anxiety and, at times, panic for the one imposing the faulty gaze. This act of seeing without really knowing engenders a crisis in white racial consciousness that Faulkner's novel lays bare. Significantly, Faulkner's imagery also exposes how this destabilizing force is transformed into a productive one for the established social order—the state of imperiled whiteness produced by images of miscegenation becomes a means of bolstering the white power structure's imperative to preserve a status quo reliant on the conceptual and material integrity of racial difference.[2]

In recent years, some of the most compelling scholarly work on race has focused on whiteness as a racial category in America and as a trope in forms of cultural expression. Responding to a longstanding emphasis on victims of racial oppression depicted in cultural works, some scholars have called for a shift in critical attention from the oppressed to the oppressor, specifically the societal structures, assumptions, and silences that have allowed whiteness to remain woefully unexamined and thus all the more potent as an instrument of social order in American society. This line of critical inquiry is responsive to a tendency in American society and culture to assume a correlation between blackness and race, essentially exempting whiteness from racial categorization altogether.

Thus, a key aim of this approach is to expose how whiteness, like gravity, works as an intangible yet immensely powerful force—an effort not surprisingly attentive to matters of visual representation and culture. Richard Dyer asserts that in forms of cultural expression "white power secures its dominance by seeming not to be anything in particular"; however, "when whiteness qua whiteness does come into focus, it is often revealed as emptiness, absence, denial or even a kind of death." Dyer concludes that "this property of whiteness, to be everything and nothing, is the source of its representational power."[3] On these grounds, whiteness maintains its hegemony in large part through the exclusionary capability of abstraction—whiteness is the implicit assumption upon which the concept of racial difference is defined and regulated. The black/white racial binary code at the base of slavery and Jim Crow in the South is, of course, a prime example. At the heart of this model is a white obsession with *difference*—an effort to mark the Other as racial, as "colored," so as to make whiteness the "natural" condition by implication. Evidence of this obsession can be found in legal cases such as *Plessy v. Ferguson*, as well as the litany of racial categories such as "mulatto," "quadroon," and "octoroon" conceived over time to quantify allegedly "black blood" to the "precise" drop in the interest of maintaining the "purity" of whiteness.[4]

In her landmark work of literary scholarship, *Playing in the Dark: Whiteness and the Literary Imagination*, Toni Morrison builds on the foundation of theoretical treatments of whiteness by discussing its relevance to American literature. Morrison argues that for many white canonical writers—Poe, Melville, Hawthorne, Hemingway, and others—the conception of "an Africanist persona is reflexive; an extraordinary meditation on the self; a powerful exploration of the fears and desires that reside in the writerly conscious. It is an astonishing revelation of longing, of terror, of perplexity, of shame, of magnanimity."[5] Morrison analyzes representations of "black or Africanist people" juxtaposed with images of "blinding whiteness" that constitute "a meditation on the shadow that is companion to this whiteness."[6] A key consequence, Morrison concludes, is the development of racial fetishes that are "especially useful in evoking erotic fears or desires and establishing fixed and major difference where difference does not exist or is minimal." In a comment that pertains to *Go Down, Moses*, Morrison cites the fixation on blood as a case in point, calling it a "pervasive fetish" in representing encounters between whiteness and the Africanist presence.[7] Eric Sundquist rightly casts this element of Faulkner's work as a function of seeing and being: "Faulkner's novels explore the problems of race visibility—a problem centered . . . in the problem of 'blood' and physical violation."[8] More than the litany of writers that Morrison cites, Faulkner mounts an exploration into the nature of this fetish, even as his work exhibits key traits of it repeatedly. Faulkner's representation of race is more probing, I would argue, because of his willingness to go where many others fear to tread—that is, to move beyond the reductive imagery of juxtaposition into the gray areas of ambiguity that call into question the integrity of the black/white racial binary code and, as several critics have noted, expose whiteness to the light of critical scrutiny.[9] One of the most effective ways of understanding how *Go Down, Moses* works in this regard is to act in the spirit of this year's conference by mining for the returns of the text—more to the point, by closely examining Faulkner's use of imagery in depicting the complex matter of miscegenation and the chronic anxiety that it engenders in the racial category of whiteness.

In "Was," the first section of *Go Down, Moses*, Faulkner draws on comic elements in crafting an orientation to the novel's abiding concern with race and creating, in many respects, a variation on the slave narrative. Not surprisingly for Faulkner, the narrative form is unconventional, starting in the first section with a third-person narrator focusing on Ike McCaslin and then shifting in the second section to a story that Ike has heard from Cass Edmonds. In the story told by Cass, Tomey's Turl, a slave on the McCaslin estate, has escaped once again to visit his beloved Tennie, a slave on the neighboring Beauchamp estate, setting in motion an inept manhunt led by Ike's father, Theophilus (Uncle Buck) McCaslin, that fails at every initial turn to carry out its ostensible purpose (to capture the fugitive slave) as well as its symbolic one (to signify control over the individual slave body and, by extension, the whole slave population). Notwithstanding the playful tone and comic elements, the narrative of Tomey's Turl's escape resounds with broader symbolic implications that determine how it works in the context of the McCaslin-Edmonds family and as the introductory section of *Go Down, Moses*. Thadious M. Davis defines a twofold purpose for the story of the fugitive Tomey's Turl: "The interconnected narrative of memory, hearing, history, and telling functions as both an origins myth for Ike and as a familial history that introduces Tomey's Turl and his relationship to the McCaslin-Edmonds family."[10] Indeed, the story reveals this relationship to be symbiotic, dynamic, and rooted in mutual dependency. Faulkner highlights these qualities during the scene in which Buck, with the aid of a determined hound dog, momentarily corners Tomey's Turl in a cabin on the Beauchamp estate but fails to capture him. In retrospect, Buck takes full blame for letting the fugitive get away, confessing that "he had forgotten when even a child should have known: not ever to stand in front of or behind a nigger when you scare him; but always to stand to one side of him." Owing to Buck's mistake, Tomey's Turl "ran right clean over him" and then "carried him along for about ten feet . . . before he threw him away and went on" (*GDM* 18).

Faulkner's use of visual and kinetic imagery in depicting Buck's failed attempt to capture the elusive Tomey's Turl enhances the mythic components of the story as a whole, particularly how white members of the McCaslin-Edmonds clan respond to the dilemma of miscegenation. By the time he hides in the cabin, Tomey's Turl has been marked as an ambiguous and marginalized racial figure: the narrator identifies him as a slave and then Hubert Beauchamp calls him "that damn white half-McCaslin" (*GDM* 6). Later in the novel, the issue of Tomey's Turl's origin becomes even more complex when incest is added to the mix. In a shocking revelation of familial history, Ike McCaslin deduces from the commissary ledgers that his grandfather impregnated Thomasina, his daughter by a slave named Eunice, resulting in the birth of Tomey's Turl and in Thomasina's subsequent suicide. Taking these factors into account, Buck's inability to capture Tomey's Turl by, in effect, framing him in a space defined by authority and control takes on symbolic value. Confronting Tomey's Turl face-to-face imperils Buck's standing, in every sense of the word, leaving him mockingly carried away and then dropped by his slave—an image that upends the paternalistic model by underscoring the master's dependency on the slave in the socioeconomic order of the time. In mythic terms, the scene explains the origin of the McCaslin-Edmonds compulsion to apprehend—indeed, to comprehend—their mixed-race kin, as well as the consequent identity crises that they suffer from trying to do so. The anxiety attending this compulsion finds symbolic representation in the strategy that Buck fails to heed: standing to the side of Tomey's Turl rather than facing him directly or standing behind him.

Adding insult to injury, Buck finds himself coerced into an engagement to Sophonsiba (Sibbey) Beauchamp after unknowingly climbing into bed with her in the dark—a result of Hubert Beauchamp's apparent scheming to unite his family with the McCaslins. Consequently, Buck's twin brother, Amodeus (Uncle Buddy) McCaslin, must come to the rescue. Buddy, under the watchful eye of young Cass Edmonds, challenges Hubert to a game of cards to settle the outstanding disputes: the presumed engagement of Buck to Sophonsiba and the ownership of Tomey's Turl and Tennie. As Davis observes, *Go Down, Moses* "deploys games . . . as constructions both of chance and of strategy that represent the arbitrariness and the boundedness of forms of identity and of economic and social interaction as these forms intersect with the regularity, protection, and compensation of law."[11] In this instance, Faulkner's game of chance casts marriage and slavery in the antebellum

upper class as matters of economic negotiation—prerogatives of patri-
archs who transform human beings and relations into commodities.
Tellingly, at the moment before Hubert decides to pass, rather than to
call Buddy's hand, he asks with symbolic implications, "Who dealt these
cards, Amodeus?" The narrator interjects that "he [Hubert] didn't wait
to be answered. He reached out and tilted the lamp-shade, the light
moving up Tomey's Turl's arms that were supposed to be black but were
not quite white, up his Sunday shirt that was supposed to be white but
wasn't quite either, that he put on every time he ran away just as Uncle
Buck put on the necktie each time he went to bring him back, and on to
his face; and Mr Hubert sat there, holding the lamp-shade and looking
at Tomey's Turl" (*GDM* 28). The mode of visual representation in this
passage mimics the function of the stereopticon, with the gaze applied
by Hubert Beauchamp intended to reduce everything in its scope to
an image that can yield proof of verifiable racial identity from a privileged perspective. Nevertheless, the uncertainty exposed by the light—
more precisely, by the lightness of Tomey's Turl's skin—undermines the
intended aim of the gaze, resulting in an image whose meaning remains
unclear. Faulkner conveys this sense of uncertainty by accentuating the
destabilized assumptions rooted in color: the arms expected to be black
are not; the shirt expected to be white is not. In the glare highlighting
the faulty black-and-white logic, the visual frame shifts by the end of the
passage from Tomey's Turl to Hubert—in other words, from the initial
target of the gaze to the one employing it. Ultimately, the passage leaves
Hubert suspended in perplexity, *looking* at Tomey's Turl but only *seeing*
him in a confusing light inconsistent with the terms of the racial binary
model that he applies. Moreover, the visual frame leaves Hubert vulner-
ably exposed in his effort to mark Tomey's Turl with racial certainty, for
now the reader is *looking* at Hubert *looking* and seeing quite vividly how
racial consciousness shapes individual perceptions and social relations.

The visually inflected encounter between Hubert and Tomey's Turl
sets the stage for similar scenes involving one of the most forceful characters in *Go Down, Moses*, Lucas Beauchamp, the son of Tomey's Turl and
Tennie. In "The Fire and the Hearth," for example, the narrator recounts
the dispute between Lucas and Zack Edmonds over the rightful claim to
Molly, Lucas's wife. When Zack's wife dies in childbirth, he brings Molly
to the main house to take care of his newborn son, Roth, virtually cuck-
olding Lucas in the process. This turn of events, in the narrator's telling,
brings about the erasure of whiteness, calling to mind Dyer's point about
how outing whiteness as a racial marker can result in a fall into nothingness—a kind of death. In this case, the death is both literal and figurative:
"It was as though the white woman had not only never quitted the house,

she had never existed—the object which they buried in the orchard two days later . . . a thing of no moment, unsanctified, nothing." Determined to reclaim his wife, and thus to unburden himself of the cuckold role, Lucas confronts Zack. "The white man was sitting down," the narrator discloses. "In age he and Lucas could have been brothers, almost twins too." As Theresa M. Towner observes, "Faulkner's portrait of Lucas's confrontation with Zack is striking in the way it repeatedly invokes the individualized 'Lucas' in confrontation with 'the white man.'"[12] Indeed, the explicit labeling of Zack as white is important because it acknowledges that whiteness is a racial category rather than an implicitly natural condition against which being "black" or "mulatto" is deemed to be *different*. As a consequence, Zack, like Hubert Beauchamp, tries to draw on the powers of observation to maintain control: "He leaned slowly back in the chair, looking at Lucas" (*GDM* 46). Zack presses the case further by goading Lucas with pointed questions: "What kind of man do you think I am? What kind of man do you call yourself?" Lucas responds by undermining the assumption of racial difference framing the interrogation: "'I'm a nigger,' Lucas said. 'But I'm a man too. I'm more than just a man. The same thing made my pappy that made your grandmaw'" (*GDM* 46–47). Lucas's assertion that he is both a "nigger" and the same as Zack prompts a kind of special effect enabled by visual imagery. On his way out of the room, Lucas turns back to face Zack, who seems to dematerialize in the light of revealed whiteness: "The other was standing now. They faced one another, though for an instant Lucas couldn't see him" (*GDM* 47). Faced with Lucas's challenge to black-and-white logic, Zack fades out of perception in a destabilizing moment brought about by white racial consciousness. Here, as in the narrator's description of Zack's deceased wife, the use of whiteness as a racial marker threatens the very existence of those who have been oblivious to the power it derives from a covertly abstract position of authority and control.

Through Lucas Beauchamp's encounters with generations of men perched on the white branches of the McCaslin-Edmonds family tree, Faulkner dramatizes the dialectical union of African Americans and whites bound together in the context of a Southern social structure built on the foundation of defining "black" and "white" as mutually exclusive terms. Under these circumstances, as Philip M. Weinstein observes, "the blacks see in the whites, the conditions they cannot escape, the whites see in the blacks the guilt they cannot assuage. Inescapable because the traditional South is the only setting Faulkner can imaginatively endorse, even for his blacks; unassuageable because the act that Faulkner would have to legitimize (ceremonialize) for his whites to get clear of guilt, the act of miscegenation, remains within his frame of values a taboo act."[13]

Indeed, what these characters see in one another (whether in visual or symbolic terms) in the throes of this binding struggle is revealing; however, what they are unable to see is equally telling about the cultural lines of demarcation drawn and enforced by the stealthy force of whiteness but threatened by the subversive reality of miscegenation. For instance, when Roth and Lucas have a row over George Wilkins's still, which poses a threat to Lucas's longstanding bootlegging operation, the narrator says, "Without changing the inflection of his voice and apparently without effort or even design Lucas became not Negro but nigger, not secret so much as impenetrable, not servile and effacing, but enveloping himself in an aura of timeless and stupid impassivity almost like a smell" (*GDM* 58). Owing to what can be termed Lucas's impenetrable lightness of being, he seemingly possesses the capacity to glide in and out of racial categories, all the while remaining an enigma to the frustrated yet always vigilant white gaze. This exchange establishes a pattern in which Lucas, from the perspective of the white characters as framed by the narrator, is repeatedly described with the same adjective. Later, for example, Roth sees in Lucas a face "absolutely blank, impenetrable," producing once again an anxious response suggested by the italicized form. Roth speculates that he is looking "*at a man most of whose blood was pure ten thousand years when my own anonymous beginnings became mixed enough to produce me*" (*GDM* 69). The sneaking suspicion at this moment—the impetus driving the fear that whiteness will perish—is not that Lucas's mixed blood is *impure*, but that it is *more pure* than the "white" blood supposedly flowing through Roth's veins. The description of Lucas's face as "impenetrable" occurs at least three more times in "The Fire and the Hearth," further supporting the notion that Lucas, as a product of miscegenation, is enigmatic by nature and thus a perilous threat to the racial hierarchy. Furthermore, it is this threat to the racial binary code that Zack and Roth use repeatedly to justify their lording over Lucas. Confrontations with miscegenation and consequent feelings of imperiled whiteness become warrants for Zack and Roth to resist Lucas's assertions of equality.

To reinforce its authority in response to anxiety, the white gaze refocuses and intensifies as an instrument for defining the racial Other as different in no uncertain terms. Recalling an encounter between Ike McCaslin and Lucas over the inheritance that Old Carothers McCaslin intended for Tomey's Turl, the narrator describes Lucas's visage as "the color of a used saddle, the features Syriac, not in a racial sense but as the heir to ten centuries of desert horsemen." Once again, the compulsion to define Lucas in fixed racial terms is pronounced, as are the contradictions that arise from trying to do so. Consider how the narrator inexplicably contends that the description is not racial, even as the references to Lucas's skin color and "Syriac" features stand front and center. The strategy to downplay racial motivations as a means of naturalizing racial categories is ultimately fruitless, though, for the narrative spirals into a vision of destabilizing ambiguity. Lucas is now "the composite tintype face of ten thousand undefeated Confederate soldiers almost indistinguishably caricatured, composed, cold, colder than his, more ruthless than his, with more bottom than he had" (*GDM* 104–5). The imagery evokes in the mind's eye those early photographic images of the Civil War whose sepia tones obscure the racial binary code by rendering "white" skin more like, well, the color of a used saddle—that is, closer to the color of Lucas's skin. Subsequently, Roth perceives Lucas through a variation on the same imagery. Roth recollects that his burgeoning racial consciousness as a white McCaslin descendant was driven by his adolescent discovery that Lucas and Zack had fought over Molly and by his subsequently learning to draw lines of social distinction defined by race between himself and his childhood companion, Henry, Lucas and Molly's son. These ruminations lead Roth in search of what the narrator calls "the stereoptic whole"—an image, as we have now seen, captured by the white gaze for the purpose of racial verification but then overburdened with symbolic meaning when depth perception, metaphorically speaking, falters and anxiety sets in (*GDM* 285). From Roth's perspective, it seems that "he could actually see Lucas standing there in the room before him" with a face that "showed less of the ravages of passions and thoughts and satieties and frustrations than his own" and "which had heired and now reproduced with shocking fidelity the old ancestor's [Carothers McCaslin's] entire generation and thought." In a moment of reflection, Roth imagines that Ike McCaslin must have confronted the identical face forty-five years earlier as "a composite of a whole generation of fierce and undefeated young Confederate soldiers, embalmed and slightly mummified" (*GDM* 114). For Roth, as for his kinsmen, confronting an image of miscegenation produces haunting visions of death and nothingness in the white consciousness. The result is an existential crisis marked by high anxiety—an outcome signaled again by the shift to italics when Roth imagines Lucas deriving power from his ability to erase boundaries of time, space, and, most significantly, race: "*He is both heir and prototype simultaneously of all the geography and climate and biology which sired old Carothers and all the rest of us and our kind, myriad, countless, faceless, even nameless now except himself who fathered himself, intact and complete, contemptuous, as old Carothers must have been, of all blood black white yellow or red, including his own*" (*GDM* 114–15). Because Lucas defies the rigid categories of racial difference imposed on him, he undermines Roth's capacity to use visual perception as a means of reinforcing the ideological line dividing "black" and "white." Faced with Lucas, who is thought to transcend racial identity, Roth imagines his white kin as *"faceless,"* their identity seriously compromised by the reality of mixed race because their whiteness relies on the fiction of quantifiable racial difference to remain viable.

These episodes involving Lucas and his relatives resonate with historical implications, responding in fictional form to the complex familial relationships that shaped and were shaped by the "peculiar institution" of slavery in the U.S. South. In so doing, Faulkner subjects whiteness to critical exposure, revealing it as an essential—and, for that matter, essentialist—instrument of social and political control during slavery and Jim Crow. To illustrate the power of whiteness in structuring American society and culture, Morrison uses the simile of a fishbowl, describing a moment of critical awareness that offered her newfound insight into the formation of racial hierarchy. For a long time, Morrison explains in figurative terms, she was preoccupied with the contents of the bowl—the color of the fish and the movement of bubbles in the water, for example. However, after learning to refocus her critical lens, Morrison adds, "I saw the bowl, the structure that transparently (and invisibly) permits the ordered life it contains to exist in the larger world."[14] This revelation was important for Morrison because it allowed her to see not just the effects of a society delineated by racial difference but also the cause—the pervasive and covert ordering presence of whiteness. Building on Morrison's observation, Tara McPherson traces a path between two racially inflected "economies of visibility" active in the 1930s and the 1990s. Although McPherson emphasizes images of black and white femininity, her critical framework is pertinent to the racial imagery employed in Go Down, Moses to depict Lucas in conflict with his white cousins. McPherson contrasts a frame of reference more prevalent in the 1930s that "foregrounds the interdependence" of black and white images only to bolster racial difference with a "lenticular" approach more common in contemporary cultural work.[15] For McPherson, this "lenticular" logic separates images of black and white into separate fields that cannot be viewed together, thus severing the complex ties inherent to race relations in the South and erasing relevant issues of historical and cultural context.[16] These discussions of visual imagery underscore the complexity of Go Down, Moses, showing how Faulkner's novel defines a broader and more penetrating scope for delving into the complexities of racial identity in the South. Faulkner's approach is not confined to images of black and white represented in stark, reductive opposition or as mutually exclusive categories segregated by a faulty lenticular logic. On the contrary, his mode of representation captures not only the racialized images themselves but also how these images have been framed by whiteness in Southern social order, engendering a dynamic struggle of domination and resistance waged in large measure through sensory perceptions that influence individual, familial, and social relations.

On the surface, Lucas Beauchamp's forceful presence seems to fade from *Go Down, Moses* at the close of "The Fire and the Hearth." On closer reading, however, Lucas remains a resonant force in the text by virtue of foreshadowing and symbolic associations that bolster Faulkner's structural claim for *Go Down, Moses* as a novel rather than a collection of previously published material revised and loosely bound together. Under conventional aesthetic principles, validating the novelistic claim requires identifying connections between the various sections that promote an overarching sense of formal unity. One line of connection between the section that features Lucas and those that bring Ike to center stage— "The Old People," "The Bear," and "Delta Autumn"—starts with the altercation between Zack and Lucas at the end of chapter 1, section 2, in "The Fire and the Hearth." Enraged at Zack for taking Molly to the main house to care for the infant Roth, Lucas goes there with a razor in hand looking for vengeance. Locked in Zack's bedroom, the two men face off in a violent struggle. Lunging for Zack, "the white man . . . saw the whites of the negro's eyes rush suddenly with red like the eyes of a bayed animal—a bear, a fox" (*GDM* 54). In response, Zack reaches for his pistol, but Lucas restrains his foe by grabbing both wrists. The narrator explains that "the white man stared at the spent and frantic face opposite his." Characteristically, the close-up perception of Lucas threatens the viability—and, indeed, the visibility—of whiteness: "*He cant even see me right now,* the white man thought" (*GDM* 54, 55). As the conflict reaches a crescendo, Lucas and Zack are locked "almost like an embrace" and fighting for the pistol, which eventually Lucas misfires (*GDM* 56). A parallel scene can be found in "The Bear" during the dramatic final confrontation involving the bear Old Ben, the fierce tracking dog Lion, and the hunting party that includes Ike McCaslin and Sam Fathers. With Old Ben finally cornered, Lion attacks the heretofore elusive prey: "This time the bear didn't strike him down. It caught the dog in both arms, almost loverlike, and they both went down" (*GDM* 230, 231). These two life-or-death embraces are part of a broader process in which Faulkner projects issues of miscegenation raised vividly in the early sections of the novel onto the screen, as it were, of the subsequent sections that focus on Ike's tormented engagement with historical and racial consciousness in the context of ruminations on the waning big woods.

Ike McCaslin's burgeoning awareness of the past and of his identity as a white man is fostered, true to the *bildungsroman* form that Faulkner employs, by the guidance of the older and wiser Sam Fathers. Ike's initiation into this experience comes when, as a small boy, he makes his first kill on a hunt. In keeping with traditional hunting ritual, Ike must be, in effect, baptized by the blood that he has drawn from the slain deer. Faulkner relies heavily on miscegenation imagery to create the initiation scene in "The Old People," with the narrator describing Sam as "a negro for two generations now but whose face and bearing were still those of the Chickasaw chief who had been his father" (*GDM* 158). Bringing Ike into the frame, the narrator emphasizes racial difference: "They were the white boy, marked forever, and the old dark man sired on both sides by savage kings, who had marked him, whose bloody hands had merely formally consecrated him to that which, under the man's tutelage, he had already accepted, humbly and joyfully, with abnegation and with pride too" (*GDM* 159). Subsequently, the narrative has the ritual "joining him [Ike] and the man [Sam] forever" in a pact that traces symbolically through blood back to the fathers of Sam Fathers, so to speak. This imagery calls to mind the blood fetish that Morrison describes, giving the impression that the tainted bloodline in Sam Fathers—a condition suggested by the narrator's description of it as "alien" and "barren"—gives way to a ritualistically purified strain of blood in Ike. Once marked by blood, Ike comes into his whiteness by viewing Sam in the same manner that Zack and Roth perceive Lucas—that is to say, as mysteriously different. Accordingly, Ike notices how Sam responds to the white men in the camp "with gravity and dignity and without servility or recourse to that impenetrable wall of ready and easy mirth which negroes sustain between themselves and white men" (*GDM* 164). Ike and Sam are now on opposite sides of a racial divide necessary for the viability of whiteness as a privileged social category whose intangible power derives in large measure from using racial difference to mark and marginalize the "impenetrable" Other.

In the section "Delta Autumn" Faulkner employs the pathetic fallacy to expand the scope of visual imagery, projecting the impenetrable lightness of being associated with products of miscegenation onto the once expansive wilderness that framed Ike McCaslin's tutelage under Sam Fathers but now is endangered by the consuming force of modernization. Through Ike's perception, the shrinking wilderness comes into focus. Once thriving, the forest is "retreating since its purpose was served now and its time an outmoded time, retreating southward through this inverted-apex, this ▽-shaped section of earth between hills and River until what was left of it seemed to be now gathered and for the time arrested in one tremendous density of brooding and inscrutable impenetrability at the ultimate funneling tip" (*GDM* 326–27). Surveying the diminishment of the big woods prompts the old man Ike to recall the primal scene that initiated his coming-of-age as a hunter and a white man in "The Bear." In retrospect, he understands that "there was something running in Sam Fathers' veins which ran in the veins of the buck too" and, consequently, he can now articulate to the slain animal what he was "unable to phrase" as a twelve-year-old boy: "*I slew you; my bearing must not shame your quitting life. My conduct forever onward must become your death*" (*GDM* 334). For Ike, of course, this conduct involves the repudiation of his birthright because, contrary to the tenets of private ownership, he comes to believe that the land "belongs to all" and, moreover, that he and the wilderness are "coevals" (*GDM* 337). In this passage, Ike's dialectical relationship with the big woods functions symbolically, illustrating how the claim of whiteness as an inherently natural and privileged state of being is reliant upon the "impenetrable" presence of the Other. When all is said and done, Ike's anxiety stems not from the ambiguity of racial mixing per se but from the idea that it signals the demise of racial difference altogether—with the loss of the "impenetrable" forest, a space that naturalizes racial difference for Ike, he senses that his whiteness will blend into a modern landscape with no lines of racial demarcation.

Ike's ruminations about the retreating wilderness set the backdrop for a final dramatic encounter with the destabilizing reality of miscegenation. For Ike, coming face to face with the nameless granddaughter of James Beauchamp, aka Tennie's Jim, in the Mississippi Delta brings about a startling epiphany. Ike realizes that, in spite of seeming white to him, this woman is of mixed racial heritage and, compounding the shock, that she has been involved in an incestuous relationship with Roth Edmonds. Using descriptive visual imagery, Faulkner has Ike focus on "the pale lips, the skin pallid and dead-looking yet not ill, the dark and tragic and foreknowing eyes" before the anxiety sets in: "*Maybe in a thousand or two thousand years in America*, he thought. *But not now! Not now!* He cried, not loud, in a voice of amazement, pity, and outrage: 'You're a nigger!'" (*GDM* 344). Trying to capture "the stereoptic whole," Ike fails and thus finds himself confronted with images of death and nothingness. In response, he reaches out to the young woman until she matches his gesture, bringing into focus an image of "the gnarled, bloodless, bone-light bone-dry old man's fingers touching for a second the smooth young flesh where the strong old blood ran after its long lost journey back home" (*GDM* 345). The scene is reminiscent of the moment in *Absalom, Absalom!* when Clytie touches Rosa Coldfield's arm and Faulkner is able to represent with potent imagery and symbolism the inescapable tension that miscegenation produces and, as Towner argues, "how white racial privilege attempts to control challenges to its power and how precariously that privilege is situated."[17] The element of incest in Ike's encounter with the young woman calls to mind another scene in *Absalom*: Quentin and Shreve's account of Charles Bon and Judith Sutpen's relationship. That scene is telling because Shreve gleans from Quentin that miscegenation trumps incest in the game of defining cultural taboos in the South. Shreve's observation seems applicable to Ike McCaslin as well, given his parting admonition to the granddaughter of Tennie's Jim: "Marry: a man in your own race. That's the only salvation for you—for a while yet, maybe a long while yet" (*GDM* 346). The urgency to defer the end of racial difference in perpetuity suggests that the salvation would not be for the woman but for Ike himself. With her marked by marriage as "black," Ike could restore his belief in the integrity of the line dividing him from the "impenetrable" Other whose difference affords his whiteness its quiet claim to superiority.

Faulkner's rendering of Ike McCaslin as burdened by the legacy of racial oppression is part of the intricate tapestry that is *Go Down, Moses*. Repeatedly, Faulkner brings Ike and his white kin into contact with what Frederick Douglass calls "a very different-looking class of people."[18] These visual exchanges take on qualities of the embrace between Lion and Old Ben—with a profound sense of urgency, they become matters of life or death. Albeit from a different point of view, Faulkner, like Douglass, shows the endangered species to be a Southern social hierarchy founded on an ideology of white supremacy that believes in a "natural" boundary between black and white, even in the face of striking evidence to the contrary. After all, the white McCaslin-Edmondses need only look at their family tree—the intricate branches of which are found in the fading pages of the commissary ledgers and in the family chronicles preserved in individual and collective memory—to realize the impossibility of reconciling the fiction of racial difference with the reality of racial ambiguity. And yet, as Faulkner's vivid imagery reveals, they are compelled to keep looking and to keep failing in each attempt to penetrate the image of the "impenetrable" Other in the hope of finding racial essence. On some level, they need to stare into the face of miscegenation and then to experience the feelings of panic that their looking invariably produces. For these characters—and, by extension, for the social class they occupy—imagining their imminent demise fuels the desire to maintain binary opposition as the racial norm and, in turn, fortifies the resistance to integration. For anyone willing to look at this process with a critical eye, Faulkner's *Go Down, Moses* makes visible how whiteness reproduces the means of its own production, running the risk of exposure while gaining much of its power from trying to hide in plain sight.

NOTES

1. William Faulkner, *Go Down, Moses* (New York: Vintage, 1970), 284. All further references to the novel come from this edition and will be cited parenthetically in the text, using the abbreviation *GDM*.

2. See Patricia McKee, *Producing American Races: Henry James, William Faulkner, Toni Morrison* (Durham: Duke University Press, 1999) for an insightful examination of how Faulkner creates "a 'visual culture' of whiteness . . . apparent in exchanges of visual representations among characters—representations not only of images but also of characters' views" (4). Although McKee confines her discussion to *The Sound and the Fury* and *Light in August*, her theoretical approach could apply as well to *Go Down, Moses*.

3. Richard Dyer, *White* (London: Routledge, 1997), 44, 45.

4. See Valerie Babb, *The Meaning of Whiteness in American Literature and Culture* (New York: New York University Press, 1998). Babb explains how this racial terminology "attempt[s] to make distinct from whites those individuals with identical physical appearances but fractions of speciously documentable nonwhite blood." She adds that "whiteness is more than a classification of physical appearance; it is largely an invented construct blending history, culture, assumptions, and attitudes" (10).

5. Toni Morrison, *Playing in the Dark: Whiteness and the Literary Imagination* (Cambridge: Harvard University Press, 1992), 17.

6. Ibid, 33.

7. Ibid, 68.

8. Eric J. Sundquist, "Faulkner, Race, and the Forms of American Fiction," in Doreen Fowler and Ann J. Abadie, eds, *Faulkner and Race: Faulkner and Yoknapatawpha, 1986* (University Press of Mississippi, 1987), 4.

9. See, for example, Craig Werner, "Black Dreams of Faulkner's Dreams of Blacks," in Fowler and Abadie, eds., *Faulkner and Race*. In this essay, Werner contends, "Even when he fails to comprehend fully the nature of Afro-American signifying . . . Faulkner provides images capable of deconstructing the binary oppositions on which racial privilege depends" (40). Also, see Jay Watson, "Introduction: Situating Whiteness in Faulkner Studies, Situating Faulkner in Whiteness Studies," *Faulkner Journal* 22 (2006–2007): 3–23. Watson provides a comprehensive and instructive overview of scholarly work on whiteness and discusses how representations of whiteness in Faulkner's fiction interrogate and complicate reductive conceptualizations of racial identity.

10. Thadious M. Davis, *Games of Property: Law, Race, Gender and Faulkner's "Go Down, Moses"* (Durham: Duke University Press, 2003), 44.

11. Ibid., 44–45.

12. Theresa M. Towner, *Faulkner on the Color Line: The Later Novels* (Jackson: University Press of Mississippi), 31.

13. Philip M. Weinstein, *Faulkner's Subject: A Cosmos No One Owns* (New York: Cambridge University Press, 1992), 62.

14. Morrison, *Playing in the Dark*, 17–18.

15. Tara McPherson, *Reconstructing Dixie: Race, Gender, and Nostalgia in the Imagined South* (Durham: Duke University Press, 2003), 25.

16. Ibid., 26.

17. Towner, *Faulkner on the Color Line*, 16.

18. Frederick Douglass, *Narrative of the Life of Frederick Douglass, an American Slave* (New York: Penguin Books, 1982), 50.

Intertextual Geographies of Migration and Biracial Identity: *Light in August* and Nella Larsen's *Quicksand*

Martyn Bone

This essay provides a comparative analysis of William Faulkner's *Light in August* (1932) and Nella Larsen's *Quicksand* (1928). My starting point is that Faulkner and Larsen have more in common than one might assume if reading them only as exemplars of the Southern Renaissance and Harlem Renaissance respectively. More specifically, reading Faulkner alongside Larsen may help to resituate Faulkner's "Southern" writing about race in wider national and transnational contexts.

In *Dirt and Desire: Reconstructing Southern Women's Writing, 1930–1990,* Patricia Yaeger makes the parenthetical observation that "Nella Larsen's reflections on the South in *Quicksand* (1928) and *Passing* (1929) offer still wider reference points for gendered remappings of the New South's racial coordinates."[1] Yaeger does not pursue the point, but *Quicksand* remaps Southern "racial coordinates" via a narrative geography that is structured around multiple migrations. *Quicksand*'s protagonist Helga Crane travels not only between the South and the North, but also back and forth across the Atlantic between New York and Copenhagen. During these migrations, Helga also crosses the color line of U.S. racial ideology. Helga's biracial identity and transnational triple consciousness (Negro, American, and Danish) challenge the rigid definitions of race that so restrict her life in the United States. My claim is that Joe Christmas's peregrinations across regional, national, and racial boundaries in *Light in August* can usefully be read alongside Helga Crane's.

At least since Alfred Kazin's 1958 essay "The Stillness of *Light in August*," Faulkner critics have been alert to the intersecting racial and spatial dimensions of the novel.[2] Only more recently, however, have critics such as Leigh Anne Duck and Joanna Davis-McElligatt more fully explored the intersection of race and space with region, nation, and migration. In a recent essay Duck claims that, "by subjecting local understandings of race to comparison" with Spanish America in *Light in August*, "Faulkner prepared himself . . . to question the bipartite social structure of the U.S. South" in similar but more thorough fashion in *Absalom, Absalom!* (1936). For Duck, Mexico's role as the putative birthplace of Joe Christmas's father and a site of emigration for Joe himself anticipates Haiti's status in *Absalom, Absalom!* as a space south of the U.S. South where "race is constructed differently."[3] Similarly, Davis-McElligatt reads Joe's "ambiguous and indeterminate ethnoracial identity" in relation to Southern regional *and* U.S. national anxieties about both miscegenation and immigration.[4] Duck and Davis-McElligatt "engage with Joe not only in the Southern context, but in the American and global context" in order that our "readings of Faulkner's *oeuvre* can be enriched."[5]

While I agree with Duck that *Light in August* gestures beyond "the U.S. southern model of clear racial divisions" by turning south of the border, this essay will emphasize that Faulkner, like Larsen, also interrogates the U.S. *national* model of racial categorization.[6] In *Who Is Black? One Nation's Definition* (1991) sociologist F. James Davis observes that the definition of blackness based around the "'one-drop rule,' meaning that a single drop of 'black blood' makes a person black," was developed in the South during slavery and Jim Crow. However, Davis emphasizes, "this definition emerged from the American South to become the nation's definition, generally accepted by whites and blacks alike."[7] In the urban North, both Joe Christmas and Helga Crane discover that what Duck calls "a bifurcated local paradigm" of racial identity premised upon the one-drop rule has become a fully blown national ideology of racial classification.[8]

If criticism of *Light in August* has been enriched by closer attention to the novel's transnational dimensions, something similar has happened in recent scholarship on *Quicksand*. In the past, Larsen critics tended to miss the full significance of Helga's maternal Danish heritage and the section of *Quicksand* that takes place in Copenhagen. Recently, however, George Hutchinson's groundbreaking work on the Danish dimensions of Larsen's life and fiction has made it imperative for critics to address "the significance of biracial and Danish-American identity to *Quicksand*."[9] Hutchinson and like-minded scholars such as Jessica Wegmann-Sánchez have demonstrated how Larsen uses the Copenhagen section of *Quicksand* to develop an "argument against American modes of racial classification."[10] Here, then, Faulkner and Larsen dovetail: the narrative geographies of their novels take a transnational turn in order to question U.S. racial ideology. As such, reading *Light in August* alongside *Quicksand* may allow us to see more clearly how Faulkner too began to interrogate race at the national as well as the regional level.

Before proceeding to a closer analysis of the two novels, I should make clear that I am not suggesting that Faulkner must have read and been influenced by *Quicksand*, which was published four years before *Light in August*. It is likely that Faulkner was unaware of Larsen and her work. In juxtaposing the two novels, I am drawing on the flexible conception of intertextuality adumbrated by Roland Barthes, whereby every text is "a tissue of quotations drawn from the innumerable centers of culture."[11] For my purposes here, the cultural center or master narrative that both Faulkner and Larsen "quote" from and critique in their fictional counter-narratives is the system of racial classification that defines Joe and Helga as "Negro." I am also indebted (as my title indicates) to Anna Brickhouse's assessment of the "intertextual geography of *Quicksand*." Brickhouse argues that textuality itself is "the self-referential subject of *Quicksand*" because Larsen revises a wide range of anterior texts to construct a "literary genealogy that is unmistakably biracial," as well as fluidly geographical.[12] In my analysis, the intertextual geographies of *Quicksand* and *Light in August* emerge from Larsen and Faulkner's mutual and almost simultaneous exploration of the ways in which the nationalized master narrative of racial classification—reified in and as law—denies the very notion of *bi*racial identity (let alone the possibility of transcending racial categories altogether). This denial prompts Helga Crane and Joe Christmas to keep moving physically across regional and national borders. Ultimately, however, neither Joe nor Helga can find a place in which to fully explore and work out an alternative (bi)racial or cultural identity. This is partly because the "U.S. southern model of clear racial divisions" also prevails in the North, but it is also because Joe and Helga themselves internalize the logic of the one-drop rule—as dramatized in their respective emigrations to Mexico and Denmark.

Both Joe Christmas and Helga Crane are orphans. In both cases this is a direct result of their (in Joe's case, putative) biracial parentage and of an ideology that pathologizes biracial identity—not least within the family. Before I proceed, it is worth periodizing the lives of Joe and Helga. Davis-McElligatt remarks that Joe's life "spans from, roughly, the middle-to-late 1890s . . . to the middle-to-late 1920s," while Hutchinson observes that *Quicksand* "seems to be set in the 1920s."[13] Given that Helga Crane is identified in the second paragraph of the first chapter as a "slight girl of twenty-two years," we can surmise that, like Joe, Helga was born in the late 1890s.[14] Joe and Helga are thus born around the time that the 1896 Supreme Court decision *Plessy v. Ferguson* provided "'judicial notice' of what it assumed to be common knowledge: that a Negro or black is any person with any black ancestry."[15] Hutchinson explains how national thinking about "race" operated at the domestic level of "family" before finding legal sanction in the Court's landmark decision: "The regime of race in the United States was set up precisely to ensure a 'natural' correlation between race and family identity. . . . The family was the basic unit in the reproduction of race. So-called mixed families thus became 'unnatural,' as new theories promulgated by the most prestigious natural and social scientists in the United States and Europe seemed to prove on objective scientific grounds. These theories, in turn, became the intellectual bulwark for judicial opinions—most crucially *Plessy v. Ferguson*—affirming racial segregation."[16] Having been born in the slipstream of a legal decision that reified "the 'naturalness' of racial separation in the making of Americans throughout the twentieth century," Joe and Helga grow to adulthood during a period when, as Davis-McElligatt emphasizes, "fear of miscegenation . . . was rampant."[17] F. James Davis notes that "the animus against miscegenation and mulattoes in the South . . . reach[ed] a peak by 1907" and "this hostility was expressed in heightened concern about the number of mulattoes, who was and was not a Negro, and about passing as white."[18] It is hardly surprising, then, that already as children Helga and Joe become the objective correlatives on to which Southerners project such fear of miscegenation.

I should acknowledge here that there are differences between Helga and Joe's familial histories and biracial identities. Though the personal history of Helga's father, "that gay suave scoundrel" (*QS* 26), is shrouded in mystery, Helga knows that he was black. By contrast, there is no conclusive evidence that Joe has any black parentage. It is only toward the end of *Light in August* that the reader finally learns—as Joe himself perhaps never does—that Eupheus "Doc" Hines is Joe's grandfather and murdered Joe's father because "old Doc Hines could see in his face the black curse of God Almighty." Yet for all Hines's racist and religious conviction, his victim may not have been African American at all—indeed, he may not even have been American. Joe's mother, Milly, told Hines "that he [Joe's father] was a Mexican."[19] The epistemological uncertainty over Joe's race (and nationality) is compounded when Joe's grandmother recalls that her husband escaped a murder charge only because "the circus owner [and employer of Joe's father] come back and said how the man really was a part nigger instead of Mexican"; even then, though, "it was just that circus man that said he was a nigger and maybe he never knew for certain" (*LIA* 377–78).[20]

Nevertheless, Hines's rabid conviction that "the fellow had nigger blood" (*LIA* 374) accords with and is bolstered by the naturalization of regional mores into national law via *Plessy v. Ferguson*. Hence, Hines not only escapes trial for the murder but is able to remove Joe from his mother (Milly dies while or shortly after giving birth) and place him in a Memphis orphanage. The whole scenario enacts and exemplifies what Hutchinson calls "the law of the color line—[that] Race Trumps Family."[21] Because Joe's father allegedly has "nigger blood," Joe too is defined by the one-drop rule and, as a "black" person, cannot possibly remain part of the Hines family. Denied any relationship with his white mother, and (as yet) having and feeling no "racial" connection to African Americans, Joe necessarily becomes an orphan.

Crucially, Joe himself comes to believe that he has "black blood." Despite this lack of knowledge about his father and his racial/national identity (and despite being visually identified by other characters as variously "white," "wop," and "foreigner"), Joe accepts and internalizes the logic of the one-drop rule. This process begins at the Memphis institution when the other "orphans in identical and uniform blue denim" (*LIA* 119) mysteriously distinguish and deride Joe as "Nigger" (*LIA* 127). How and why this happens is not clear: quite possibly the other children classify Joe at the covert instigation of Hines, who keeps a panoptical eye trained on the boy through his job as the orphanage janitor. Or it may be that in the 1890s South even orphaned children know that "Nigger" is the ultimate insult—a powerfully performative sign of otherness and inferiority. Whatever the case, Joe carries the belief that his core identity is "black" from orphanhood into adulthood.

Unlike Joe Christmas, Helga Crane spent at least part of her childhood with her white mother. Like Joe's childhood, however, Helga's was fraught with anxiety related to her racial classification—not least within her own family. When Helga's father disappeared, Helga's desperate mother, Karen Nilssen, remarried "a man of her own race": "Even foolish, despised women must have food and clothing; even unloved little Negro girls must be somehow provided for" (*OS* 26). From birth, then, Helga is, like Joe, defined as "Negro," even though Karen Nilssen is, like Milly Hines, white. While Joe encountered the racial taunts of his fellow orphans, Helga experienced "the savage unkindness of her stepbrothers and sisters, and the jealous, malicious hatred of her mother's husband" before she too was orphaned at age fifteen by "her mother's death" (*QS* 26).

Ostensibly Helga is rescued from her wicked white stepfather when her mother's brother, Peter Nilssen, pays for her to attend Devon, "a school for Negroes" (*QS* 26) in Nashville. However, this apparent act of charity serves to reaffirm Helga's classification as "Negro." It ignores the fact that Helga has grown up in a white family in Chicago; that she is even more likely to be categorized as "Negro" in the South, ground zero of the one-drop rule; and that she has no familial or ancestral connection to black Southerners. Indeed, Helga "became gradually aware of a difference between herself and the girls about her" at Devon: "They had mothers, fathers, brothers, and sisters of whom they spoke frequently, and who sometimes visited them" (*QS* 26-27). Helga's lack of black Southern family is painfully apparent again when, at age twenty, she becomes a teacher at another black Southern school, Naxos. Discussing the generation of African American leaders dominated by Booker T. Washington—whose Tuskegee transparently provides the model for Naxos—Hutchinson notes that they "were committed to [an idea of] 'race' as extended 'family' and the focal point of personal identity."[22] Helga, however, is unable to enter this racial neofamily because of her biracial and non-southern background. As at Devon, so at Naxos Helga is seen as "a solitary girl with no family connections" (*QS* 9); moreover, she begins to see herself as such. Eventually, Helga's conflicted feelings about her biracial and non-Southern lineage lead to her breach with Naxos: she tells the principal Robert Anderson that "I haven't any [family]. I was born in a Chicago slum. . . . My father was a gambler who deserted my mother, a white immigrant. It is even uncertain that they were married. . . . I don't belong here" (*QS* 24).[23]

Joe too appears to be rescued from orphanhood when he is adopted by the McEacherns, a white family that, in its rural southern religiosity, recalls the Hines clan. On the surface, Joe's adoption as a white child may seem to contrast with Helga's growing isolation among the black Southern pupils of Devon. Yet Joe never truly feels part of the McEachern family because he has already accepted the notion—fostered at the Memphis orphanage and facilitated by the wider culture's adoption of the one-drop rule—that really he is black. Joe's barely conscious acceptance that Race Trumps (adopted) Family is apparent in his malicious repudiation of Mrs. McEachern's maternal care and his yearning to make her "tell [Simon McEachern] what he has nursed . . . a nigger beneath his own roof" (*LIA* 168). The extent to which Joe has internalized the pseudoscientific idea of racial "blood" so central to the one-drop rule is evident in his declaration to his lover Bobbie that "I got some nigger blood in me" (*LIA* 196). Much as Eupheus Hines's assertion that Joe's "Mexican" father had "nigger blood" was sufficient to summon the Southern fear of miscegenation and legitimize the murder of an innocent man, so the possibility that Joe is *"really a nigger"* (*LIA* 219) is enough to ensure that, as Donald Kartiganer notes, Bobbie furiously "revert[s] to the categorizations of her society" ("Me f . ing for nothing a nigger son of a bitch" [*LIA* 218]) and that Joe is savagely beaten by Bobbie's pimp, Max, and an accomplice.[24]

By young adulthood, then, both Helga and Joe have already been ostracized from their respective "white" families and repeatedly classified as "black"; moreover, they have begun to see themselves as black, rather than as white or biracial. These profoundly racialized histories of orphanhood mark the adult personalities of Joe and Helga. When Joe in his early thirties arrives at the sawmill in Jefferson, the other workers quickly sense that "there was something definitely rootless about him, as though no town nor city was his, no street, no walls, no square of earth his home. And that he carried this knowledge with him always as though it were a banner, with a quality ruthless, lonely, and almost proud" (*LIA* 31–32). By the time that Helga reaches Naxos at the age of twenty, her lack of familial or regional roots has generated a similar lonely pride (albeit more sensitive and brittle than Joe's). Helga emanates "that faint hint of offishness which hung about her and repelled advances, an arrogance that stirred in people a peculiar irritation"; the narrator states explicitly that Helga has "adopted [it] instinctively as a protective measure for her acute sensitiveness, in her child days" (*QS* 37). All told, Joe and Helga are orphaned not so much by the death or disappearance of their parents as by the ways in which their personal histories are inextricable from an ideology in which the specter of *racial* blood (especially "black blood") trumps *familial* blood ties.

Following Helga's repudiation of Naxos at age twenty-two and Joe's rejection by Bobbie at age eighteen, their experiences relate more clearly in their respective migrations across regional and national borders. After leaving Naxos, Helga travels north to Chicago and Harlem, across the Atlantic to Copenhagen, back to Harlem, and finally returns to the rural South. These migratory trajectories compare quite strikingly with Joe's movements once he enters the "thousand savage and lonely streets" (*LIA* 220) through which he travels "for fifteen years" (*LIA* 223) before arriving in Jefferson, Mississippi. Like Helga, Joe goes "back north"—in his case, "to Chicago and Detroit" rather than Chicago and New York—and also travels abroad. Whereas Helga goes to Denmark, Joe turns south of the U.S. South to Mexico. Eventually, though, Joe, like Helga, ends up "back south again" (*LIA* 224).

During their transregional and transnational travels, both Joe and Helga search for a place where they might be able to escape the prejudice they have experienced previously and renegotiate their racial identity. Neither Joe nor Helga is successful, partly because they encounter the same racial classifications in the North as in the South and among blacks as well as whites. More than that, though, Joe and Helga's physical migrations are rendered largely redundant by their own mental acceptance of the one-drop rule that defines them as essentially "black."

In a limited sense, Joe does live out a biracial identity during his travels across and between the rural South and urban North. Thadious Davis argues that "Faulkner maintains Joe Christmas is both black and white" and that "Joe lives both existences, contrary to the accepted standards of the South. During his wandering, he exists as a black man with other blacks and also as a white man with other whites."[25] Yet Joe is never really able to live as "both black and white" at the same time, or in the same place. Even when Joe lives as white in the South, he continues to believe that really he is black; because Joe has been subjected to "the accepted standards of the South" since childhood, he is never able to overcome the belief that he is fraudulently passing as white. And while Joe's decision to live as black among "other blacks" in the urban North may seem transgressive, it actually conforms to the inexorable logic of the one-drop rule—an originally Southern ideology that has been nationalized.

Joe defines himself by the one-drop rule throughout his travels. Still moving through what the narrator calls "the (comparatively speaking) south," Joe is shocked and repulsed to encounter a white prostitute who is rather blasé about his racial identity. When Joe declares "that he was a negro," the woman bemusedly responds, "You are? . . . I thought maybe you were just another wop or something" (*LIA* 225). Up until this point, the standard response of white Southern women to declarations of Joe's "black" identity has been incredulity: both the orphanage matron and Bobbie declare "I dont believe it" (*LIA* 132, 197). The idea that a white Southern woman (the prostitute) might not cleave to the one-drop rule, as Joe himself does, and even have sex with a *visibly* "black" man ("You ought to seen the shine I turned out just before your turn came"), leaves Joe "sick for two years" (*LIA* 225). This scene bears out John Matthews's point that "Joe falls victim to the South's refusal to admit the open secret of racial hybridity"—despite plentiful evidence of sexual contact across the color line.[26]

However, both Joe and Helga discover that the urban North proves little more open to racial hybridity. Joe moves to Chicago and Detroit where he very deliberately embraces a "black" identity and everyday life: "He lived with negroes, shunning white people" (*LIA* 225). Helga does something similar—though in a less aggressive fashion—when she moves from Chicago to Harlem. As Hutchinson notes, in Chicago "'race' trumps 'family'" once again when uncle Peter's new wife makes a "completely specious denial" that Helga is any relation to her husband.[27] Helga is thus even more alienated from her white Danish-American family and inclines further to the idea that she is fundamentally a "Negro." That Joe and Helga identify themselves as black is historically consistent with "the racially polarized nation of the early 1920s." By this time, F. James Davis notes, biracial and black Americans had followed whites by "accept[ing] the one-drop rule completely" so that "by 1925 mulattoes and blacks in general were convinced that no alternative definition was possible."[28] Indeed, Helga's self-identification as "Negro" is encouraged by not only a white Northern woman (uncle Peter's new wife), but also a black Northern woman. Jeanette Hayes-Rore, a prominent spokeswoman on race issues who employs Helga as her private secretary, recommends that Helga repudiate her white family history in order to smooth her entry into Harlem: "I wouldn't mention that my people are white, if I were you. Colored people won't understand it" (QS 44). So, much as Joe in Chicago and Detroit "live[s] with negroes, shunning white people," Helga moves to "teeming black Harlem" (QS 46) and takes on a black identity while ignoring "white New York" (QS 48).

Nevertheless, for all that Helga and Joe try to convince themselves that they are black, they are both performing an identity that conforms to U.S. racial ideology. Helga's complicity in the erasure of her matrilineal heritage means that, as Jessica Wegmann-Sánchez nicely puts it, "Helga is passing in Harlem, except that she passes as Black, not White."[29] Much the same might be said of Joe Christmas in Chicago and Detroit, except that (leaving aside the fact that Joe may not actually have a black father) his lighter skin means that he cannot pass as black in the way that Helga can. The tragicomic result is that Joe ends up fighting with "the negro who called him white" (LIA 225). Ultimately, by trying to pass as (only) black, both Joe and Helga recapitulate "the South's refusal to admit the open secret of racial hybridity"—but they do so in the urban North. They demonstrate their allegiance to the one-drop rule, which has expanded from regional origins to become the national model of racial classification.

Yet neither Helga nor Joe can entirely deny their "white" heritage. Though Joe follows the one-drop rule by defining himself through his supposed "black blood," he also believes that his body contains "white blood" and that this "white blood" must be repressed if he is to live as "black" in the urban North. The narrator describes Joe lying awake one night in Detroit "trying to expel from himself the white blood." However, Joe can never fully slough off his "white" identity because, at some level, he knows that it is cultural as well as biological. Joe has not discovered his "blood" kinship to Milly Hines, but he does dimly recognize that his upbringing in the McEachern family, and in the white South more generally, has shaped him—hence his desperation to "expel" not only the "white blood" but also the "white thinking and being" (LIA 226).

As Thadious Davis observes, "Larsen avoids the stereotypical depiction of the 'tragic mulatto,' the passive victim of two different bloods warring in her veins."[30] Thus Helga never demonstrates Joe's intense anxiety about "black blood" competing with "white blood." Still, when Helga in

Harlem feels unable to continue repressing her white heritage, she does figure it as a physical presence within her body that, like Joe's "white blood," struggles to reassert itself against the presently ascendant black identity: "Somewhere, within her, in a deep recess, crouched discontent." So where Joe abandons "liv[ing] with negroes" in Detroit and returns to the South, Helga more tentatively begins to embark on "lonely excursions to places outside of Harlem." More disturbingly, Helga begins to feel physically repulsed by Harlem's black masses, whom previously she has tried to embrace (notwithstanding her experiences at Devon and Naxos) as her racial neofamily: "She recoiled in aversion from the sight of the grinning faces and from the sound of the easy laughter of all these people who strolled, aimlessly now, it seemed, up and down the avenues" (*QS* 50). It is important to recognize that this is not simply hatred of the urban black folk; rather, it is a projected expression of Helga's interior "discontent" that living as "black" has required her to so thoroughly abandon her matrilineal heritage and biracial identity. Helga goes from feeling she has "found herself" (*QS* 46) in Harlem to feeling "self-loathing" for identifying entirely with blacks as "my own people" (*QS* 57). This correlates to Joe's conflicted (but characteristically more compressed) feelings when entering Jefferson's black district after his return to the South. Punningly depicted as "passing still between the homes of white people" before entering Freedman's Town,[31] Joe is at first "lost" before "he found himself," only then to feel enclosed and repulsed by the black masses and their "bodiless voices murmuring talking laughing in a language not his" (*LIA* 114). Joe and Helga's well-nigh schizophrenic responses to black life and culture derive from that rigid binary logic that makes their racial identity—in the small-town South *and* the metropolitan North—either black or white, but never both.

Helga escapes Harlem and migrates once more when Uncle Peter sends her a substantial check accompanied by a letter suggesting that she use the money to visit her extended Danish family in Copenhagen. The representation of Helga's two years or so in Denmark constitutes about a quarter of *Quicksand*. By contrast, *Light in August* says very little explicitly about its protagonist's time abroad. While it is fairly clear that Helga travels to Denmark in order to escape U.S. racial attitudes and reclaim her maternal heritage, it is less apparent why Joe goes to Mexico. One might venture that Joe, like Helga, seeks to escape the Southern model of racial classification that, he now knows, has spread throughout the United States. One might also speculate that in an ironic parallel to or parody of the way in which Eupheus Hines "knew somehow" (*LIA* 374) that Joe's father was "black," so Joe "knew somehow" that his father was

Mexican and so, like Helga, traveled abroad to reclaim his family history. There is no textual evidence for such motives, however. Moreover, Joe's experiences in Mexico do not seem to have transformed in any way his understanding of race. Indeed, neither Joe nor Helga is able to escape the usual racial categories by moving abroad. This is because they have now so internalized U.S. racial ideology that it continues to color the way they see themselves even beyond the nation's borders.

Joe seems to have experienced Mexico much as he did Oklahoma, Missouri, Chicago, Detroit, and Mississippi: as interchangeable sites along that same "street" he travels for fifteen years. As Leigh Anne Duck points out, towards the end of his life Joe reconfigures the metaphorical "street" of migration as "a circle," concluding resignedly that "I have never got outside that circle" (*LIA* 339). Joe has thus come to see himself as trapped within what Duck calls "a closed system in which he has intentionally moved from one racially demarcated neighborhood to another, consistently exploring his own body to see whether it conforms more fully to 'blackness' or 'whiteness' as he imagines them."[32] Joe's cognitive remapping of the street as "a circle . . . he is still inside of" occurs during his wagon ride into Mottstown (where he will be arrested for the murder of Joanna Burden) and is tellingly juxtaposed with a vivid depiction of how, even after fifteen years on the road, Joe still sees himself as essentially black: "'I have never broken out of the ring of what I have already done and cannot ever undo,' he thinks quietly, sitting on the seat, with planted on the dashboard before him the shoes, the black shoes smelling of negro: that mark on his ankles the gauge definite and ineradicable of the black tide creeping up his legs, moving from his feet upward as death moves" (*LIA* 339). Here we see how, for all his physical migrations, Joe remains mentally trapped within the "closed system" of U.S. racial classification. He "cannot ever undo" the racial identity imposed on him as an orphaned child; indeed, he has so thoroughly internalized it that he figures even one drop of "black blood" as a "black tide" marking his whole body and being as "black."

Given that Joe has so completely accepted U.S. racial categories, it is perhaps not surprising that he proved unwilling or unable to distinguish Mexico's social and racial structures from those he grew up with in the South. Yet Joe's incorporation of Mexico into his mental map of race as a predetermined, prisonlike "circle" contrasts with another passage from *Light in August* in which, Duck argues, other journeys "out of the U.S. Southeast into Spanish America" suggest that "race is constructed differently in different places."[33] These journeys are undertaken by Joanna Burden's grandfather Calvin and father, Nathaniel. Nathaniel lives in "Old Mexico" (*LIA* 243) itself for some time around 1863; three years later he married a Mexican woman, Juana (Joanna's namesake), with whom he already had a child, Calvin (Joanna's half-brother).

The Burden family history of mixed or *mestizo* identity enables further comparative reflection on Joe's biracial and transnational subjectivity. For example, old Calvin Burden defines his own half-Mexican grandson and namesake as a "damn black Burden" while Nathaniel "listened quietly, not even attempting to tell his father that the woman was Spanish" (*LIA* 247). This anticipates Eupheus Hines's fervent conviction that *his* grandson is "black," despite his daughter's insistence that Joe's father was "Mexican." Put simply, both Calvin Burden and Doc Hines try to make partly Hispanic family members conform to the rigid black-white binaries of U.S. racial classification.[34] Neither the younger Calvin Burden nor Joe Christmas would be defined in this way in Mexico. In *Who Is Black?* F. James Davis notes that during the Spanish colonization of Mexico "there was massive miscegenation between the Spanish and the Indian populations, and some that involved African blacks." While Spanish colonial policy ranked Mexicans in racial categories, it did not define any individual with "Negro" parentage or ancestry as fundamentally "Negro" himself, as per the practice in the United States.[35] In Mexico, then, Joe Christmas would not be defined as black. Joe, however, seems to have been unaware of this—or unable to accept it—during his sojourn south of the border. By a grim irony, Joe has inherited from his grandfather—if nothing else—the U.S. Southern model of racial classification based on the one-drop rule. As Duck puts it, "Joe, like his grandfather, encounters Mexicans without recognizing that they configure race differently from U.S. southerners."[36]

Already on the Atlantic crossing between New York and Copenhagen, it becomes apparent that Danes will configure race differently from the Americans (whites and blacks, northerners and southerners) whom Helga Crane has known. On her first evening aboard the ship taking her to Denmark, Helga is invited to dine with the "purser, a man grown old in the service of the Scandinavian-American Line, [who] remembered her as the little dark girl who had crossed with her mother years ago." The purser's insistence that Helga "must sit at his table" (*QS* 65) contrasts with scenes of white and black resistance in the U.S. to such easy socializing between a "Negro" woman and a white man.[37] Thus we begin to see how Larsen, like Faulkner, uses the novel's transnational turn to develop an "argument against American modes of racial classification."[38]

Throughout the Copenhagen section of *Quicksand*, there are, as Hutchinson remarks, "many instances in which Larsen dramatizes the differences between Danish and American perceptions of racial identity."[39] I will cite one more example here that demonstrates just how much Helga herself remains mired in U.S. racial thinking. During one of her strolls through Copenhagen, Helga encounters a fishwife in the market at Gammelstrand who "asked her to what manner of mankind she belonged." When Helga responds, "'I'm a Negro,'" the old fishwife "become[s] indignant, retorting angrily that, just because she was old and a countrywoman she could not be so easily fooled, for she knew as well as everyone else that Negroes were black and had woolly hair" (*QS* 78). The Danish fishwife's perception of "Negroes" may be comically crude, but she shifts from friendliness to fury with good reason: she perceives that Helga's self-identification is questionable. By telling the fishwife that she is "a Negro," Helga reveals her inability to abandon U.S. racial categories, claim the Danish "birthright" she has been seeking in Copenhagen, and affirm a *bi*racial and *trans*national subjectivity.

Helga Crane's experiences in Copenhagen thus intone the transnational geographies of migration and racial classification that Faulkner traces in *Light in August*. On one hand, Larsen, like Faulkner, uses the foreign setting to suggest that U.S. racial categories are not universal, but rather culturally specific and intensely ideological. On the other hand, the narrative demonstrates that, like Joe Christmas, Helga Crane has so thoroughly internalized U.S. racial definitions—especially her own status as "Negro"—that she cannot entertain an alternative conception of "race."

If Joe and Helga's childhoods in the South—Joe in the Memphis institution, Helga at the black school in Nashville—revolved around the racial politics of orphanhood, their adult returns to the South are marked by the racial politics of marriage and parenthood. On the outskirts of Jefferson, Joe becomes involved in a relationship with a white woman, Joanna Burden. Again, Joe seems poised to transgress the law of the color line. But when Joanna begins "discussing children" (*LIA* 264) and Joe perceives that "*[s]he wants to be married*," he says "No at once." Joe reckons that marriage and procreation with Joanna "will deny all the thirty years that I have lived to make me what I chose to be" (*LIA* 265). Yet as we have seen, Joe has never been able to decisively choose his identity because he has long since acceded to the notion that a drop of "black blood" determines his whole being. Joe cannot accept the possibility of having a child with Joanna because it would reproduce his racial anxieties—and his supposed "black blood"—all over again. Joe's adherence to the one-drop rule is seconded by Joanna herself. For all her locally notorious Yankee heritage, Joanna accords with Southern racial ideology by abstracting Joe as "Negro! Negro! Negro!" (*LIA* 260). Evidently Joanna has learned no more from the story of her family's mixed Mexican/

American lineage than Joe does.[40] Even Joanna's charitable plan to send Joe to a black school in the South (*LIA* 276) recalls Peter Nilssen firmly classifying Helga by sending her to "a school for Negroes" in Nashville.

Joe's repudiation of marriage and parenthood across the color line is reminiscent of Helga's striking stance against miscegenation during her time in Denmark. Helga tells her aunt, Katrina Dahl, that "there's nobody here for me to marry," by which she means that there are no black men; Helga explicitly clarifies that "'she didn't . . . believe in mixed marriages, 'between races, you know'" (*QS* 80). When the Danish painter Axel Olsen asks Helga to marry him, Helga responds that "I couldn't marry a white man. I simply couldn't. It isn't just you, not just personal, you understand. It's deeper, broader than that. It's racial" (*SQ* 90). As non-Americans, neither Dahl nor Olsen can comprehend Helga's "racial" rationale; as Olsen puts it, "I have offered you marriage, Helga Crane, and you answer me with some strange talk of race and shame. What nonsense is this?" (*QS* 90). Dahl and Olsen do not understand that for Helga, as for Joe Christmas, the idea of an interracial marriage and procreation is inextricable from a fraught "personal" history that is imbricated with a national "racial" ideology.

Helga's racialized position on marriage and parenthood reaches its logical conclusion when she returns to the U.S. South via New York. In Copenhagen, Helga again begins to long for and identify herself with "Negroes," even empathizing for the first time ever with her father's "facile surrender to the irresistible ties of race" (*QS* 94). Though Helga's neofamilial sense of reconnection to Harlem's "dark-eyed brown folk . . . her people" (*QS* 97) is damaged after her romantic rejection by Robert Anderson, Helga's reclamation of a decisively black identity is effected through her marriage to an Alabama preacher, Pleasant Green, and a return to the rural South. Helga now embraces—at least initially—the possibility of parenthood because Reverend Green, unlike Olsen, is black. Gradually, however, Helga realizes that her own "facile surrender to the irresistible ties of race"—more specifically, to a highly romanticized black Southern folk identity—has meant repressing once again her biracial and transnational heritage. Moreover, Helga's final desperate embrace of a singular "black" identity accords with the way U.S. society has always wanted to define her. This is expressed in a variation on the novel's titular metaphor as Helga belatedly perceives "the quagmire in which she had engulfed herself" (*QS* 134).

Ultimately, both Joe Christmas and Helga Crane make a final, doomed return to the South because they have finally accepted an identity as "Negro." There is a certain grim logic in these final southward migrations given that the South was the original site of that national system of racial classification that has repeatedly defined them as "black." But perhaps the grimmest tragedy is that both Joe and Helga have internalized that definition. In case there is any doubt, I should make clear that I am not critiquing Joe and Helga's fluctuating identification, at different points in their lives, with the quotidian reality of black Southern culture. Rather, I am arguing that Joe and Helga have accepted and recapitulated a nationalized narrative of "race" that defines them as "Negro" at the expense of their hybrid and transnational family histories.

It is bleakly ironic that when Joe is finally captured in Mottstown, white Southerners still cannot make him fit their binary model of racial identity: "He never acted like either a nigger or a white man. . . . That was what made the folks so mad" (*LIA* 350). For however threatening Joe's ambiguous racial identity might yet remain to others, Joe himself has finally and fully accepted his status as "black." Joe has—to quote Joanna Burden in another context—learned "to understand that a man would have to act as the land where he was born had trained him to act" (*LIA* 255). In rural Alabama, Helga yet retains a residual desire for an alternative existence, and dreams of one last migratory escape. It is too late, however: Helga and her ever-expanding family will remain "all black together" (*QS* 136) in the South. At the end of *Quicksand* Helga is, as Thadious Davis remarks, "symbolically dead."[41] Meanwhile, Joe Christmas is murdered by Percy Grimm in a ritual that ensures that, as Davis puts it, "his ultimate racial classification is . . . as a black person."[42] Joe's own acceptance of a black identity may be more resigned and complete than Helga's, but his sense of submitting to the one-drop rule is expressed in a metaphor strikingly similar to the quicksand or "quagmire" of racial classification that has "ruined [Helga's] life" (*QS* 134): "It seemed to him that he could see himself being hunted by white men at last into the black abyss which had been waiting, trying, for thirty years to drown him" (*LIA* 331). Joe's eschatological vision supports Edouard Glissant's claim that throughout Faulkner's fiction the South's "refusal of Creolization" leads to "the abyss."[43] In the fractured chronology of *Light in August*, Joe first associates black Southern life with the "abyss" during his previously discussed brief encounter with Freedman's Town (*LIA* 116). Joe first imagines *himself* "like a man being sucked down into a bottomless morass" during the final phase of his fraught relationship with Joanna. Though this metaphor strongly suggests Joe's gynophobic terror that he will be emasculated/castrated by Joanna's vagina, it is also significant that it comes only one paragraph (but "six months") after Joanna has started abstracting him as "Negro! Negro! Negro!" (*LIA* 260). Even before Joanna's death, then, Joe has begun to figure (Joanna's conformity to) the regional-national system of racial classification as a "black abyss"

(*LIA* 261) in a way that resembles Helga's conception of that same system as a "quicksand" or "quagmire" to which Helga, too, has conformed.

My insistence throughout this essay that Joe internalizes regional cum national racial categories may seem pessimistic to readers persuaded by critical readings of *Light in August* that emphasize those moments where Joe seems to subvert racial binaries or destabilize white Southern attempts to fix him as "black." But part of my aim in juxtaposing *Light in August* with *Quicksand* has been to amplify just how thoroughly Faulkner, like Larsen, critiques American modes of racial classification. Both writers demonstrate just how pervasively and perniciously racial categories inform the lives and thoughts of so many Americans—whites and blacks, Southerners and Northerners, as well as "rootless" hybrid individuals like Joe Christmas and Helga Crane. This analytic thoroughness does generate a fairly grim assessment of the role of race in U.S. society. Still, by sending Joe abroad, Faulkner joins Larsen in suggesting that "one nation's definition" of racial identity between the 1890s and the late 1920s is neither natural nor universal. And though neither Joe nor Helga can fully "imagine an identity that is not defined by blackness and whiteness," their stories dramatize how and why such rigid binary definitions of identity represent a collective—indeed, *national*—failure of imagination.[44] In doing so, *Light in August* and *Quicksand* compel readers to start thinking against and beyond race.[45]

NOTES

1. Patricia Yaeger, *Dirt and Desire: Reconstructing Southern Women's Writing, 1930–1990* (Chicago: Chicago University Press, 2000), 51.

2. Alfred Kazin, "The Stillness of *Light in August*," in Frederick J. Hoffman and Olga W. Vickery, eds., *William Faulkner: Three Decades of Criticism* (New York: Harbinger, 1963), 247–64.

3. Leigh Anne Duck, "Race, Labor, and Hispanic Migration in *Light in August*," in Beatriz Vegh and Eleonora Basso, eds., *William Faulkner y el mundo hispànico: diàlogos desde el otro Sur* (Montevideo: Linardi y Risso, 2009), 57–69. My thanks to Leigh Anne Duck for providing me with a manuscript copy of her essay. All citations are from the English manuscript, 9.

4. Joanna Davis-McElligatt, "Race, Nation, Miscegenation: William Faulkner's *Light in August* and Fear of Blacks and Immigrants in the Postwar Era," conference paper presented at the biannual conference of the Society for the Study of Southern Literature, College of William and Mary, Williamsburg, Virginia, 19 April 2008. My thanks to Joanna Davis-McElligatt for providing me with a manuscript copy of her paper.

5. Davis-McElligatt, "Race, Nation, Miscegenation," manuscript.

6. Duck, "Race, Labor, and Hispanic Migration," manuscript, 2.

7. F. James Davis, *Who Is Black? One Nation's Definition* (Pennsylvania: Pennsylvania University Press, 1991), 5.

8. Duck, "Race, Labor, and Hispanic Migration," manuscript, 1.

9. George Hutchinson, "Nella Larsen and the Veil of Race," *American Literary History* 9 (Summer 1997): 345. In the mid-1990s Hutchinson uncovered the first definite proof that Larsen traveled to Denmark at least twice during her youth (in 1898 and 1909).

10. Jessica Wegmann-Sánchez, "Rewriting Race and Ethnicity across the Border: Mairuth Sarsfield's *No Crystal Chair* and Nella Larsen's *Quicksand* and *Passing*," *Essays on Canadian Writing* 74 (Fall 2001): 136.

11. Roland Barthes, "The Death of the Author," in Seán Burke, ed., *Authorship: From Plato to the Postmodern* (Edinburgh: Edinburgh University Press, 1995), 128.

12. Anna Brickhouse, "Nella Larsen and the Intertextual Geography of *Quicksand*," *African American Review* 35 (Winter 2001): 535.

13. Davis-McElligatt, "Race, Nation, Miscegenation," manuscript; George Hutchinson, *In Search of Nella Larsen: A Biography of the Color Line* (Cambridge: Belknap Press of Harvard University Press, 2006), 69. Hutchinson qualifies, however, that "Larsen's physical descriptions of [Copenhagen] pertain to an earlier decade," suggesting that she had "fairly extensive experience" of Copenhagen during her youth.

14. Nella Larsen, *Quicksand* (1928), ed. and intro. Thadious M. Davis (New York: Penguin Classics, 2002), 5. All further references to *Quicksand* are to this edition and will be cited parenthetically in the main text with the abbreviation *QS*.

15. Davis, *Who Is Black?*, 8.

16. Hutchinson, *In Search of Nella Larsen*, 29.

17. Ibid., 29; Davis-McElligatt, "Race, Nation, Miscegenation," manuscript.

18. F. James Davis, *Who Is Black?*, 54. It was also during this period (1890–1920) that the U.S. Census honed and narrowed its definition of "black" in accordance with the one-drop rule. Finally "in 1920 the mulatto category was dropped, and black was defined to mean any person with any black ancestry" (12).

19. William Faulkner, *Light in August* (1932; New York: Vintage International, 1990), 374. All further references to *Light in August* are to this edition and will be cited parenthetically in the main text with the abbreviation *LIA*.

20. This scene exemplifies what Edouard Glissant identifies as a pattern of "deferred revelation" in Faulkner's work: "an accumulating mystery and a whirling vertigo—gathering momentum rather than being resolved, through deferral and disclosure—and centered in a place to which he felt a need to give meaning." Knowledge of Joe's paternity and "race" remains deferred even as it is revealed: though Mrs. Hines tells about Joe's father, readers (like the Hines family) still "never kn[o]w for certain" the man's racial identity and, by extension, whether or not Joe himself is "black." Yet this ambiguity only compounds the accumulation of "meaning" around Joe's racial identity. See Edouard Glissant, *Faulkner, Mississippi* (1996), trans. Barbara Lewis and Thomas C. Spear (Chicago: University of Chicago Press, 1999), 9.

I qualify that Joe *perhaps* never learns about his father's parentage because, as Davis-McElligatt helpfully points out, Mrs. Hines visits Joe in the Mottstown jail shortly before his escape and murder by Percy Grimm. Though readers are not "privy to their conversation," it seems likely that Mrs. Hines informs Joe of his family history during this encounter (Davis-McElligatt, personal communication with the author, 24 July 2008). However, Joe's racial identity would remain deferred even if Mrs. Hines revealed his parentage to him.

21. Hutchinson, *In Search of Nella Larsen*, 30.

22. Ibid., 28.

23. In *Who Is Black?* F. James Davis emphasizes that biracial individuals with "no family connections" could be ostracized by "the black community." Using singer Lena Horne as a case study, Davis notes that "when satisfactory evidence of respectable black parents is lacking, being light-skinned implies illegitimacy and having an underclass white parent and is thus a disgrace in the black community" (3).

24. Donald M. Kartiganer, *The Fragile Thread: The Meaning of Form in Faulkner's Novels* (Amherst: University of Massachusetts Press, 1979), 45. That Joe *"don't look like one,"* as Max's accomplice puts it, demonstrates both the heightened importance and fundamental absurdity of ideas of racial "blood" underpinning the one-drop rule. That Joe is not visibly "black" generates the desperate need to *"see if his blood is black"* (*LIA*, 219). Jay Watson has argued persuasively that *Light in August* repeatedly foregrounds "the literal and material fact of blood"—especially violent assaults on bodies that cause bleeding—in order to interrogate the metaphor of "black blood": "By repeatedly bringing blood to the surface of the human body, cutting in *Light in August* mobilizes the power of literal meaning and the natural world as a rejoinder to the discursive system that puts 'blood' in service of racial exploitation and violence." See Watson, "Writing Blood: The Art of the Literal in *Light in August*," in Donald M. Kartiganer, ed., *Faulkner and the Natural World: Faulkner and Yoknapatawpha, 1996* (Jackson: University Press of Mississippi, 1999), 87, 69.

25. Thadious M. Davis, *Faulkner's "Negro": Art and the Southern Context* (Baton Rouge: Louisiana State University Press, 1983), 135.

26. John T. Matthews, "This Race Which Is Not One: The 'More Inextricable Compositeness' of William Faulkner's South," in Jon Smith and Deborah Cohn, eds., *Look Away! The U.S. South and New World Studies* (Durham: Duke University Press, 2004), 206.

27. Hutchinson, *In Search of Nella Larsen*, 229.

28. Davis, *Who Is Black?*, 58.

29. Wegmann-Sánchez, "Rewriting Race and Ethnicity Across the Border," 143.

30. Thadious M. Davis, *Nella Larsen: Novelist of the Harlem Renaissance: A Woman's Life Unveiled* (Baton Rouge: Louisiana State University Press, 1994), 253.

31. It is one of the subtler ironies of the novel that Joe is better able to pass as white than as black, despite his underlying conviction that really he is black.

32. Duck, "Race, Labor, and Hispanic Migration," manuscript, 10.

33. Ibid., manuscript, 2,

34. Duck qualifies, however, that Calvin Burden and Doc Hines "ultimately configure race very differently—the latter suggesting that ideas of race and blood may reflect individual passions" (4). She also notes that the Burden family narrative, with its multiple encounters in the contact zone between the U.S. South and Mexico, depicts an "engagement with alternate constructions of identity [that] contrasts sharply with Doc Hines' conviction"—deriving from his static rootedness in Mississippi—"that there is no possibility of a Mexican identity" (6). Duck, "Race, Labor, and Hispanic Migration," manuscript.

35. Davis, *Who Is Black?*, 88.

36. Duck, "Race, Labor, and Hispanic Migration," manuscript, 10. See also Matthews's wry observation that, even if Joe's father was "part Negro," this "does not rule out being Mexican" too ("This Race Which Is One," 215–16).

37. White resistance to the social mixing of blacks and whites is dramatized in Helga's Jim Crow train journey from Naxos to Chicago (*QS* 28); black resistance to such social mixing is memorably personified in Anne Grey's rant against Audrey Denney "giv[ing] parties for white and colored people together. . . . It's worse than disgusting, it's positively obscene" (*QS* 62–63).

38. The scene intones Larsen's own experience on the S.S. *C. F. Tietgen*, the ship that carried her back from Copenhagen to New York in 1909. Though Larsen's nationality was listed in the ship manifest as "American," "the ship's surgeon, Dr. C. A. Larsen, identified her 'race or people' as 'Scandinavian,' despite explicit instructions that anyone with a visible 'admixture of Negro blood' was to be listed as 'African' (black)." Hutchinson suggests that Dr. Larsen "felt that identifying Larsen as African was absurd" (*In Search of Nella Larsen*, 66). In *Quicksand*, the purser's refusal to define Helga by her visibly "dark" skin similarly throws into relief the absurdity of U.S. racial categories.

39. Hutchinson, *In Search of Nella Larsen*, 70.

40. See also Davis, *Faulkner's "Negro,"* 137, and Kartiganer, *The Fragile Thread*, 55, on how (as Kartiganer puts it) "Joanna must now nail Joe down as Negro."

41. Davis, *Nella Larsen*, 271.

42. Davis, *Faulkner's "Negro,"* 167.

43. Glissant, *Faulkner, Mississippi*, 98. It is noteworthy that Joe's nemesis Percy Grimm is described as having "been for a long time in a swamp in the dark" until his emergent "belief that the white race is superior to any and all other races" provides him with a cast-iron conviction that is expressed through another spatial metaphor: "He could now see his life opening before him, uncomplex and inescapable as a barren corridor" (*LIA* 450–51). Grimm's racialized uplift from "dark" swamp to the "bright" (*LIA* 451) corridor of white supremacy inverts and is premised upon Joe's descent from the circular "street" into the "black abyss" of racial classification that finally defines and destroys him.

44. Duck, "Race, Labor, and Hispanic Migration," manuscript, 9.

45. Reading my argument about *Light in August* in conjunction with Ted Atkinson's essay on *Go Down, Moses* elsewhere in this volume, one might plausibly argue that Faulkner subsequently extended his criticism of U.S. racial classifications by depicting Lucas Beauchamp as a "black" character who is more successful than Joe Christmas in "def[ying] the rigid categories of racial difference imposed on him." Moreover, Lucas's words and actions go beyond Joe's in generating a profound and *ongoing* "anxiety of whiteness" among white Southerners. Atkinson argues persuasively that "Faulkner's representation of race is more probing" than that of other white American writers "because of his willingness . . . to move beyond the reductive imagery of juxtaposition into the gray areas of ambiguity that call into question the integrity of the black/white racial code and . . . expose whiteness to the light of critical scrutiny." See Atkinson, "The Impenetrable Lightness of Being: Miscegenation Imagery and the Anxiety of Whiteness in *Go Down, Moses*," in this volume.

"I Sees De Light, En I Sees De Word": Black Female Transcendence of Racial and Gendered Boundaries in *The Sound and the Fury* and "That Evening Sun"

ETHEL YOUNG-MINOR

Personally, I respect genius, and I respect sincerity. I believe Mr. Faulkner is an excellent writer and a sincere citizen. He is not a political demagogue talking for votes. So when he says what he says, he really means what he says. But WHY he says what he says is not clear.

—*Langston Hughes*[1]

Langston Hughes's 1956 comment that it is difficult to clarify why William Faulkner "says what he says" about race continues to ring true; in spite of Noel Polk's pronouncement that the majority of Faulkner's canon is comprised of works that are not specifically about race, Faulkner's portrayals of African American characters and culture generate energetic and contentious textual debates among historians and literary critics.[2] While we will never definitively answer "why" any writer constructs particular characters and content, examining Faulkner's racial discourse in the first half of the twentieth century can yield new and meaningful ways of understanding how some white Southerners grappled with the changing positioning of African Americans. Thadious Davis asserts that "Faulkner (born September 25, 1897) never knew or wrote about 'black' people as we today know and understand the term. He wrote about 'the Negro,' the white man's own creation."[3] Reading in Faulkner's fiction his attempts to discuss race at a time when Southern notions of race were rapidly changing, we can see that Faulkner does more than capture an imperialist vision of "the negro"; his fiction provides arresting insights into how one white, male citizen-writer used his artistic vision to navigate an intricate web of racial ideologies that permeated the South that he knew. Examining his characterizations of race in this vein can help us move beyond simple discussions of what he does, and into the complex motivations of *why* this writer would spend so much time grappling in his fiction with confrontations between Southern whites and "the negro."

More specifically, close examination of the narrative movements of Faulkner's "negro" women within the world of Yoknapatawpha opens up our ability to understand how Faulkner attempts to empower black women in his fictive world. Surprisingly, one can even read "the negro women" of his fiction as women who are cocreators or agents in constructing Southern belief systems. This empowerment of the black Southern woman who is trapped inside the cultural modes of the South is especially important because many fiction writers in the first half of the twentieth century thought that the most important examinations of black women were those placed in urban-progressive contexts. Even Elise Johnson McDougald, a prominent African American sociologist and teacher of the Harlem Renaissance whose "Double Task of Negro Womanhood" provides one of the most complex discussions of black womanhood to appear in the nonblack press in her discipline, suggests that the best indicator of black female progress was to be found by examining black women in the city. McDougald proclaims that "from grace to strength, they [black women] vary in infinite degree, with traces of the race's history left in physical and mental outline on each."[4] Faulkner attempts to give voice to how this racial history outlines the physical and mental characteristics of black rural women as he contemplates the thoughts and feelings of black women who had the opportunity to leave for the urban North, but decided to remain in the South and fill subservient positions in the white South as he knew it. Faulkner moves beyond the work of his well-meaning contemporaries who often described black mammies as loyal and simple subjects, happy to attend to the needs of maintaining the South's oppressive social order. Instead, Faulkner manipulates stereotypical images of blacks in the kitchen and in the church. In doing so, he develops characters that emerge, in the words of Craig Werner, "capable of deconstructing the binary oppositions on which racial privilege depends."[5] As "negroes" Faulkner's characters often participate in the cultural practices that white people associate with "blackness"; however, instead of being bound up in these practices, these characters often choose to engage in practices that privilege liminality that allows them to temporarily escape the trappings of race. In this essay, I will examine how black cultural practices activate a sense of empowerment for two black female characters: Dilsey in *The Sound and the Fury* and Nancy in "That Evening Sun." As both characters engage in cultural practices, they are able find ways to transcend white limitations for "the negro" and successfully maneuver the cultural tools that will help them determine the course of their own black narratives.

Assessing states of liminality can have vital implications for the transformation of culture in the development of national literature. Victor

Turner identified liminal states in cultural rites of passages as "a period of special and dangerous power, which had to be constrained and channeled to protect the social order."[6] But, liminality can do more than maintain social order—as Homi Bhabha argues in *The Location of Culture*—it can also be a powerful state for helping oppressed cultures move beyond the boundaries of identity that their oppressors have used to contain and control them.[7] When we turn to the life and legacy of William Faulkner, his contemplations of race and region consistently explore liminality— or the inclusion of dual ideology—as a method of advancing his narrative concerns. In both his personal life, and in the life of his characters, Faulkner promotes the power and validity of ideas that are generally discussed by others in oppositional terms. This can be seen in many of his personal sociopolitical statements. For example, when one interviewer asked how he would want his grandson, as an inheritor of the Southern legacy, to treat his regional heritage, Faulkner said, "I hope of course that he will cope with his environment as it changes. And, I hope that his mother and father will try to raise him without bigotry as much as can be done. He can have a Confederate battleflag if he wants it but he shouldn't take it too seriously.'"[8] His argument that one can preserve the symbols of the Old South tradition, without assigning power to such symbols, is evidence of a liminal position: people generally preserve a cultural object because it wields some form of power. The symbol is kept and displayed because they do, in fact, "take it seriously."

Faulkner's ability to ride the liminal line between criticizing and affirming markers of the "Old South" comes to life in *The Sound and the Fury* (1929), as he calls attention to dual realities of race, region, and religion.[9] John C. Hoffman argues that "literature can use liminal figures from history or pure fiction as instruments to subvert the social order."[10] In Faulkner, dualities allow notions of social order in the U.S. South to be both inscribed and subverted. As we look at the dualities in *The Sound and the Fury*, we see Faulkner's engagement with historical and fictional liminalities that offer one "negro" woman a small window of dangerous power through which she may be able to move beyond the racist constraints of Yoknapatawpha. My reading of the dualities of the novel complement interpretations initiated in Thadious Davis's *Faulkner's "Negro,"* where she considers racial binaries in the development of Dilsey's character. I offer, as a complimentary piece, a discussion that considers this split as a positive rather than negative quality. In Davis's readings the novel ends unsatisfactorily for Dilsey: "Black life remains a foil to emptiness, the loss of value and meaning, in white southern life" (126). While I concur that blackness remains devoid of real meaning for most members of the white community that Faulkner crafts in *The Sound and the Fury*,

I believe that by the end of the novel Dilsey is able to create her own definitions of blackness. As the novel progresses, Dilsey has the opportunity to define herself within a number of contexts, and through each contact she gains a better understanding of her power to become an agent of change in her community. Even though Dilsey's status in the community does not shift in the course of the narrative, I do believe that she gains a clearer sense of self and more desire to speak back to oppressive forces. While Dilsey's split reality enables her spiritual and material survival in Yoknapatawpha, and helps her to support her family, it is not until after Reverend Shegog's sermon that she gains the intellectual power and transcendental experience necessary to use liminality as an agent of change.

When asked about the symbolism of setting the narrative in April 1928, Faulkner denies any real symbolic meaning of the dates: "I'm sure it was quite instinctive that I picked out Easter, that I wasn't writing any symbolism of the Passion Week at all. I just—that was a tool that was good for the particular corner I was going to turn in my chicken house and so I used it."[11] Even so, setting the narrative in the early days of April 1928 certainly places readers in the middle of a world filled with transitional moments and liminal states. The month of April is typically considered a liminal month, where one day presents weather reminiscent of winter and the next day has the conditions of spring. T. S. Eliot captures April's multiplicities in "The Burial of the Dead" where he declares: "April is the cruelest month, breeding / Lilacs out of the dead land, mixing / Memory and desire, stirring / Dull roots with spring rain."[12] The Compson family's story is riddled with examples of how the month of April brings awareness of how such "breeding," "mixing," and "stirring" have complicated their understandings of race, religion, and regional identity. Caddy's "breeding" outside the Southern social norm of marriage causes the family so much shame that Quentin commits suicide, Jason is haunted by his need to continually control and punish Caddy, and Mrs. Compson is overly concerned with controlling her offspring. The "mixing" of black/white realities at work and home blurs distinctions of authority and power so much that Dilsey, who serves in a domestic position often considered void of power, ultimately becomes the center of power and stability in the family. Jason is also pulled between urban and rural realities when trying to understand his value or worth in the community: the novel calls attention to the tension between the assessment of the value of cotton by members of the New York stock exchange and own visual assessment of the landscape; this dynamic keeps him on a pendulum that swings between trusting the scientific/economic predictors of his future, or the more immediate markers available in his home community.

In addition to the month of April resting in two distinct states of seasonal reality, in the year 1928 the state of Mississippi was also experiencing its own sociopolitical liminality as its citizens struggle to embrace its traditional past, while at the same time embracing ideologies and technologies that would secure a solid economic future. Blyden Jackson points to the significance of evaluating the role of Mississippi as a backdrop for understanding Faulkner's texts in his warning that "it is anything but an environmental fallacy to attribute to Faulkner . . . a decided impact from Mississippi of his youth."[13] Faulkner's Mississippi was in a state of flux and many members of the community struggled with ways to adapt to change. As Theodore Bilbo assumed the governor's office in January 1928, he announced three significant changes he would like to see take place in the state: (1) moving the University of Mississippi from small Oxford to thriving Jackson, (2) establishing a state-owned printing plant for publishing school textbooks, and (3) selling $53,000,000 worth of state bonds to transform Mississippi muck into motor roads.[14] This third goal is the one that is of most import in understanding how the changing landscape of Mississippi impacted the cultures that Faulkner lived in and wrote about: the transformation of Mississippi muck into motor roads would provide more opportunities for communication and contact with people from different geographical areas. The state was attempting to recover from the 1927 flood with a 1928 statewide recovery plan supported by the federal government; as the state pursued recovery efforts, lawmakers were especially interested in the roadway as a tool for providing better access to more remote parts of the state and a step towards industrialism over agriculture. While many leaders in Mississippi argued for the need of mechanical progress, the slow and deliberate speed of many of these changes kept many citizens mired in the muck of their tradition and closed community. This need to embrace the past, while slowly awaiting the promise of the future, kept citizens swinging on a liminal pendulum between the values of the past and the values of the present. In May of 1928 George Coad of the *New York Times* described Mississippi's dual sociopolitical climate as one embracing progress, while still remaining trapped in the constrictions of the past. He says of Mississippi that many changes have been made: "An overt act has been committed; a legalized boxing match has been held. Baseball is played on Sunday in three towns on the coast and at Vicksburg on the Mississippi. Golf tournaments, schooner races and fishing are among the day's amusements." At the same time that he reports these radical and progressive shifts in ideology, Coad reminds his readers that in Mississippi, "viewing a film is still too sinful for the police to condone." He also calls attention to the duality of Mississippi by describing the polarities between the

North and the South. Coad says, "It is a notorious fact that the Gulf Coast does not carefully observe the laws of the State, and there are those who predict that it will observe ever fewer of the restrictions upon personal liberty in the future."[15]

Mississippi was also in a state of racial transformation in this era when African Americans reached new heights of nationhood and self-suffi-ciency in a region that sought to suppress these notions. In 1928 a frater-nal organization named Afro-American Sons and Daughters founded a hospital in Yazoo City, Mississippi, that was reported to have some of the best healthcare available to blacks in the South.[16] Governor Bilbo cre-ated a stir by accusing Herbert Hoover of dancing with a "negro woman" in Mound Bayou during his visit to Mississippi. All of these movements background Faulkner's conception of race and region and help us to bet-ter understand the world that Faulkner invites readers to enter in *The Sound and the Fury*. The narrative calls upon notions of duality in the discussions of race and religion as a way of opening up ways for readers to grapple with the historical dualities alive in Mississippi in 1928. Faulkner realizes that in this world of changing racial ideologies, Dilsey has more opportunity to take control of her own narrative and her own destiny as a black woman in Mississippi than any black woman would have had in any previous generations. While Dilsey may not have been able to create real change in her life, she could have definitely been a transformative force for the generations to follow her. The image of senior African American women as the "midwives" of change in the first decades of the twentieth century is mirrored in texts written by African American authors contem-porary with Faulkner. Granny in Zora Neale Hurston's *Their Eyes Were Watching God* acknowledges her inability to teach the "great sermon from on high" that she aspired to preach; so, she chooses as an alternative to "build a pulpit" for her granddaughter to preach from. In Langston Hughes's poem "Mother to Son" a mother tells her son that life has dark places and difficult terrain, but he is not allowed to sit down because "he finds it kind er hard." Rudolph Fisher's "Madjuta and Learnin" features parents who migrated out of the South to provide opportunities for their offspring; though they often have little chance for change for themselves, their offspring are expected to bring the change into being.

In order for Dilsey to advance, though, she needs a teacher to guide her to discover the power of her own duality in order to take control of her destiny. Faulkner brings Dilsey's teacher to church in the body of Reverend Shegog. Reverend Shegog's Easter sermon in *The Sound and the Fury* provides an interesting key to Faulkner's understanding of the power of liminality as a tool for religious and cultural transformation. The celebration of Easter stands as a celebration of dual positioning in religious traditions. When Christ rises on Easter morning he affirms his position as a liminal embodiment of both man and God. Reverend Shegog, the character who has been called upon to lead the congregants in the celebration, is a liminal member of the community that we have become acquainted with in the earlier chapters of the novel. He is both insider and outsider. He is an insider because he is an African American who, when examined visually, appears to have little power in his community. Jason continually derides Dilsey's appearance and treats her as if she has no power because in his eyes she is an "old half dead Nigger" (185); in the same way, the black community of Yoknapatawpha derides Shegog's "insignificant looking" appearance and assumes that he will have little power because he appears "dwarfed and countrified" when sitting next to the community minister. He is a participant in an institution long considered to be the center of African American life, but he is an outsider because he does not come from this area of the South. He is brought in from St. Louis, Missouri, a region of the country that enjoyed its own liminal status. At times the state identified with the West and at other times with the South. Christopher Phillips says that the people of Missouri held mixed feelings about their regional placement: even though "their culture might have derived largely from a slaveholding heritage . . . 'peculiar' to the South, Missourians still considered themselves and their state part of the West."[17] This border state, the place that Shegog travels from, signals his role as a person who stands between cultures. Because he comes from a landscape of interstitial positioning, he is able to "stand in between two worlds" of a community that was divided into two distinct worlds: the black world of Dilsey and the white world of he Compson family.

Because of Shegog's background, he can assume the preacherly role that David Hein describes: to bring church worshippers to a state where they stand in a "moment of *kairos*—of time out of time." Hein argues that in this moment "worshipers may experience the divine reality contemporaneously in meaning-filled past, ecstatic present, and blessed future."[18] In doing so, they will be able to occupy a liminal relationship with time; Shegog is only able to lead them to this space by embodying and displaying the ability of one who looks almost just like them but who moves beyond the limitations of how they appear on the surface. Shegog begins his movement into liminal spaces as soon as he assumes the roster. Rather than standing in one position to deliver his sermon, Shegog moves back and forth between the crumpled paper and the bell. The paper can be seen as a representation of man's attempt to immortalize words and time. The words are concretized for future generations to probe and explore, just as we continue to probe Faulkner's words many years after his own death. The bell, however, represents the movement of time and the mortality of all. The erection of church bells was important for Faulkner's contemporaries. In reading the history of one of the local churches captured in Martin Dain's *Faulkner's World*, Mt. Hope of Taylor, Mississippi, we find very few details about church repairs recorded. The historians, however, recorded the erection of a bell tower in the 1920s. According to the church records, the bell was used to signify the beginning of church services and the death of a member of the community.[19] So, Shegog's movement between the paper and bell moves him between the symbols of eternal life (paper) and death (bell) in the Old South.

The words of the sermon capture Shegog's ability to literally "stand in the gap" between two worlds. He uses the language of the educated *and* the uneducated to make sure that all classes of blacks are reached in his community. In the sermon, Shegog declares that he "sees the light" and he "sees the word." Shegog's ability to see both the light and the word signifies his ability to stand between two worlds: the natural and the supernatural. To see the light is to be able to see the supernatural presence of God's active work in humanity. Biblical narratives associate the Christian presence as that of light. Christians are told that Jesus is The Light, but they are the light of the world. Matthew 5:15 gives specific directions about how the light is to be treated once it is received: "Neither do men light a candle, and put it under a bushel, but on a candlestick; and it giveth light unto all that are in the house." Luke 1:78, 79: "Through the tender mercy of our God; whereby the dayspring from on high hath visited us, to give light to them that sit in darkness and [in] the shadow of death, to guide our feet into the way of peace." As the congregants share in Shegog's ability to see the light, they now have an obligation to take the power of that light into the world and guide the feet of the community members into pathways of peace.

Shegog takes the community of churchgoers on a supernatural ride with intellectual prescience. His ability to see the word signifies mastery of intellectual and material realms. The word represents intelligence, rational being, and civilization. Those who can manipulate words in the European tradition assume a locus of power in their community. Shegog knew the daunting task of black Americans in the South who reckoned with the racist signifiers that controlled their daily existence. But when the supernatural light is put into play alongside the traditions and symbols of the natural world, the community can make steps towards liberation. When we read of his ability to see the light and the word along with his recollection of the blood of the lamb we get to the root of power in Shegog's transformative sermon. The recollection signifies Shegog's awareness of the long march of history that has led his congregants to their present states; at the same time, the blood of the lamb is able to erase the power of the stifling past in determining their reality and provide them with the power to create a new future.

By standing between spaces, Shegog is able to escort Dilsey to new understandings of her own dual positioning as a member and servant to the Compson family. David Hein suggests that it is through Shegog's sermon that Dilsey "receives her orientation."[20] But to what is Dilsey becoming oriented? Hein joins legions of critics in suggesting that the Dilsey who exits the church after the Easter sermon will go on serving as a maid to the Compson family, understanding that while she is devalued in the daily narratives of the family, her work will have important value in the eternal narrative of the Bible. He believes that since Benjy is God's child, Dilsey will continue the work of assisting God in caring for this child/man who, too, lives in his own liminal world of being both adult and child. I want to suggest, however, that Dilsey's orientation is to a more radical worldview than most critics have given Faulkner credit for in their analyses of the closing strains of the text. Because she has watched Shegog, who appeared insignificant in his alpaca coat, gain power over his audience by seeing the light and the word, Dilsey understands the power of duality in transforming and transfixing community. After Shegog's sermon, Dilsey is able to examine her history critically and spiritually in a way described by Erskine Peters: "She may be a victim of the historical past and present; however, she is not tyrannized by them."[21] Dilsey is depicted as liminal throughout the narrative. At times she is part of the Compson family; at other times she is not even a part of the black family. At times she is able to order the actions of the Compson family; at other times they order her around. At the beginning of Dilsey's section even her dress embraces two worlds. Her "black straw hat" connects her to the American legacy of slavery and fieldwork in the South, while the "turban" she wears beneath the hat represents a connection to her African heritage. The "maroon velvet cape" and "dress of purple silk" signify the regality of her womanhood, while the "mangy and anonymous fur" reminds us that the regality has been altered by time and the beastlike desires of her oppressors. She does not understand the power of her duality, however, until Shegog's sermon models liberational pedagogy and orients her to seeing her world in new ways. It is only after Shegog announces his ability to see in dual realms—the word and the light—that Dilsey understands the inherent power of her cultural liminality; when she understands her own power, she leaves the church crying, yet "walking with her head up" (297). These tears are not tears of resignation to a horrible fate or grief; instead Dilsey's tears should be seen as the cleansing waters that wash away the dust from her eyes. These tears purge her visual spectrum of the old perspectives that inhibited her vision as a liminal community member. She now understands the power she has gained over the white community by observing the Compson family through the DuBosian veil of culture; to state it more precisely, Dilsey realizes that her service in the Compson household has served her in accumulating decades of knowledge that helps her see their twisted family values. In her words, "I've seed de first and de last. . . . I seed de beginning, en now I sees de endin" (297).

Dilsey is able to transcend oppression with a renewed vision of community, whereas the Compson family is still blinded and unable to see Dilsey as a human being who is valuable beyond the functional needs that they call upon her to carry out in their day-to-day lives. When she returns to the Compson household, she continues to function as a domestic, but in the last few pages of the novel she begins to show the stirrings of her new self. She picks up Miss Quentin's undergarment and stocking from the floor and places them in a closed drawer. Next, she visits Mrs. Compson's room and places her Bible on the bed as she is ordered to, but as she gives her the Bible, Dilsey says, "You can't see to read, noways" (300). Dilsey knows that she is able to see her reality differently because of Shegog's sermon. Because Mrs. Compson has not gained insight from any cultural seers, she will continue to operate in "the room in halflight" (299): Dilsey, however, is no longer trapped in the white narratives of black culture. Faulkner has taken her narrative as far as he is able to as a writer. Dilsey must write the next chapter of her life, without the lens of whiteness that has accompanied, if not imprisoned, black narratives in America since the slave narrative. Because of Shegog's liberatory sermon, she is well-equipped to see, define, and control the parameters of this new narrative.

In one of the novel's visions of Dilsey, she sets the table for a new kind of relationship across racial lines when she tells the white man (Benjy) and the black man (Luster), "Ya'll kin g'awn en eat. . . . Jason aint comin home" (301). After dinner, she connects their destinies even more intricately by sending them on a tour of the graveyard alone. Unfortunately, neither Luster nor Benjy has been equipped to see their connections to one another, so they are irresponsible with the power. Even though they were both in church with Dilsey, they did not experience the same transcendence as Dilsey did through the sermon. Luster is still abusive and trying to grasp power through violent means, as he hurls antagonizing words at Benjy and beats the horse with a switch. Benjy, too, remains static as he continues to moan for Caddy.

Only after Jason returns from his journey in search of Quentin and his treasure, his perceptions are altered; even though he was looking for his money, the signs tell him to keep his eye on Mottson. In this new territory, Jason must reevaluate his vision of blackness. The Negroes Jason attempts to order around in the next town know the value of their labor and refuse to reduce their value simply because Jason wants to haggle with them. When Jason tells a black driver to take him home to Jefferson for two dollars, the nameless man replies, "cant go fer no less'n fo. . . . You want me er not?" Jason acquiesces and the "negro took the wheel," both literally and figuratively. He has to submit to the will and direction of a black man to find his way home. Jason's abuse and assertion of power over Luster and Benjy have little real value at the end of the narrative. This beating is full of "sound and fury," but we know that it means nothing because Luster and Benjy are both considered "boys" in the community. Jason is reduced to controlling the lives of people who have no power. He could not control the black men that he met beyond the boundaries of Jefferson, and we suspect that he will no longer control Dilsey with the same force that he did before her Easter transformation.

The Compson family's continued blindness when it comes to the diversity of black culture is carried on in the short story "That Evening Sun."[22] This 1931 narrative opens new understandings of how critically nuanced liminality can provide Nancy with a new vision of her own power. Just as Dilsey is developed through dualities, Nancy is also a character who continually embodies polarized cultural norms. She is both a wife to her black husband, Jesus, and whore to local white men. She is a servant and free—she only serves as a maid for the Compson family as Dilsey's relief. Robert Slabey even argues that we should view Nancy as a mulatto character who is neither black nor white.[23] In this world of dualities, Nancy is like the "warm and golden brown" protagonist in Langston Hughes's poem "Ruby Brown," who works in the white people's kitchen until she asks herself one day, "what can a colored girl do on the money from a white woman's kitchen?" Evidently the answer is very little, because Ruby Brown turns to prostitution and by the end of the poem the white men "pay more money to her now / than they ever did before, / when she worked in their kitchens."[24] Nancy also embodies the strains of both blues and religion. She is linked to the blues in that she, like W. C. Handy, hates to see the evening sun go down. She is linked to religion in that her use of language imitates the tremor of the traditional black preacher as her speech rests between talking and singing. Even though Nancy has inherent power, it is untapped because she continues to block her own progress by repeating the phrase, "I aint nothing but a nigger" (87). She uses this language to absolve herself of any responsibility in the creation of her current predicament. She defines herself as a figment of the white man's imagination, until, through a series of events in the narrative, Nancy finally realizes that the Compson family cannot see her. This revelation seems to come during the four-year-old Jason's questioning of what it means to be "a nigger." Jason provides three lines about whom he sees as a nigger. Jason says in succession "Jesus is a nigger" "Dilsey's a nigger too," and "I aint a nigger" (87).

Although Jason's utterance that "Jesus is a nigger" is certainly a reference to Nancy's absent husband, it is also a sermonic text that aligns Nancy's religious God with a new sense of shared culture. Jesus, who commands power over the darkness of sin that marks the Compson landscape, is also a nigger. This declarative statement reminds us that perhaps the textual visions of race and religion in the United States captured in the writings of Langston Hughes and William Faulkner were more similar than we might initially imagine. Jason's assertion that "Jesus is a nigger" parallels the narrator's proclamations in Langston Hughes's 1931 poem "Christ in Alabama":

> Christ is a Nigger,
> Beaten and black—
> *O, bare your back.*
>
> Mary His Mother
> Mammy of the South,
> *Silence Your Mouth*

Jason's statement catalyzes Nancy's understanding that she can relate to the supernatural. The rest of the story shows her grappling with ways to exercise this power. She attempts to gain power and safety in the Compson home until Mrs. Compson is fed up with her. She then seeks refuge in the company of the Compson children, bringing them to her home and hoping that they will save her. Eventually, Nancy must own her own liberation. She resigns herself to facing the future alone without the white Compson filter by telling them "I reckon it belong to me. I reckon what I going to get aint no more than mine" (98). In spite of her new self-determination, Mr. Compson is not able to recognize Nancy's radical future and tells her "you'll be the first thing I'll see in the kitchen tomorrow morning" (99). She refutes his statement by saying "you'll see what you'll see" (99). By the end of the narrative, Nancy's declaration that she is just a nigger may be her own vehicle of transcendence. As the narrative ends she preaches her own story and tells her story in a liminal voice that the narrator describes as "not singing and not unsinging" (100). She is prepared to face Jesus and speak her story in the face of violence from any source.

Trudier Harris suggests "the image of the maid is certainly one with which the majority of black women can identify and empathize, and it is one with which many blacks have personal ties. A large percentage of blacks in the current generation who are doctors of philosophy or medical doctors or lawyers—or writers—are so because black women in their pasts scrubbed floors or washed or cooked for whites."[25] I have to admit that my own positioning as a black woman from the South has compelled my search for liberatory strains in the experiences of Dilsey and Nancy. On my mother's side, I am a descendant of blacks in Springfield, Tennessee, who emerged as a privileged class of blacks in the nineteenth century. On my father's side, I am a descendant of a family whose history is much more sketchy and difficult to follow. I do know that my paternal grandmother worked in the kitchen of a white doctor in order to provide for her family and was said to be a woman who could "turn a church out" with her singing of the traditional long-metered hymns. This grandmother's discussions of how it felt to work in the kitchens of Southern whites does not line up with the images Faulkner gives us of Dilsey and Nancy in the Compson kitchen, so I have a certain amount of inherited "disease" with Faulkner's characterizations of black women. And, I am always hyperaware of my frustrations as the singular black graduate student in a Faulkner seminar, when my professor and fellow graduate students raved about Faulkner's *authentic* depictions of the black South. To me, when they chose Faulkner's blackness as real, they devalued multiple realities of the black South that I know and embody. Though I must admit that I still feel much discomfort with Faulkner, considerations of his use of liminality have escorted me into new respect for his attempts to grapple with his understandings of race through his characters. Much like Langston Hughes said, "I respect genius and I respect sincerity. I believe Mr. Faulkner is an excellent writer and a sincere citizen."[26] Faulkner's complex visions of race will always be muddied with the soil of his sociocultural realities. Even so, he attempts to pull some of his characters out of the mud, by allowing these characters culturally liminal moments in time that hold the possibility for a self-defined future. By providing his black female characters with a small opportunity for self-determination, Faulkner cracks the door open for self-determined racial aesthetics for the black community. Faulkner's willingness to create a racial world that embodies the pains of the past and that projects a better future is the true sermon on race that he passes to us. Sometimes the real truth about how race operates—textually or in the real world—is not fully understood by standing on one side, or the other. Sometimes to walk in the truth of race, we must stand right in the liminal middle.

NOTES

1. Langston Hughes, "Concerning a Great Mississippi Writer and the Southern Negro: May 26, 1956," in Christopher De Santis, ed., *Langston Hughes and the" Chicago Defender": Essays on Race, Politics, and Culture, 1942–62* (Urbana: University of Illinois Press, 1995), 91.

2. Noel Polk, *Children of the Dark House* (Jackson: University Press of Mississippi, 1996), 43.

3. Thadious Davis, *Faulkner's "Negro": Art and the Southern Context* (Baton Rouge: Louisiana State University Press, 1983), 2.

4. Elise Johnson McDougald, "The Double Task: The Struggle of Negro Women for Sex and Race Emancipation," *Survey Graphic* 53 (1 March 1925): 689.

5. Craig Werner, "Minstrel Dreams: Black Dreams of Faulkner's Dreams of Blacks," in *Faulkner and Race: Faulkner and Yoknapatawpha, 1986*, ed. Doreen Fowler and Ann J. Abadie (Jackson: University Press of Mississippi, 2007), 4.

6. Victor Turner, *The Forest of Symbols* (Ithaca, N.Y.: Cornell University Press, 1967), 288.

7. Homi Bhabha, *The Location of Culture* (New York: Routledge, 1914), 213–14.

8. William Faulkner, *Faulkner in the University: Class Conferences at the University of Virginia, 1957–58*, ed. Frederick L. Gwynn and Joseph L. Blotner (Charlottesville: University of Virginia Press, 1986), 13.

9. William Faulkner, *The Sound and the Fury* (New York: Vintage, 1990).

10. John C. Hoffman, *Law, Freedom, and Story: The Role of Narrative in Therapy, Society, and Faith* (New Jersey: Humanities Press, 1986), 81.

11. William Faulkner, *Faulkner in the University*, 68.

12. Erskine Peters also aligns Dilsey's environment with the aesthetics of T. S. Elliot. He argues that when Dilsey is looking for Luster, "We seem to be also in the world of T. S. Eliot's 'Preludes,' which close with the image of 'ancient women/Gathering fuel in the vacant lots.'" See Peters, *William Faulkner: The Yoknapatawpha World and Black Being* (Darby, Penn.: Norwood Editions, 1983), 138.

13. Blyden Jackson, "Faulkner's Negroes Twain," in *Faulkner and Race*, 58.

14. "Mississippi's Governor," *Time Magazine* (30 January 1928), 9.

15. George Coad, "Mississippi Loses Fear of Capital," *New York Times* (Sunday, 18 May 1928), Editorial Section, 47.

16. Davit Beito and Linda Royster Beito, "Let Down Your Bucket Where You Are," *Social Science History* 30.4 (Winter 2006): 551–69, 559.

17. Christopher Phillips, "The Crime against Missouri," *Civil War History* 48 (March 2002): 63.

18. David Hein, "The Reverend Mr. Shegog's Easter Sermon: Preaching as Communion in Faulkner's *The Sound and the Fury*," *Mississippi Quarterly* (Summer–Fall 2005): 562.

19. Martin J. Dain, *Faulkner's World* (Jackson: University Press of Mississippi, 1997), 81–84.

20. Hein, 559.

21. Peters, 37.

22. All quotations refer to the 1993 edition of "That Evening Sun," in *Selected Short Stories of William Faulkner* (New York: Modern Library, 1993), 76–99.

23. Robert Slabey, "Faulkner's Nancy as 'Tragic Mulatto,'" *Studies in Short Fiction* 27 (Summer 1990): 409–13.

24. Langston Hughes, "Christ in Alabama," in *The Panther and the Lash* (New York: Knopf, 1967), 37.

25. Trudier Harris, *From Mammies to Militants: Domestics in Black American Literature* (Philadelphia: Temple University Press, 1982), 5.

26. Langston Hughes, "Concerning a Great Mississippi Writer and the Southern Negro," 91.

The Weird Stuff: Textual and Sexual Anomalies in Faulkner's Fiction

THERESA M. TOWNER

—for Ann Abadie

I bring you tidings of great joy: The text is back.

For ten or fifteen years now, some scholars of Romantic and Renaissance literature have been offering up ideas about studying poems to discover the sources and structures of their beauty. In other words, they have rediscovered aesthetics—the study of the beautiful—and recovered the third of Aristotle's broad categories of human endeavor—*poiesis*, the process of making the beautiful, or as Martin Heidegger called it, the "bringing forth," an evanescent yet undeniable moment of transformation. Dubbed "the New Formalism" and making its way through the academy, this "movement" "seeks to reinstate close reading at the curricular center of our discipline and as the opening move, preliminary to any kind of critical consideration." In the heavily contoured prose that one usually finds in the pages of our professional organization's flagship magazine, Marjorie Levinson goes on to explain the importance of this activity that the New Critics loved so dearly:

> Reading, understood in traditional terms as multilayered and integrative responsiveness to every element of the textual dimension, quite simply produces the basic materials that form the subject matter of even the most historical of investigations. Absent this, we are reading something of our own untrammeled invention, invariably less complex than the products of reading. That complexity . . . , which is attributed to the artwork and recoverable only through a learned submission to its myriad textual prompts, explains the deep challenge that the artwork poses to ideology, or to the flattening, routinizing, absorptive effects associated with ideological regimes."[1]

She also notes that one strain of this new movement "makes a strong claim for bringing back pleasure as what hooks us on and rewards us for reading."[2]

Those of us who spend our academic careers and personal time reading the works of William Faulkner—whether any of the nineteen novels,
or the one hundred-plus collected and uncollected short stories, or the
essays and speeches and public letters, and even the poetry and illustrated fables that he left us—*begin* with the premise that reading for
pleasure and coming to a full appreciation of a beautifully made text
are not merely complementary or corrective activities. Indeed, they are
required behaviors in Faulkner's world. Who among us, upon looking
into *The Sound and the Fury* for the first time, did not gasp at the sight
of the bellowing Benjy quieting as Luster finally got him back in the right
direction and "cornice and façade flowed smoothly once more from left
to right, post and tree, window and doorway and signboard each in its
ordered place," even as we still wondered whether one of the Quentins
was a girl?[3] Readers of Faulkner understand negative capability, and we
feel pleasure in following Faulkner's sentences, meeting his characters in
them, walking alongside as they live and die and enter the evanescent yet
undeniable moment of transformation. In short, we know beautiful when
we read it.

In the midst of all this beauty, though, are not a few instances of just
plain weirdness. Often the weird is rendered beautifully, as in the story
of Ike Snopes's deep love for Jack Houston's cow:

> They go first to the spring. He found it on the first day—a brown creep of
> moisture in a clump of alder and beech, sunless, which wandered away without
> motion among the unsunned roots of other alders and willows. He cleaned it
> out and scooped a basin for it, which now at each return of light stood full and
> clear and leaf by leaf repeating until they lean and interrupt the green reflec-
> tions and with their own drinking faces break each other's mirroring, each face
> to its own shattered image wedded and annealed. Then he rises and takes up
> the rope, and they go on across the swale, toward the woods, and enter them.[4]

It might not be an exaggeration to say that most of Faulkner's work is
weird in some way. It was certainly unconventional enough upon its
appearance to throw book reviewers into general confusion, and M.
Thomas Inge has recently suggested that such confusion was at least
partly because "Faulkner wrote as if there were no literature written
in English before him, no century and more of convention and literary
tradition established before he put pen to paper."[5] "Weird" could also
describe his prose style. However, for my purposes in this essay, "the
weird stuff" will refer to several stories, episodes, and characters that
stand out in Faulkner's canon as oddities—things that upon reading one
might well think "*Faulkner* wrote that?" In particular, I will treat "Hair,"

"Artist at Home," "Divorce in Naples," and "The Leg" as deliberate textual and sexual anomalies.

Bad Narrators

Many people try to tell stories in Faulkner's fiction and fail miserably for one reason or another. Doing so is one of his great recurring themes. For example, with V. K. Ratliff and Chick Mallison, Gavin Stevens tries to tell Snopes stories and to manipulate their outcome, but his complete misunderstanding of his original material cripples him with grief at the end of *The Town*. Wishing to have foreseen the end of Eula's story, he thinks, "always and ever that *was* remains, as if what is going to happen to one tomorrow already gleams faintly visible now if the watcher were only wise enough to discern it or maybe just brave enough."[6] In other words, had he been a better narrator, her story would have had a better ending. On another point in the scale of narrative skill stands the reporter of *Pylon*, a literary wannabe who cannot for the life of him produce either good literature or good journalism, which his editor describes as "an accurate account of everything that occurs out there tomorrow that creates any reaction excitement or irritation on any human retina."[7] Other narrators may be said to fail because they have some personality trait or psychological obstacle that impedes their telling: Jason Compson's anger in *The Sound and the Fury*, Quentin Compson's childhood terror in "That Evening Sun," Georgie's youth and overweening greed in "That Will Be Fine," Harry Wilbourne's self-delusion as a writer of "moron's pap" in *If I Forget Thee, Jerusalem*,[8] Rosa Coldfield's outrage in *Absalom, Absalom!* Yet it seems to me that in all of these examples Faulkner's target is not to expose a bad narrator per se but to reveal the high stakes involved in our attempts to tell our own stories, to figure our identities for ourselves and the world. In "Hair" and "Artist at Home," however, he represents bad narrators in the act of producing bad narratives. "Hair" comes to us in the words of a misognynist salesman, "Artist" through a nebulous presence who needles us to get "it," or the important point of the story. In the former, our understanding of plot and character is obscured by the obsessive attention the narrator pays to minutiae; and in the latter, we are left palms upturned and outward wondering what just exactly happened and why we should care about it.

"Hair" is divided into three parts, each with a rather complicated internal chronology. Part 1 tells the story of Susan Reed growing up an orphan in a little Mississippi town called Jefferson. Gossip circulates around and about her constantly. The first of this concerns her adoptive parents: "Some said that Susan was a niece or a cousin or something; others cast the usual aspersions on the character of Burchett and even of Mrs. Burchett: you know."[9] As an aside, our traveling salesman narrator adds, "Women mostly, these were" (131). This remark tells us at least three things about him:[10] he talks about people to other people; he talks to enough people about Susan Reed, who is only five years old when he takes up her story, to be able to quantify by gender the gossip he hears; and he will generalize from his gossip about one individual to explain the behaviors of a group (and later he also reverses this process). The section goes on to relate the escalation of the gossip about Susan as she grows up and begins to experiment with makeup and clothing "pulled and dragged to show off what she never had yet to show off, like the older girls did with their silk and crepe and such" and "all the talk began" about her loose morals (134) and her truancy. Section 2 relates the narrator's history of watching and asking questions about the barber known in Jefferson as Hawkshaw, who lost his fiancée to fever thirteen years before and paid to bury both her and her mother and has spent two weeks every year since cleaning up their homestead, paying the mortgage too. In this section he reveals that Hawkshaw's fiancée, Sophie, and Susan Reed have the same color hair: "straight, soft hair not blonde and not brunette" and "brown-yellow" describe Susan's (131, 135); "straight hair not brown and not yellow" describes Sophie's (139). He reveals this information but never once connects the two women or sees significance in the fact that a barber who had cut his own dying fiancée's hair would coax a five-year-old girl child with the same color hair to have her first haircut. We also see in these two sections that the narrator has strong opinions about women and about "backwoods folks" like Sophie Starnes:

> Girls are different from boys. Girls are born weaned and boys don't ever get weaned. . . . It's not that she was bad. There's not any such thing as a woman born bad, because they are all born bad, born with the badness in them. The thing is, to get them married before the badness comes to a natural head. . . . She just grew up too fast. She reached the point where the badness came to a head before the system said it was time for her to. I think they can't help it. I have a daughter of my own, and I say that. (133)

> These backwoods folks: you know how it is. No doctors, or veterinaries, if they are. Cut them and shoot them: that's all right. But let them get a bad cold and maybe they'll get well or maybe they'll die two days later of cholera. (139)

Section 2 closes with the oddly reticent admission that the narrator has only told one person what he knows about Hawkshaw—Gavin Stevens, "the district attorney, a smart man: not like the usual pedagogue lawyer and office holder" (144), friendly enough with the narrator to have been the one who got him his present job. Together they speculate on what Hawkshaw will do once he's paid off the Starnes mortgage:

> "Maybe he'll just go off and die," I said.
> "Maybe he will," Stevens said.
> "Well," I said, "he wont be the first man to tilt at windmills."
> "He wont be the first man to die, either," Stevens said. (144)

The allusion to Cervantes establishes that the narrator is educated, like Stevens, but the latter seems to have a reserve of sympathy for humanity that the narrator lacks.

We see that sympathy again in section 3, when the narrator tells Stevens that Hawkshaw has paid off the mortgage. The narrator smugly finishes Hawkshaw's story by saying "That's what I told Bidwell." But when Stevens muses aloud that Hawkshaw must have felt "time and despair rus[h] as slow and dark under him as under any garlanded boy or crownless and crestless girl," the narrator reverts to his opinion that "only the girl went bad on him" (147). He seems finished with the pair of them, convinced that he has comprehended them fully. In the final lines of "Hair," however, Stevens blindsides him with a piece of information that his disposition, experience, and prejudice would never have allowed him to entertain. After paying off the Starnes mortgage, Hawkshaw married Susan Reed and left town with her. Because we have been so closely imprisoned in his view of the world, we too are surprised—and probably not a little pleased that the two have escaped the prying eyes and loose tongues of this little town, anyway. By adding Stevens's coda to the narrator's neat and cynical vision of Hawkshaw exploited and abandoned, Faulkner calls our attention to a different way to read the welter of dates, places, times, and commentary with which the narrator fills his own account of Hawkshaw and Susan.[11] We can see a young girl abused by gossip and truly cared for only by a man who sees in her a vision of the fiancée he has sought for "six or eight" years in "different towns in Alabama and Tennessee and Mississippi." "I was just looking around," he says (142). Yes, he was, for that hair, and when he saw Susan the first time, "Be durn if it didn't look like Hawkshaw had been waiting for her to come along" (131), as his boss says. Yes, he had been; but we know these things because of a minor character in the story and not because of our narrator.[12]

If "Hair" succeeds as a story in spite of the person entrusted with telling it, "Artist at Home" examines narrative in the process of going bad almost from the beginning. The story describes an incident in the life of novelist Roger Howes and his wife, Anne. Their home in the Valley of Virginia is routinely descended upon by vagabond artists in search of a free ride. The most recent of these, poet John Blair, falls in love with Anne; their brief affair ends with Blair mooning outside their house during a torrential rain storm. Six months later he's dead. The central oddity of the story is that when Blair confesses to Roger, "Tonight I kissed your wife. I'm going to again, if I can" (637), Roger almost immediately begins typing, breaking a long-term writer's block. He writes, and quickly sells, a novel about "Him, and Anne, and the poet. Word for word, between the waiting spells to find out what to write down next, with a few changes here and there, of course, because live people do not make good copy, the most interesting copy being gossip, since it mostly is not true" (644). As I've argued elsewhere, this "highly metafictional passage . . . blurs the distinctions between 'live people' like John and Anne, who are 'real' only on paper, and the creations of Blair and Roger Howes, which are ostensibly art. Moreover, the reminder that this story is a fiction further interrogates the role and stance of the narrator. Since the story has such a gossipy tone, and '[gossip] is mostly not true,' why should we believe what the narrator says?"[13] Several critics have argued that this unnamed narrator is Roger himself,[14] and that "Artist at Home" is a highly autobiographical, perhaps Freudian representation of Faulkner's own transition from poet to novelist.[15] I find those arguments compelling, but what I find fascinating is the sheer amount of bad narrative techniques in the story, so many of them as not to be accidental but so as to constitute Faulkner's representation of how to tell a story badly.

A few examples will illustrate that claim. First, tenses shift for no apparent reason and to inconsistent effect. This happens first with the appearance of John Blair, after two pages of straightforward, slightly ironic, description of Roger's life with Anne and the visiting bohemians. "So when this poet in the sky-blue coat gets off the train," we read, and as good readers of Faulkner we can take this in stride and feel a cinematic, fade-in effect. We have to get used to this kind of changeup because it happens without warning throughout the rest of the story. Second, the narrator interrupts passages of dialogue to give us information we don't really need, as happens when Anne complains bitterly about Blair's unannounced visit and the narrator lets us know that "Pinkie was the Negro cook" and someone else "was a farmer that lived across the creek from them" (630, 631). Third, Blair and Anne are caricatures rather than fully developed characters, Roger only marginally less so. Fourth, the narrator rather airily implies the inferiority of his characters to himself. During John and Anne's first conversation, for instance, "Then she tells him to come on into the house and live there forever. Except she didn't say exactly that"; "Then she went to find Roger and tell him to bring down the pram from the attic. Of course she didn't say exactly that, either" (630). After condescending on the story's first page to "those gaunt and eager and carnivorous tymbesteres of Art" (627), the narrator moves in on his artist at home: Anne at her dressing table "is not doing anything, which any husband, even an artist, should know is a bad sign. When you see a woman sitting half dressed before a dressing table with a mirror and not even watching herself in the mirror, it's time to smell smoke in the wind" (632–33). Fifth, the denouement is almost impossible to follow. With the money from the sale of his novel, Roger pays Blair's hospital and funeral bills and buys a fur coat for his wife and winter underwear for himself and their two children; Anne gives the coat to a neighbor woman, and Roger and Anne "go into a clinch on their own account," after which they both "feel better" (for different reasons) (645). Finally, the narrator keeps nudging us, like a chatty neighbor in a movie theater, telling us to notice something apparently important. "Now get this. This is where it starts," he notes in introducing the part where John kisses Anne and, after a token protest, she kisses him. Then he tells us "But that's not it. That can be seen in any movie. This is what it is, what is good" (636), by which he means that Roger has seen the second kiss. But you could see *that* in any movie, too, and besides, he has another heads-up for us: "Now get this. This is it," by which he means Roger beginning his novel about the three of them, and after telling us about that, he begins the denouement with, "Anyway, here's the rest of it, what they did next" (645). "Artist at Home" literally and deliberately writes the book on how not to write a book.

Pink Teddies

"Divorce in Naples," the penultimate story in both *These* 13 and *Collected Stories*, opens with the first-person narrator's striking equation of language with sex:

> We were sitting at a table inside: Monckton and the bosun and Carl and George and me and the women, the three women of that abject glittering kind that seamen know or that know seamen. We were talking English and they were not talking at all. By that means they could speak constantly to us above and below the sound of our voices in a tongue older than recorded speech and time too. Older than the thirty-four days of sea time which we had but completed, anyway. Now and then they spoke to one another in Italian, the men in English,

as if language might be the sex difference, the functioning of the vocal cords the inner biding until the dark pairing time. (877)

The men need only three prostitutes because Carl and George have each other. "They came into the ship together at Galveston," the narrator says, and they have spent the subsequent "thirty-four evenings" on ship "in pants and undershirts, dancing to the victrola on the after well deck above a hold full of Texas cotton and Georgia resin" (879). The bosun refers to Carl as George's "wife" and his "girl" (877, 878), and from the second page of the story we know that Carl's virginity stands at the very center of George's life; he has dedicated himself to preserving it, literally holding it close in his arms while they dance. On the night the story opens, Carl disappears with the third prostitute, who knows Carl is "*Éin-nocente*" (878), and George, drunk, ends up in jail. When he returns to the ship to find Carl gone, he feels as betrayed by Carl as Joe Christmas does by Bobbie Allen in *Light in August*:

> "I never thought he'd a done it. I never thought he'd a done me this way. It was her. She was the one made him done it. She knew what he was, and how I . . ." Then he began to cry, quietly, in that dull, detached way. . . . "And I never suspicioned. She kept on moving her chair closer and closer to his. But I trusted him. I never suspicioned nothing. I thought he wouldn't a done nothing serious without asking me first, let alone . . . I trusted him." (883–84)

Not for nothing, then, does the pun-conscious Faulkner call his characters "seamen" rather than "sailors," and these two seamen who "came into the ship together" have one of the weirdest lover's quarrels (and ambiguous reconciliations) in all of his fiction.

Critics of the story focus on its homosexual elements and the clear contrast between Carl and George.[16] The former is slightly built, blonde, and only eighteen years old; he launders his own clothes and favors tight-fitting garments. George "was a Greek, big and black, a full head taller than Carl" who "cursed us all with immediate thoroughness and in well-nigh faultless classic Anglo-Saxon" (877). His eloquent swearing sets George apart from the others; after one volley, Monckton says, "you're by way of being almost a poet" (881). Not just an aside, the comment highlights again the narrator's focus on sexuality and textuality as indicators of one another: George tries to protect Carl's virginity with profanity; when Carl abandons him, he returns to the ship "dazed," with a "blank look" (887); when he tries to hurt Carl by going on a bender himself, he returns to the ship "a little drunk at three and four o'clock, to waken everyone by hand, save Carl, and talk in gross and loud recapitulation of recent and always different women before climbing into his bunk" (890). Robert Dale Parker has analyzed the shifting "homosexual-heterosexual binary" in this story;[17] the speech-silence binary is just as carefully applied and even more significant when we consider that Carl and George have not been having a sexual affair. Carl's virginity is George's *raison d'être et de parler*—reason for being and speaking. The narrator, a rather voyeuristic sort who feigns sleep to watch Carl after he comes back to the ship, would have told us had he observed any sexual activity, even though none of the seamen really seems either to care or to take offense at the idea of it. They mostly enjoy watching the two men dance, ribbing them a little sometimes, and listening to George swearing in response. This is why it's important that when George forgives Carl, he tries to talk to him and receives in turn the silent treatment until Carl is ready to "look back that way" toward Naples and ask George about women and how "a man treat[s] them" (891). He gets a typically vulgar assessment that includes the information that "if she was going to be your girl, you'd give her something," "like something to wear or something" (891). He also explains heterosexual prostitution in terms that make Carl physically ill (891–92). Even after they resume their evening dancing, "They didn't talk; they just danced," until "Carl spoke for the first time after almost twenty days":

> "George," he said, "do me a favor, will you?"
>
> "Sure, bud," George said, stamping on the deck each time the needle clucked, his black head shoulders above Carl's sleek pale one, the two of them in decorous embrace, their canvas shoes hissing in unison: "Sure," George said. "Spit it out."
>
> "When we get to Galveston, I want you to buy me a suit of these pink silk teddybears that ladies use. A little bigger than I'd wear, see?" (892–93)

Resuming speech signals their full reconciliation, but what does that speech signify? Is Carl asking George to buy him the lingerie so he can send it to the Neopolitan prostitute? I doubt it, because at the suggestion that he might see her again, Carl "looked like he was fixing to jump off the boat and swim on ahead and wait for us at Hatteras" (891). How does the former virgin even know about teddies? Presumably, he saw the prostitute wearing them. Is he simply curious about how it would feel to wear this exotic kind of close-fitting clothing? This seems the most likely explanation for the request that ends the "Divorce in Naples." When Carl asks George to buy him "something to wear," he asks for a customary token of a heterosexual relationship as George has explained it to him and thus seals his status as George's "girl." The two of them have survived what the narrator calls "the most difficult moment in marriage: the day after your wife has stayed out all night" (889).

Dead Poets

John Blair of "Artist at Home" writes two poems during the course of that story, one before his affair with Anne begins and one right after it ends. He uses Roger's typewriter to write the first one, and Anne imagines how he does it: "He enters the room which the children are absolutely forbidden and puts one finger on that typewriter which Pinkie is not even permitted to touch with a dust-cloth, and writes a poem about freedom and flings it at you to commend and applaud" (633). The full significance of this act of appropriation emerges during the scene in which Blair tells Roger he has kissed Anne and will do so again. They talk in Roger's office, "the room where he writes his books" (637), and Roger sits behind the typewriter while Blair confesses; after Blair leaves the house, Roger starts his novel. In a sense, then, Blair has stolen not only Roger's wife but his means of literary production, and in telling the story of the affair Roger takes both of them back. In the town, meanwhile, Blair has "crashed through" (634) and written "Something with an entrail in it," "the shot," the good poem that Roger sends to the little magazines (632, 643). He writes it on the back of a flyspecked menu, mails it to Roger and Anne, and leaves town without seeing either of them again. As long as the two men remain under the same roof, impasse prevails. In the rainstorm that brings on Blair's fatal illness, Faulkner tells us that they're both all wet: "Both gentlemen, being artists: the one who doesn't want the other to get wet; the other whose conscience won't let him wreck the house from the inside" (642). If, as Noel Polk has suggested, we read the last name "Howes" as Faulkner's pun on "house,"[18] we see that Blair must leave the home he would wreck in order to produce his art, just as Roger must inhabit and revivify it with his own.

Faulkner wrote "Artist at Home" early in 1931. It was rejected by the *Saturday Evening Post* and *Scribner's* before he had his agent Ben Wasson take over the submissions process,[19] and *Story* published it for its customary twenty-five dollars in August 1933. "Hair" and "Divorce in Naples" also appeared during this immensely productive time in Faulkner's career. "Hair" was published in the May 1931 issue of *American Mercury*, after five rejections, and Faulkner also submitted "Divorce" five times to various magazines, at last including it in *These 13.*[20] It would seem that contemporary editors were also wary of Faulkner's weird stuff—"Hair" is at least recognizable for its Jefferson setting. Slightly predating these three and also tracing an improbable plot, "The Leg" makes use of an unstable narrator to represent sexual anxiety and violence, and starting in 1928, four editors passed up the chance to publish it; Faulkner finally included it in the collection *Doctor Martino* in 1934. The story describes the friendship of two Oxford University students, the American Davy and the British George. One day in 1914 they punt down the Thames, and in an attempt to impress a lockkeeper's daughter, George quotes Milton's *Comus* to compliment her "divine Inchanting ravishment";[21] still quoting, George falls into the lock and has to be fished out by her father and brother. Over the course of this first section, he quotes or alludes to the poetry of Walt Whitman, Shakespeare, Thomas Campion, Homer, Keats, Edmund Spenser, Christopher Marlowe, Alexander Pope, and the New Testament—a veritable anthology of verse. "We were twenty-one then," Davy says, "we talked like that, tramping about that peaceful land where in green petrification the old splendid bloody deeds, the spirits of the blundering courageous men, slumbered in every stone and tree" (828). Their usual subjects were "courage and honor," "love," "death," and of course poetry (829). Yet in the next year George is killed in the Great War and Davy's leg is amputated, and the story changes tone completely. Gone are the elaborate phrases and quotations, replaced by short, disjointed conversations between Davy and George—the dead George—about Davy's lost leg.[22] He fears that it still lives, and he turns out to be right. The missing leg eventually sprouts a body, and that body seduces the lockkeeper's daughter and abandons her to madness and death.

As is the case with other instances of the genre we now call magical realism, readers of "The Leg" don't get to deny that such a transformation could happen. Like the rain of butterflies or the baby with the pig's tail in Gabriel García Márquez's *One Hundred Years of Solitude*, Davy's doppelganger is undeniable. We even have a photograph of it: "it was my own face that looked back at me. It had a quality that was not mine: a quality vicious and outrageous and unappalled, and beneath it was written in a bold sprawling hand like that of a child: 'To Everbe Corinthia' followed by an unprintable phrase, yet it was my own face" (841–42). While Davy has been learning to use his new leg, George has seen the doppelganger twice, yet Davy comes to believe that the leg is dead and "perhaps in killing it [George] had lost his own life: the dead dying in order to slay the dead" (835). With the revelation of his double's role in the destruction of Everbe Corinthia's entire family, Davy can only think, "I told him to find it and kill it. . . . I told him to. I told him" (842). George's theories and practice of poetry have completely disappeared from a text now deeply mired in concerns of sexual predation, attempted murder, frustrated desire, guilt, and no small amount of physical pain— all of which Davy tries to deflect finally onto George, who unwittingly predicted Davy's fate after he fell into the lock: "That which you have saved from death or disaster will be forever dear to you, Davy; you cannot ignore it. Besides, it will not let you" (827). George and Davy's leg remain together "somewhere in the mazy corridor where the mother of dreams dwelt" (834), intangible but real, and destructive.

The four stories I've discussed in this essay did not appear on Robert Haas's original list of suggestions for a volume of Faulkner's collected stories; Haas does not appear to have had copies of *These* 13 or *Doctor Martino* with him when he made the list.[23] Faulkner wrote Haas in April 1948 that he would "go over your list carefully later; think a few changes to your starred list, one or two on it I don't consider first rate and I think one or two omitted which I do."[24] By late September of that year, Faulkner had replied to Haas's suggestions and included several of the stories that now appear in *Knight's Gambit* (*SL* 274–75). In fact, thinking about the collected stories project led him to conceive *Knight's Gambit*. "Maybe we are too previous with a collected Faulkner," he wrote his publisher, "I am thinking of a 'Gavin Stevens' volume, more or less detective stories" (*SL* 280). The same principle thus guided his *Gambit* that Faulkner had articulated a few weeks earlier in a letter to Malcolm Cowley: "The only book foreword I ever remembered was one I read when I was about sixteen I suppose . . . something like 'This book written in . . . travail (he may have said even agony and sacrifice) for the uplifting of men's hearts.' Which I believe is the one worthwhile purpose of any book and so even to a collection of short stories, form, integration, is as important as to a novel—an entity of its own, single, set for one pitch, contrapuntal in integration, toward one end, one finale" (*SL* 277–78). Faulkner's organization of *Collected Stories* came to him easily and he settled on it quickly: "suddenly the whole page stood right, each noun in character and tone and tune with every other word" (*SL* 277). The only "Gavin Stevens" story he included was "Hair," one of Gavin's earliest appearances in Faulkner's canon, where he is an important foil to the bad narrator who introduces him. Faulkner placed "Artist at Home" in the volume some time after he made his original list, along with two other oddities, "Pennsylvania Station" and "The Brooch," appearing on either side of it. As it did in *These* 13, "Divorce in Naples" stood second-to-last,[25] with yet another oddity between it and "The Leg." Despite the stories' fates with publishers, Faulkner's weird stuff kept its maker's good opinion, and he didn't abandon Susan Reed or John Blair or George and Davy any more than he abandoned that other child of his imagination, his "heart's darling,"[26] Caddy Compson. As he wrote in another context, "you dont love because: you love despite; not for the virtues, but despite the faults."[27] The protagonist in "Carcassonne" could have spoken for Faulkner's own desire *"to perform something bold and tragical and austere"* in the margins of his canon as well as its center. Beautifully and unapologetically weird, this fiction challenges us. It will not leave quietly but instead picks at the very bedrock of our understanding of Faulkner.

And that's another story.

NOTES

1. Marjorie Levinson, "What Is New Formalism?," *PMLA* 122:2 (2007): 558–69. A review essay, this article contains an excellent working bibliography of New Formalist works on subjects as diverse as Shakespeare, pedagogy, contemporary poetry, and of course New Formalist theory itself. See also *Aesthetics and Ideology*, ed. George Levine (New Brunswick: Rutgers University Press, 1994); *Beauty and the Critic: Aesthetics in an Age of Cultural Studies*, ed. James Soderholm (Tuscaloosa: University of Alabama Press, 1997); and *Renaissance Literature and Its Formal Engagements*, ed. Mark David Rasmussen (New York: Palgrave, 2002).

2. Levinson, 562. Joseph Urgo has explained these pleasures very elegantly in *In the Age of Distraction* (Jackson: University Press of Mississippi, 2000): "Literary critics use the present tense when they discuss texts because literary enactment always exists in the present, in the now. And what else is pleasure but a heightened sense of one's physical existence in the now? . . . In a prolonged and extensive now is where literary texts place the minds of those who can read their language, not in the name of attending to the present but with the purpose of exploring underneath, beyond and past it. . . . Once we read past historical fiction, science fiction, comedy, tragedy, romanticism, and the rest, the single, universal object of literary study is the present in all its limitlessness and expansion. Anything less trivializes our lives as readers, the vocations of literary scholars, and the purpose of literary study. Above all else, we read literature to extend the present, to fill the now as fully as possible, paying no attention to the tendency of human institutions and information technologies to trivialize the now by insisting that memory or management define it essentially. In the literary now, between the curling flower spaces, time will always tell what we get when we make room for the desires of literary employments. This is what feels right, feels good" (156–57).

3. William Faulkner, *The Sound and the Fury* (1929; New York: Vintage International, 1990), 321.

4. William Faulkner, *The Hamlet* (1940; New York: Vintage International, 1991), 202.

5. M. Thomas Inge, *William Faulkner* (New York, Woodstock, London: Overlook Duckworth, 2006), 1.

6. William Faulkner, *The Town* (1957; New York: Library of America, 1999), 293.

7. William Faulkner, *Pylon* (1935; New York: Vintage, 1987), 48.

8. William Faulkner, *If I Forget Thee, Jerusalem* (1939; New York: Vintage International, 1995), 103.

9. William Faulkner, *Collected Stories* (1950; New York: Vintage International, 1995), 131. Subsequent quotations from Faulkner's short stories are from this edition and cited parenthetically in the text.

10. I take a dimmer view of the narrator than do most critics. James B. Carothers, for example, gives him credit for changing: "'Hair' shows the narrator telling a story on himself, a story which suggests that he has been mistaken in his assessment of Hawkshaw, of Susan Reed, and of the human condition." See *William Faulkner's Short Stories* (Ann Arbor: UMI Research Press, 1985), 96. Lisa Paddock argues that his "harshness" sets him apart from an otherwise fairly gentle community; see *Contrapuntal in Integration: A Study*

of Three Faulkner Short Story Volumes (Lanham: International Scholars Publications, 2000), 156. Like Hans H. Skei before him, James Ferguson claims that the narrator reminds him of "Suratt-Ratliff," and he "regards Hawkshaw with the proper degree of wonder and compassion"; see *Faulkner's Short Fiction* (Knoxville: University of Tennessee Press, 1991), 109. Skei's final assessment of the narrator lies close to my own: "The narrator's propensity for guesswork and approximations proves that he does not try hard to reach an understanding of the significance of his own story. Thus the narrative inconsistency underscores the theme of the story, which also proves the narrator's inability to grasp the meaning of his own experience, observation, and narration." See *William Faulkner: The Novelist as Short Story Writer* (Oslo: Universitetsforlaget, 1985), 177.

11. Edmond L. Volpe argues the opposite, that the "sudden introduction" of Gavin Stevens's character is "certainly awkward" and "causes a dissonance that severely violates the story's unity." See *A Reader's Guide to William Faulkner: The Short Stories* (Syracuse: Syracuse University Press, 2004), 133.

12. Judson D. [Jay] Watson III has argued for Gavin's strong "credentials as a storyteller," even in the "few lines he speaks"; see "'Hair,' 'Smoke,' and the Development of the Faulknerian Lawyer Character," *Mississippi Quarterly* 43 (1990): 349–66.

13. Theresa M. Towner and James B. Carothers, *Reading Faulkner: "Collected Stories"* (Jackson: University Press of Mississippi, 2006), 352.

14. See Joseph Reed, *Faulkner's Narrative* (New Haven: Yale University Press, 1973), 41–42; Stephen M. Ross, *Fiction's Inexhaustible Voice: Speech and Writing in Faulkner* (Athens: University of Georgia Press, 1989), 240–41.Ferguson disagrees (115–16). Paddock calls the story "a self-referential work" (183).

15. See, for example, Noel Polk, *Children of the Dark House: Text and Context in Faulkner* (Jackson: University Press of Mississippi, 1996), 137–65; Lothar Hönninghausen, "'Pegasusrider and Literary Hack': Portraits of the Artist in Faulkner's Short Fiction," in *William Faulkner's Short Fiction: An International Symposium*, ed. Hans H. Skei (Oslo: Solum Forlag, 1997), 275–80; Volpe, 170.

16. Paddock, 58; Ferguson, 66; Volpe, 7, for example.

17. Robert Dale Parker, "Sex and Gender, Feminine and Masculine: Faulkner and the Polymorphous Exchange of Cultural Binaries," *Faulkner and Gender: Faulkner and Yoknapatawpha. 1994*, ed. Donald L. Kartiganer and Ann J. Abadie (Jackson: University Press of Mississippi, 1996), 79.

18. Polk, 153.

19. Diane Brown Jones, *A Reader's Guide to the Short Stories of William Faulkner* (New York: G.K. Hall, 1994), 440.

20. Jones, 142; Skei, *William Faulkner: The Short Story Career* (Oslo: Universitetsforlaget, 1981), 37.

21. Towner and Carothers, 431–32.

22. Several commentators read this story in Freudian terms, with Davy's lost leg symbolizing a fear of castration or an aversion to female sexuality (or both). See Ferguson, 66–67 and 203, n9–11; Volpe, 60–61. Michael Grimwood offers an extensive analysis of the place of "The Leg" in Faulkner's personal life, tracing its origins to the back brace that Maud Falkner had young William wear and examining its implications for Faulkner's anxiety about his own vocation; see *Heart in Conflict: Faulkner's Struggles with Vocation* (Athens: University of Georgia Press, 1987), 55–60.

23. I am indebted to Jim Carothers for this information.

24. *Selected Letters of William Faulkner*, ed. Joseph Blotner (New York: Vintage, 1978), 266. Further citations appear parenthetically in the text with the abbreviation *SL*.

25. For an analysis of how the organization of this collection "addresses the readerly desire to discern structural patterns," see Judith Bryant Wittenberg, "Synecdoche and

Strategic Redundancy: The 'Integrated Form' of *These 13*," in Skei, *William Faulkner's Short Fiction*, 281–88.

26. *Faulkner in the University*, ed. Frederick L. Gwynn and Joseph L. Blotner (1959; Charlottesville: University of Virginia, 1995), 6.

27. *Essays, Speeches, and Public Letters*, ed. James B. Meriwether (New York: Random House, 1965), 42–43.

Contributors

Ted Atkinson is assistant professor of English at Mississippi State University. His publications include a book, *Faulkner and the Great Depression: Aesthetics, Ideology, and Cultural Politics*, and articles in *Mississippi Quarterly*, *Studies in American Culture*, *Faulkner Journal*, and *Southern Literary Journal*.

Serena Haygood Blount is an instructor in the Department of English at the University of Alabama where she received Outstanding Dissertation awards for "Faulkner's Graphophone." She is the recipient of an Andrew Mellon Research Fellowship from the Harry Ransom Humanities Center at the University of Texas for her research in chronologizing and evaluating early Faulkner manuscripts.

Martyn Bone is associate professor of English at the University of Mississippi. He previously taught at the University of Nottingham in England and the University of Copenhagen in Denmark. He is the author of *The Postsouthern Sense of Place in Contemporary Fiction* and editor of *Perspectives on Barry Hannah*. His work has appeared in *American Literature*, *Comparative American Studies*, *Mississippi Quarterly*, and other journals.

James B. Carothers, professor of English at the University of Kansas, has published and lectured widely on Faulkner. He is the author of *William Faulkner's Short Stories* and coauthor, with Theresa M. Towner, of *Reading Faulkner: "Collected Short Stories."*

Thadious M. Davis is Geraldine R. Segal Professor of American Social Thought and Professor of English at the University of Pennsylvania. She is the author of *Faulkner's "Negro": Art and the Southern Context*, *Nella Larsen, Novelist of the Harlem Renaissance*, and *Games of Property: Law, Race, Gender, and Faulkner's "Go Down, Moses."*

Taylor Hagood is associate professor of English at Florida Atlantic University. He is the author of two books, *Faulkner's Imperialism: Space, Place, and the Materiality of Myth*, and *Secrecy, Magic, and the One-Act Plays of Harlem Renaissance Women Writers*. Additionally, he has published articles and reviews in numerous journals, including *African American Review*, *European Journal of American Culture*, *Faulkner Journal*, and *Studies in Popular Culture*.

James Harding is associate tutor and D.Phil. candidate at the University of Sussex in the United Kingdom. His thesis on "Semanticising the Body in William Faulkner and John Dos Passos" explores the ways in which two distinctive regional modernisms are shaped and how formal literary components—for example, syntax, rhythm, parataxis, narrative silence, blank spaces—become carriers of meaning.

Arthur F. Kinney is Thomas W. Copeland Professor of Literary History and director of the Center for Renaissance Studies at the University of Massachusetts, Amherst. He is the author of *Faulkner's Narrative Poetics: Style as Vision*, *"Go Down, Moses": The Miscegenation of Time*, and editor of four volumes on Faulkner's fictional families.

Owen Robinson is lecturer in United States literature in the Department of Literature, Film, and Theatre Studies at the University of Essex. He is the author of *Creating Yoknapatawpha: Readers and Writers in Faulkner's Fiction* and coeditor of *A Companion to the Literature and Culture of the American South*.

Theresa M. Towner is professor of literary studies in the School of Arts and Humanities at the University of Texas at Dallas. She is the author of *Faulkner on the Color Line: The Later Novels* and *The Cambridge Introduction to William Faulkner*.

Annette Trefzer is associate professor of English at the University of Mississippi. She is the author of *Disturbing Indians: The Archaeology of Southern Fiction* and coeditor with Ann J. Abadie of several volumes of critical essays on William Faulkner, including *Global Faulkner*, *Faulkner's Sexualities*, and *Faulkner and Formalism: Returns of the Text*. She is also coeditor, with Kathryn McKee, of "Global Contexts, Local Literatures: The New Southern Studies," a special issue of *American Literature*.

Ethel Young-Minor is associate professor of English and African American studies at the University of Mississippi. She is the author of essays on pedagogy and performance in African American literature. Her book on female playwrights is forthcoming with Mercer University Press.

Index